Strategies for Helping
Parents of
Exceptional Children

Strategies for Helping Parents of Exceptional Children

A Guide for Teachers

Milton Seligman

THE FREE PRESS
A Division of Macmillan Publishing Co., Inc.
NEW YORK

Collier Macmillan Publishers
LONDON

The Free Press
A Division of Macmillan Publishing Co., Inc.
866 Third Avenue, New York, N.Y. 10022

Collier Macmillan Canada, Ltd.

Library of Congress Catalog Card Number: 78–24764

Printed in the United States of America

printing number

1 2 3 4 5 6 7 8 9 10

Library of Congress Cataloging in Publication Data

Seligman, Milton.
    Strategies for helping parents of handicapped children.

    Includes bibliographical references.
    1. Handicapped children--Education--Handbooks, man-
uals, etc. 2. Handicapped children--Family relationships
--Handbooks, manuals, etc. 3. Parent-teacher relation-
ships. I. Title.
LC4015.S4   371.9   78-24764
ISBN 0-02-928420-1

Passages from Alan O. Ross's *The Exceptional Child in the Family*
(New York: Grune & Stratton, Inc., 1964) used by permission
of the publisher and the author.
Passages from Alfred Benjamin's *The Helping Interview*, 2nd ed.
(Boston: Houghton Mifflin Company) copyright
© 1974 by the publisher and used by permission.

This book
is affectionately dedicated
to Pat

Contents

Preface

This book is for and about two groups of people who must work together often in the face of adversity: parents of children who are handicapped, and teachers. As a parent of an exceptional child, a consumer of the literature on parents of handicapped children, and an educator of teachers and counselors, I have become increasingly aware of the significant challenges faced by both groups. It is most unfortunate that, because of the burdens of parenting a handicapped child and the pressures that teachers face in assuming broader role functions, parents and teachers often find themselves at odds with each other—engaged in adversary relationships instead of in collaborative efforts. This situation, which to me cries out for change, has prompted me to write this book.

My own parenting involvement aside, I have gained important insights into parent-teacher relationships as a result of teaching a course designed to help preservice and practicing teachers work more effectively with exceptional parents. Each time the course has been taught I have become more aware that gross deficiencies in knowledge and skill exist in this vital area of what should be a mutual endeavor. It has become clear to me that, in order to achieve a greater understanding of these parents and to be able to assess, recognize, and anticipate behavior unique to exceptional families, it is essential for teachers to become more knowledgeable about them—about their hopes, joys, disappointments, frustrations. Awareness and appreciation of the paths often taken when a disabled child is born, of the dynamics operating both within the family and between family and community, and of the attitudes and behaviors of professionals, seem to me necessary and significant contributions to a more incisive understanding of the life circumstances confronting such parents.

Teachers often feel uncomfortable in the presence of these parents—anxious, negative, unable to relate with ease and in a useful manner. These reactions, signs not only of a lack of understanding and compassion but also of an inadequate development of interpersonal skills, often result in what might generously be called "non facilitative encounters." The unfortunate fact of the matter is of course that changes in relationships come about slowly at best, and then only with the aid of the good will and sincere positive action of the concerned parties. For teachers I believe this translates into a dual commitment: to become more knowledgeable about the exceptional parents they confer with, and to augment this increased awareness through the improvement of their own communication abilities.

Chapter 1 of this book proposes that the teacher's traditional pedagogical role be broadened by acquiring facilitative communication skills vis-à-vis parents of exceptional children. Compelling arguments support a broadened role, with the strongest impetus coming from legislation requiring teachers to interact more with parents. With the passage of the Education for All Handicapped Children Act of 1975 (PL. 94–142), there was mandated a more individualized approach to realizing educational goals for handicapped children. Under the terms of this Act, learning abilities and deficiencies are to be evaluated, and an individualized educational program written, for each handicapped child. The goal is to place children in the least restrictive educational setting. This evaluation and placement process is perhaps the most impactful aspect of PL. 94–142. Particularly germane is that it is now incumbent upon the schools to include the parent as one of the members of the educational team that approves the educational program and decides on educational placement. Thus, parental contacts with school personnel are becoming much more frequent. Irrespective of legislative mandate, good practice dictates that productive and friendly parent-teacher relationships must prevail to the ultimate benefit of the exceptional children whom both are obliged to help.

Chapter 2 explores some of the reciprocal expectations and stereotypes that teachers and parents of exceptional children may hold which can contribute to negative relationships.

The goal of Chapter 3 is to provide the reader with an understanding of exceptional families, particularly of their realities and their means of coping with them. Such issues as family dynamics, stages of acceptance, defense mechanisms, professional attitudes, and parental attitudes, as well as other related topics, are examined.

Chapters 4 and 5 highlight interpersonal factors which contribute to facilitative parent-teacher relationships. Among other topics Chapter 4 discusses: teacher values, the setting of the conference, establishment of goals, interviewing models, the art of listening, barriers to listening, defensive behavior, silences, and termination.

Chapter 5 includes: establishing rapport, nonverbal behavior, helpful teacher leads, attending behavior, paraphrasing, timing, how to and when to be supportive or firm, the proper use of questions, pros and cons of interpretation, home conferences, referring parents, and bibliotherapy.

Chapter 6 covers a series of critical incidents commonly encountered by teachers. The situations depicted in this chapter are included to stimulate discussion and role-playing of these incidents toward the ultimate goal of preventing unproductive and anxiety-ridden relationships.

Chapter 7 addresses in some detail a number of potentially troublesome parent-teacher encounters. The primary aim of this chapter is to explore and understand factors which motivate parents of exceptional children to respond in ways not necessarily apparent during conferences. A second goal is to discuss alternative strategies which teachers may wish to consider in dealing with challenging situations. Ethical concerns in conducting conferences, and teacher burn-out, are also discussed. The latter issue in particular is currently receiving considerable attention.

In the Appendix the reader will find a variety of resources useful to assist parents of exceptional children. These range from information and psychological referral sources to appropriate reading material for exceptional children and their parents.

Acknowledgments

Writing a book may be likened to producing a play. The successful culmination of either endeavor necessitates the aid of persons who are not obvious contributors. For their typing help I would like to thank Mary Jane Alm, Nancy Blatnica, and Irene Petrovich. Drs. Mary Moore and Ralph Peabody and Ms. Mary Garvey often, and with short notice, provided me with important references, and for their help I am most grateful. I am indebted to Drs. June Mullins and Dvenna Duncan for their support and encouragement throughout, and particularly for their conscientious reading of portions of the manuscript and supplying me with constructive and useful comments. Finally, from her perspective as teacher and parent, my wife, Patricia, contributed numerous insights and made herself available during a desperate month when typing assistance was limited—to her go my warmest thanks.

CHAPTER 1

The Teacher as Facilitator

The Teacher as Counselor: A Dilemma

Books designed to acquaint prospective teachers with their roles and specific functions focus on activities related to curriculum and how effectively to communicate subject matter to their students. In recent years, authors have sought to broaden the context within which children may acquire knowledge by suggesting that teachers actively seek the help of parents to extend and enrich learning beyond the classroom. Without question educators are supporting the active involvement of parents in the education of their handicapped child (Calvert 1971; Kelly 1973; Kingsley 1971; Feldman *et al.* 1975; Reynolds and Birch 1977; Losen and Diament 1978).

Few would argue that parental involvement in education is important, if not crucial; however, little effort is being directed toward how teachers might engage parents in coordinated educational endeavors. Although teachers convey subject matter to chil-

1

dren, they have been given little if any training in working cooperatively with parents.

> Unfortunately, many teacher training programs do not provide
> an opportunity to students to learn the skills and techniques of
> conferring with parents. The importance of effective teacher/
> parent relationships can not be overemphasized. Teachers who un-
> derstand the children in their environment can make appropriate
> educational plans in the classroom. Parents who are provided with
> information about the school setting and their child's progress can
> be strong supporters and assistants in the child's educational
> growth and development. Parents and teachers who recognize
> each other's capabilities can join together in successful problem
> solving. [Kroth 1975, p. 155]

Barsch (1968) made the following observations regarding the lack
of expertise available for working effectively with parents of exceptional children:

> One may look hard and long before any listing of courses de-
> voted to understanding of parenthood of a handicapped child is
> found to be a formal part of the professional preparation. Not
> only do professionals from hundreds of university programs hold-
> ing varying and differing orientations enter the fields of rehabili-
> tation and special education each year but they also enter the
> fields with little or no preparation for their encounters with
> parents. [p. 15]

Buscaglia (1975) believes that a gold mine remains untapped
when teachers of exceptional children fail to work with parents:
"Teachers . . . who do not use parents as at least one-third of the
learning team are utilizing only two-thirds of their potential effectiveness" (p. 298). And Reynolds and Birch (1977) contend that
teachers are currently asked to assume a number of roles in relation
to parents:

1. Supervise parents who are employed or volunteer to assist
   teachers.
2. Evaluate the educational progress of pupils and report and interpret the evaluation to parents.
3. Participate with parents in planning and decision making regarding school policies and practices.
4. Consult with parents about the problems of and with their
   children.
5. In effect, *be* the child's parent when it is necessary and proper.
   The teacher role under the doctrine of *in loco parentis* has been

eroding in recent years in a legal sense but remains strong in less formal ways.

6. Explain the work of the schools to parents in general as well as to other citizens in the school area whose taxes support the school.

7. Take part with parents in organizing and conducting general community improvement and maintenance activities. [p. 173]

To add to the multiplicity of roles and responsibilities expected of teachers, Ulin (1977) presents a convincing case for the inclusion of education about death and dying. It is apparent that teachers are sharing or are expected to share many of the responsibilities previously assigned exclusively to parents. This trend may reflect an uneasiness with perceived gaps in adequate parenting and/or suggest that what children learn from their parents can be reinforced and expanded upon in the classroom.

From the perspective of the parent, Leigh (1975), in his review of the literature related to exceptional children and their parents, uncovers an important omission:

Noticeably absent in any type of literature are comparable articles written *for* parents on what to expect from an interview or conference with a teacher. . . . This is especially unfortunate since many parents approach the initial . . . conference with no idea of what kind of questions they will have to answer, or equally important, what questions they can and should ask about their children. [p. 42]

Engaging parents to collaborate *on educational issues* is a concern of some importance and one that is often dealt with effectively, but as Barsch (1969) notes, "What would at first glance appear to be a relatively mechanical, simple encounter is in truth a very complex situation" (p. 12). Dealing with parents *around more problematic concerns* is another issue often subject to considerable frustration and anxiety on the part of both teacher and parent. How this relationship develops has major implications for the following reasons. A "healthy" parent-teacher relationship ultimately affects significantly the future academic and emotional growth of the child. The relationship itself is affected by how the teacher is viewed by the parents, and conversely, how the parents are perceived by the teacher. A constructive, candid, focused encounter (meeting) with a facilitative teacher (supportive, nonjudgmental, interested, and sensitive) can do a great deal toward realizing some of the most ambitious goals for handicapped children and their parents.

The achievement of facilitative relationships with parents often is difficult, and the variables in parent-teacher conferences are many. In unraveling the ingredients of such a relationship, consider the following:

1. the personality of the parent(s)
2. the personality of the teacher
3. the problems presented by the nature of the child's handicap
4. parental reactions to their handicapped child
5. the relationship between the spouses of the handicapped child and between the parents and the child
6. the stereotypes teachers may have of parents of exceptional children
7. the anxieties teachers experience (often related to 6 above)
8. how parents have been received (treated) by other professionals

A teacher may ask, "Am I supposed to be a teacher of children, a 'counselor' of parents, or both?" Given the discussion thus far the response would be "both," with the qualification that teachers should be considered facilitators and not "counselors" as the term is used in a traditional sense. Furthermore, the training of teachers as facilitators to parents must be an integral part of any training program for prospective teachers. In reference to the general climate between parents and school personnel, Feldman et al. (1975) believe that "It is imperative that something be done to alter the negative conditions that have traditionally been present when parents and school officials are together" (p. 551).

It is disheartening to learn that recent publications designed to help regular school teachers work with handicapped students in their classes omit discussion of the importance of parenting in general and parent-teacher conferences in particular. In contrast, McWilliams (1976) builds a convincing case that all professionals who work with children and their parents should be well versed in counseling skills, and Schmid et al. (1977) believe that teachers cannot avoid some aspects of guidance work and urge teachers to become familiar with the rudiments of counseling. Of particular concern is that parents be encouraged to augment the learning that takes place in the classroom. The creative use of parents to further develop and reinforce what children learn in school is receiving considerable support (Reynolds and Birch 1977; Barsch 1969; CEC undated).

No matter how resistant teachers and parents may be to parental conferences, sooner or later the teacher will be faced with parents who carry the burden of the day-to-day responsibility for the care and development of their handicapped child. Since parent-teacher conferences are inevitable and because it would be most desirable to have them often, it is to the teacher's advantage to be adequately prepared. This text, then, is an effort to help teachers deal as effectively with parents of children they teach as they deal with the children.

Parent–Teacher Conferences

A particularly important focus in parent-teacher meetings is on the cooperative *educational* venture, that is, parents and teachers working together on a child's educational program. In this regard, Reynolds and Birch (1977) note that "There is increasing evidence that a child's educational progress is accelerated when teachers and parents work in close partnership . . ." (p. 175).

The educational program generally focused upon during a conference is that which is carried out in the home. The teacher may wish to schedule a conference with parents to generally discuss the child's progress and how to help the child at home or to communicate specific concerns related to the child's behavior, attendance, etc. Conversely, parents may on their own initiative ask for a meeting to discuss the child's progress; to inform the teacher of changes perceived in their child's behavior at home; for support, encouragement, or information; or because they are upset or angry at the school. Other professionals in the school (e.g., the school social worker) may recommend that a meeting be held among the worker, parents, and teacher to discuss problems of which the parent ought to be aware.

Meetings, then, may be initiated by a number of different involved persons for a variety of reasons. Again, adequate preparation for teachers is essential so that they can deal effectively and confidently with parent conferences. Because such conferences are inevitable as well as desirable, time and energy must be devoted to coping with this aspect of the total education of an exceptional child. Reynolds and Birch (1977) put the responsibility for the liaison squarely on the shoulders of the teacher:

> . . . communicating with and guiding parents is now an integral part of the teacher's responsibility. Other school staff members (counselors, social workers, principals, psychologists, supervisors) may assume some of the responsibility, but in the final analysis it is the teacher-parent interaction that is essential. [p. 183]

The reality that parent-teacher conferences are necessary requires the development of facilitative interpersonal skills by the teacher. Acquiring such skills takes determination and commitment as they are numerous and may appear to be difficult to learn (see Chapters 4 and 5). However, providing a supportive and encouraging atmosphere vis-à-vis parents can in itself be truly helpful.

Support and Encouragement

Teachers may be confronted with completely dispirited parents having considerable doubt, confusion, and anxiety about their handicapped child. A troubled parent may enlist the help of a teacher to discuss problems that are indirectly related to a child's performance at school. A parent's reaction to or inability to cope effectively with a handicapped child is often a motivating factor in seeking some source of help. A person may feel embarrassed to engage a qualified psychologist or psychiatrist or be unable to afford one. Easy access to a church-affiliated counselor may not be possible. Other services may not be known to parents, or they may feel that the teacher is most knowledgeable about their child; thus, the teacher may find the distraught parent at her doorstep.

A teacher's initial reaction to parent meetings might justifiably be one of anxiety. For most teachers, this anxiety is rooted in the partially realistic fear that they may not be able to cope with the situation. Through increased understanding of families of handicapped children, the development of facilitative interviewing skills, and the accumulation of experience in parent-teacher conferences, one's initial anxieties will generally give way to understanding, a genuine desire to be helpful within the constraints of one's abilities, and a feeling of comfort in dealing with parents.

Once the teacher achieves some degree of comfort, using the skills acquired she can proceed to work with parents. When parents are obviously distressed, the strategy of actively listening and being supportive and encouraging may be (and often is) all that is necessary. When someone is troubled, often the treatment is an attentive, understanding, nonjudgmental listener. Of course, when it is obvious that some sort of outside intervention is needed, the communication of support and encouragement may be augmented by some concrete suggestions of where assistance may be sought. The suggestion of some sort of therapeutic intervention, for example, should be accompanied by an explanation of why this assistance seems to be necessary. Although some resistance may be encountered when it is suggested that another professional should be consulted, it should be substantially diminished when the referral is made by a competent and understanding teacher.

Effect of Teachers

Until the mid- to late 1960s, in the field of counseling, it was generally thought that counselors and psychotherapists had either a positive influence on their clients or none whatsoever. Eysenck's (1955) landmark rebuttal to a number of research studies which he examined on psychotherapy outcomes revealed that people improved or remained essentially the same regardless of psychotherapeutic intervention. The assertion that psychotherapy had little effect on people shocked the professional community, but the point to be made here is that no mention was made of the possible deleterious effect intervention might have had.

In a later examination of the same studies that Eysenck had reviewed, Bergin (1963) discovered that the statistical variances of the groups that were treated suggested that although some people did indeed improve and others did not change, a number of the treated group actually *declined in their social-emotional adjustment*. This was the first empirically based conclusion that clients under psychotherapeutic treatment may improve, remain essentially unchanged in any significant way, or get worse. Carkhuff (1969), after conducting a number of studies, concluded that as a consequence of therapeutic treatment, client outcomes may be "for better or for worse." Indeed, Truax (1970) extends the above commentary and observes that "the . . . mass of evidence suggests that the therapeutic endeavor is, on the average, ineffective (p. 6)." As

Wittmer and Myrick (1974) note, the idea is frightening that people are harmed in a situation that was theoretically designed to bring about growth. These revelations, along with recent evidence that participants in small psychotherapeutic groups find themselves less well off after than before the experience (Yalom and Lieberman, 1971), has made the counseling profession examine more carefully the variables that account for effective therapeutic change.

Although the effectiveness of counseling has been severely attacked during the past ten to fifteen years, the criticism has served the profession positively. Practicing clinicians and graduate training programs are responding by evaluating counseling outcomes more diligently and by explaining the process by which they are achieved. Interestingly, those who have been most vociferous in their attack on counseling practice and training are the ones who are intensely involved in related research.

What implications do these observations have for teachers? For one thing, the question of teacher effectiveness has to be addressed in a much more serious fashion than it has in the past. The possibility that teachers, like counselors, may have a negative effect on children must be examined, and careful attention must be given to certain characteristics or behaviors that co-vary with effective or ineffective teaching.

A study by Branan (1972) presents some compelling evidence that teachers must be aware of the relationships they establish with their pupils in the classroom. Branan asked 150 college-age students to describe in detail what they considered the two most negative experiences in their lives. Negative experiences were considered to be those that the respondents felt made their lives worse or were a negative force in their development. Responses were divided into two categories: interpersonal and nonpersonal experiences. Two hundred and fifty-seven responses (out of 300) involved interpersonal relationships, and the largest subcategory was interaction with teachers. Recentness of experience was not an important variable; more negative experiences occurred in high school than in college, and more in elementary than in junior high school. Teachers were involved more often than any other persons in the most negative experiences reported, with parents a poor second. Individual situations included humiliation in front of class, unfairness in evaluation, destruction of self-confidence, personality conflicts, and embarrassment. Branan concludes that "human relations training and skill should be as important a prerequisite for teachers as any other requirement. Human relations knowledge and skill should become a prerequisite to teacher credentials at any level. The damage resulting from sarcastic, insensitive, and non-caring teachers at any level must be decreased" (p. 82).

Although it obviously is important for a teacher to be skilled in the methods of instruction, in the past there was an overemphasis on instructional methods and an underemphasis on the development of proper learning climates (atmospheres, or interpersonal relationships) that are related to learning. Recent years have witnessed an increase in publications addressed to the social and psychological impact teachers have on their charges (Brown 1971; Fantini and Weinstein 1970; Kohl 1969; Ringness 1968; Wittmer and Myrick 1974). Nonetheless, university curricula still emphasize teaching methodology, and facilitative interpersonal skills are in some cases tolerated and in others completely ignored.

Even though training institutions and supervisors are lagging behind some of the more innovative and creative thinkers in the field, Replogel (1950) gives us some insight into what those on the firing line, namely teachers, consider to be important but unfulfilled needs: utilizing principles of group dynamics; providing for individual differences; meeting the needs of atypical students; relating the ongoing class activities to the problems, concerns, and tensions of the pupils. It appears that teachers are more concerned about the quality of life in the classroom than those who have the responsibility for training them, although some evidence to the contrary is beginning to appear.

Combs and Soper (1963) revealed that both effective and ineffective teachers felt that the helping relationship was important in the classroom. Most teachers apparently know and can talk about the importance of being a helping person, but according to Wittmer and Myrick (1974), few are capable of putting theory into practice. Based on a number of published studies, Combs *et al.* (1974) conclude that good teachers

1. perceive others as having the capacity to deal with their problems successfully
2. do not regard others as threatening [to themselves] but rather [see them] as essentially well-intentioned . . .
3. see other people as being worthy rather than unworthy
4. see people as creative and dynamic rather than passive or inert

5. regard [people's] behavior as understandable rather than capricious, unpredictable, or negative
6. regard people as important sources of satisfaction rather than sources of frustration and suspicion [p. 63].

Wittmer and Myrick (1974) weren't satisfied with published reports about good versus poor teachers by investigators who used a variety of research procedures but did not necessarily include the perceptions of students. Over a period of four years the authors proceeded to collect open-ended responses from undergraduate and graduate students regarding their experiences with teachers, from which the authors were able to compile lists of adjectives that characterized good and poor teachers.

The following describe the most ineffective teachers:

1. insensitive
2. cold
3. disinterested
4. authoritarian
5. ridiculing
6. arbitrary
7. sarcastic
8. demanding
9. punitive
10. disciplinarian

The effective teachers had the following qualities:

1. good listeners
2. empathetic
3. caring
4. concerned
5. genuine
6. warm
7. interested
8. knowledgeable
9. trusting
10. friendly
11. sense of humor
12. dynamic
13. able to communicate [p. 39]

David Aspy and his colleagues have spent the past ten to twelve years studying the effect teachers who manifest certain characteristics have on their students. Aspy was particularly intrigued with Carl Rogers' conception of the ingredients required for the successful conduct of individual psychotherapy. Rogers believes that if the psychotherapist could communicate high levels of empathy, congruence, and positive regard, constructive personality change would follow. Rogers, by the way, was one of the first prominent theoreticians to put his conception to empirical test. The dimensions of empathy (e), congruence (c), and positive regard (pr) were operationally defined by Rogers, who then proceeded to develop ways to measure them. Others, namely Charles B. Truax and Robert R. Carkhuff, developed even more precise instruments that are currently in wide use.

Empathy may be defined as one's ability to perceive and recognize the inner feelings and experiences of another. It has been characterized as "walking in another person's shoes." In addition to sensing a person's feelings, empathy includes the ability to *respond* to someone else so as to communicate that the nature and intensity of the emotion is understood.

Congruence refers to the consistency between one's beliefs, attitudes, feelings, and values and one's behavior. For example, an illustration of incongruence would be a teacher saying, "I really love working with the parents of the children I teach," yet experiencing considerable apprehension before and during parent conferences.

Positive regard refers to accepting another person unconditionally no matter what his behaviors or characteristics. For example, a teacher is as accepting of a parent who dresses, talks, and has a belief system different from hers as she would be of a parent who more closely resembles her.

Because teaching, like counseling or psychotherapy, resembles a therapeutic meeting or encounter, Aspy was persuaded to use these three constructs to determine the effect low and high e, c, and pr teachers have on their students.

One study investigated the relationship between the teacher's level of facilitative interpersonal conditions (e, c, pr) and the cognitive growth of third-grade students (Aspy 1969). The results indicated that teachers who provide high levels of facilitative conditions tend to increase students' cognitive growth, but those who provide low levels of these conditions may retard learning. A replication of the study confirmed the findings. The data also revealed that low functioning teachers reported significantly more student absences than high functioning ones, which led the authors to speculate that there may be some relationship between school phobia and the interpersonal skills of the teacher.

Another study indicated that students' use of their higher cognitive processes (e.g., problem solving) is significantly and positively related to the teacher's levels of interpersonal conditions (Aspy and Roebuck, 1967). This relationship was particularly strong for positive regard, prompting the authors to speculate that since thinking aloud is a kind of interpersonal risk, a person tends to do it more frequently when he feels valued.

Additional studies by Aspy and others indicate that for teachers to improve in their interpersonal skills they must have supervisors and professors (trainers) who are high in these skills themselves. Trainers whose level of skills is low have a deleterious effect on those they train, just as teachers who have poor facilitative skills have a negative impact on their pupils. This conclusion appears to be as true in teaching as it is in counseling (Carkhuff 1969).

Thus, one might hypothesize that teacher-parent relationships may likewise be positive or negative. Given the fact that teachers receive little formal training in interpersonal processes, and unless one is a naturally gifted facilitator, there is better than an even chance that teachers, on the whole, are relatively ineffective in dealing with parents. Teachers who work with parents of exceptional children, in particular, often are confronted by difficult and complex situations. Hence, the need to develop good interpersonal skills is apparent. Carl Rogers, as quoted by Lyon (1971), makes this point most poignantly.

> Better courses, better curricula, better coverage, better teaching machines will never resolve our dilemma in a basic way. Only persons acting like persons in their relationships with their students [and parents] * can even begin to make a dent on this most urgent problem of modern education. [p. 251]

Administrators' View of Teachers as Facilitators

Perhaps the most potent source of support for teachers are principals and other administrative personnel responsible for the management of a school. The point of view (philosophy or theoretical orientation) of the administration trickles down through the hierarchy to staff and faculty employees. Powerful norms † emerge in

* Words in brackets are the author's.
† "At a group level, norms [or the normative system] are the organized and largely shared ideas about what members should do and feel, about how

a school setting, or any organization for that matter, which reflect the conscious or unconscious desires of the administration.

For the sake of the children, parents, and teachers in any given school, one would hope that administrative support exists for cordial and helpful relationships between the school and parents. It is important for administrators to sanction and indeed encourage teachers to work collaboratively and facilitatively with parents. Such an attitude (or norm, if you will) will do much to further the teacher's feeling that what she is doing is condoned by the school and reinforces the idea that good parent-teacher relationships are beneficial. Lyon (1971) comments:

> If our schools and our educational systems are managed by less than human managers, we can not expect our teachers to be humanistic in their orientation. Accordingly, emphasis on people-oriented management must begin at the top echelons and flow down if it is to have any positive effect on teachers. [p. 251]

Some cues that reveal whether or not a particular school projects a facilitative climate include the following:

1. Is the school a positive and exciting place to be by oneself, to learn, and to be with others?

2. Do the children make positive or negative comments about the school, the teacher, the principal, and themselves?

3. Do teachers and administration discuss their school and the students in a positive fashion, or are there suggestions of a serious morale problem?

4. Does the rapport among teachers and between teachers and the administrator seem poor or good?

In a study using the School Survey of Interpersonal Relationships (SSIR) with 211 elementary and secondary schools in Florida, Wittmer (1971) showed that a school's climate of learning is largely determined by the relationship between (1) the teacher and the principal, (2) the teacher and other teachers, (3) the teacher and other helping personnel, and (4) the teacher and students.

The atmosphere of a school is dependent on the administration, and the central figure in promulgating a facilitative climate for other administrators, staff, teachers, and students is the principal.

---

these norms should be regulated, and about what sanctions should be applied when behavior does not coincide with the norms" (Napier and Gershenfeld 1973, p. 80).

A facilitative principal knows the need for close communication between himself and the teachers. He knows that teachers need support and reassurance. He senses that there is a time to evaluate and a time to respond to feelings as well as ideas and products. He is eager to communicate with teachers in time of excitement and satisfaction, as well as in time of crisis. A facilitative principal has all of the characteristics of a facilitative teacher. [Wittmer and Myrick 1974, p. 150]

Several major studies reveal that the principal has an enormous effect on "schooling," a reality that has only recently gained wide recognition (*The Pitt News* 1978). Blake (1977) singles out the principal for having a major impact on a school's philosophy, stating unequivocally that "The principal is the greatest determinant of the character of the school" (p. 120).

The influence of those who have achieved positions of leadership is, of course, crucial in areas other than education. In a study of the management of 5,000 corporations throughout the country, Likert (1961) analyzed those managers found to be either extremely productive or exceptionally nonproductive. Personality traits or characteristics common to the former and not to the latter were isolated. Managers who were of average or questionable productivity were eliminated from the study. An adaptation of Likert's summary statement might be presented as follows:

Low Producers	*High Producers*
1. production oriented (people considered tools to get the job done)	1. people oriented (people considered to be unique individuals)
2. little two-way personal communication (relatively inaccessible to workers)	2. good two-way personal communication (is accessible to workers)
3. autocratic	3. allows subordinates to participate in decisions
4. poor delegator	4. good delegator
5. punitive	5. relatively nonpunitive
6. identifies with only his supervisors or only his subordinates	6. identifies and relates with *both* his superiors and his subordinates
7. fails to plan ahead	7. plans ahead effectively
8. holds frequent formal meetings	8. holds few formal meetings (not necessary since communications are effective)

9. in time of crisis, pitches in with workers, thereby relinquishing his role as a supervisor

9. in time of crisis, maintains supervisory role

10. workers in his unit feel little pride toward their work groups

10. workers in his unit feel strong pride toward their work groups

11. workers feel their boss is ineffective in his relations with top management

11. workers feel their manager has good communication with top management and can effectively represent their interests

Perhaps the most important lesson to be learned from these characteristics is not whether a principal is deeply committed to the value of parent conferences but whether allowances are made for a diversity of ideas and practices, although Losen and Diament (1978) take a more adamant position: "The choice . . . is not between whether to include parents or to exclude them but whether to include them grudgingly or to develop new strategies for working with parents to achieve important mutual goals" (p. 4). An atmosphere where open communication is valued and innovation and experimentation are encouraged is one that would be conducive to facilitative and positive relationships, from administrators to teachers, to students, and ultimately to parents. A positive atmosphere is particularly critical when teachers are dealing with students who have special problems and when parents, as a consequence of these handicaps, have added burdens which are sometimes brought to the teacher.

Influencing the System

It would be quite proper to initiate a system of rewards for teachers who attend seminars and workshops to increase their interpersonal skills. The reward system, for example, may be tied in directly with evaluations of how effectively teachers deal with parents and/or how open they are to working with parents and on identified weaknesses. Such a program will only work if it has administrative support.

When the administration is authoritarian and oppressive and

considers parents to be nuisances, the teacher may wish to consider ways of convincing the administration and other teachers that working productively with parents of handicapped children is important. Faculty meetings would seem to be a particularly good place for a teacher to discuss parent conferences he has had. An astute teacher can indicate the connection between teacher-parent relationships and a child's academic and social and emotional growth. Of course, the teacher himself must be convinced of this importance if this value is to be communicated without double messages.

Reynolds and Birch (1977) suggest that social modeling is one of the best methods of influencing others when competence and self-confidence are lacking. They encourage teachers who may be reluctant to confer with parents to observe other teachers who have a reputation for conducting effective parent-teacher conferences. After observing a good model for a number of sessions, the teacher ought to ask that same person or someone else she admires and feels comfortable with for supervision as she takes on the responsibility herself.

Tape recordings of sessions can be very helpful to the teacher and will also allow others (teachers and administrators) to take part in "her" conference. This participation is easily accomplished by asking for suggestions or recommendations of colleagues after playing a recording (e.g., "How would you handle this kind of a situation?" or "Can anybody think of any alternative ways I might have handled this situation?"). Admittedly, it would take a courageous person to risk this kind of feedback, but the effort could dissipate whatever resistance existed about working with parents.

In taping a conference, the teacher must be sure to ask the parent(s) if they would mind being taped and discuss with them candidly how the tapes will be used. For example, a teacher could tell the parents that the sessions are being recorded so that she could replay the tape later for learning purposes. If others will be listening to the tape, the teacher must so inform the parents. Taping should never be done without some *training* goal in mind. The information shared between a teacher and a parent is restricted, to be discussed only in the presence of another professional. (This issue is discussed more fully in Chapter 6.)

Another strategy for convincing others of the value of parent conferences would be to involve teachers in the process, for example, by discussing one's conferences with skeptical colleagues.

A teacher's ease in working with parents may well influence her colleagues, resulting in their own attempts to hold parent conferences more often.

Characteristics and Development of the Professional Helper

A popular theory in vocational psychology is that people seek out occupations that fulfill certain psychological needs (Roe 1957; Hoppock 1967), and individuals who enter the helping professions are no exception. Teachers, like counselors, are attracted to their fields because it enables them to gratify their need to be helpful, needed, and appreciated by others. In addition, the need to be seen as knowledgeable, likeable, and having a certain amount of status and influence may be present. On a darker note, authors have speculated that the selection of a person-oriented profession is motivated by the need to know about the private lives of others from a position of authority, or the need to have clients or children make up for the emptiness that characterizes one's personal or social life.

Whatever the need, relatively few in the helping professions are what some refer to as "gifted" or "natural" helpers. Because of one's upbringing, education, or the models present during the developmental years (e.g., parents, teachers, respected peers), a minority of the professionals who work with people have a naturally warm, understanding, and generally easy-going (yet productive) manner. Such people, although they can profit by further sharpening of their interpersonal skills, have little need for extensive training. On the other hand, because of the developmental influences mentioned above, most of us have to work conscientiously at functioning optimally during interpersonal encounters. This need is particularly critical for teachers, who must work effectively with their classes of children, some of whom are handicapped, *and* the parents of these children—a most demanding job.

In summary, three ingredients must be present to help teachers work effectively with exceptional children and their parents: (1) a thorough understanding of the dynamics of families with a handicapped child; (2) a good cognitive understanding of the dimensions of effective interpersonal relationships, combined with opportunities to practice different interpersonal styles; and (3) extensive experience working with parents of handicapped children.

An analysis of family dynamics is presented in Chapter 3; and an extensive discussion, augmented by experiential exercises, of the skills that facilitate human interaction is the content of Chapters 4 and 5. A firm grasp of family dynamics combined with interpersonal skill development will provide the motivation for the third ingredient, namely, frequent, rich, fulfilling, and helpful experiences with parents. No training can take the place of the actual experience of working with parents. As experience accumulates (given a sound foundation), one's effectiveness and feelings of ease will increase.

Before moving into an examination of exceptional families in Chapter 3, Chapter 2 will briefly explore prevailing attitudes teachers have toward students. Particular emphasis will be placed on reciprocal teacher-parent attitudes, and to grasp the nature of such relationships, it is important to be aware of the needs and stresses of both parties. An analysis of what parents and teachers bring to their mutual relationship from historical, psychological, and sociological perspectives should provide a beginning to understanding and coping with a situation that sometimes is fraught with considerable anxiety.

CHAPTER 2

How Parents and Teachers View Each Other

At the risk of oversimplification, we might say that human beings respond to each other out of a combination of reality and stereotyped beliefs. Examples of behavior that reflect objective phenomena (or reality) include overt hostile responses, such as a sharp interchange between two strangers at a football game or fear shown by a snake-phobic person to the sight of a reptile. Responses indicative of attitudes based on stereotypes are represented by ascribing sexual orientations to specific occupational groups and assigning certain attitudes and behaviors to specific ethnic and minority groups or people of different socioeconomic levels.

Perceptions of reality tend to be universal; i.e., many people would perceive a physical assault as an expression of hostility; whereas stereotypes, although they may be held by groups of people, are reflections of more individualized reactions. Stereotypes are largely the product of interactions with significant others during one's formative years, and they may be reinforced by what is internalized from books, movies, radio, and television.

How teachers and students and teachers and parents perceive each other is subject to a complex combination of reality and stereotyped thinking and reactions. Because attitudes are the precursors to behavior, and because behavior often reveals underlying attitudes, it becomes imperative to study reciprocal attitudes held by school personnel and the populations they serve. Particular attention will be given to reciprocal parent-teacher attitudes and how such perceptions influence their relationship. However, this chapter will begin with a brief examination of attitudes teachers have toward students.

Teachers' Attitudes Toward Pupils

A brief overview of this topic should serve a twofold purpose: to ascertain how the attitudes of classroom teachers facilitate or impede learning, and perhaps more crucial to the focus of this book, to determine whether a relationship exists between teacher-held attitudes toward students and those toward parents.

Stern and Keislar (1977) warn that the research in this area spans a wide range of sophistication; some studies reflect questionable reliability and use often inadequate instruments for gathering data.

Although most people would agree a priori that teachers' attitudes toward students have an effect on how students feel about themselves as well as on how they view their academic development, Khan and Weiss (1972) indicate that there is very little direct evidence to demonstrate this relationship. The results of this review may be indicative of the difficulty with which teachers' attitudes and students' reactions can be measured, rather than an accurate representation of what actually occurs: "One cannot help but recognize that teachers do have emotional reactions to certain attributes of students, and that these feelings, or attitudes, predispose them to behave differently to them" (Stern and Keislar 1977, p. 66).

Stern and Keislar note that different attitudes are elicited from teachers by certain attributes of students, the most important being race or ethnicity, socioeconomic status, divergent speech patterns or language, level of ability or achievement, sex, and classroom behavior.

Related to race, there are numerous reports indicating that both white and black teachers have biased attitudes toward black students (Swick and Lamb 1972), and that their attitudes toward Mexican-American students are also extremely negative (Palomares 1970). Black children are described as being more introverted, more distractable, and more hostile than white children, and Mexican-American children are seen by teachers as possessing a negative self-concept.

Students who present behavior problems are treated differently, depending upon whether they come from middle class or poor families (Stern and Keislar 1977). Parent conferences are more generally the rule with students of higher socioeconomic status, whereas with the poor child, more emphasis is placed on punitive action.

Speech is often confounded with race and socioeconomic status, and it has particular relevance to teachers working with exceptional children who have expressive disorders. The literature supports the finding that linguistic attitudes and stereotypes affect teachers' perceptions of students (Cohen and Kimmerling 1971). Furthermore, judgments based on speech characteristics tend to be predictive of how children are graded and assigned to classrooms (Williams *et al.* 1971).

Insofar as ability is concerned, the notion that teachers respond more favorably to students who are represented as "bright"—the so-called Pygmalion effect, or self-fulfilling prophecy—has been subject to serious question, although this remains an unresolved area of study (Stern and Keislar 1977).

There are many studies indicating that sex stereotyping is an important determinant of differential attitudes. Current emphasis on sex equality may bring into question the extent to which previously reported attitudes are still extant. Nevertheless, the evidence accumulated up to recent years indicates that teachers have negative attitudes toward and expectations of boys even before they enter the classroom and that boys received more disapproval than girls (Zach and Price 1973). For the most part, however, students, whatever their sex, who are considered conforming, obedient, compliant, quiet, studious, and passive are generally preferred by teachers (Stern and Keislar 1977).

As Stern and Keislar indicate, the attitude of the teacher has been identified in many studies as the critical variable. Attitudes formed by cultural factors, socioeconomic status, sex, and ability constitute an important consideration in teaching exceptional children. Attitudes that lead to negative expectations are compounded by those generated by deviations from the norm, such as disfigurement, abnormal speaking and walking patterns, and expression of realistic dependency by sensorily handicapped students and those whose learning is impeded. To complicate the situation, these attitudinal predispositions have little chance for change because of existing pressures on the teacher, such as unfavorable class size, disciplinary problems, and inadequate preparation to deal with the wide range of students teachers are required to educate. The problems for teachers are formidable as they are being asked to take on more responsibility, assume added roles, and learn new skills.

In conclusion, it is possible to say with a high degree of certainty that negative attitudes toward students with certain characteristics exist. It is not at all clear, however, how these attitudes affect children academically or psychologically. Attitudes are often subtly expressed, and therefore, their impact is difficult to ascertain. Nevertheless, we can assume that negative attitudes by teachers toward children do little to enhance a child's confidence and self-esteem or his attitudes and accomplishments in academic areas. Moreover, it will become clear that some of the attributes teachers find distasteful in children correspond to the characteristics they find troublesome in parents.

Teachers' Attitudes Toward Parents

Teachers' attitudes toward parents vary but tend to lean heavily in a negative direction. The first step in rectifying these attitudes is to be well informed about the underlying reasons for them, whether they are rational or irrational.

It appears that a relationship exists between negative attitudes toward students and similar ones toward parents of exceptional children. However, rather than finding these parents per se difficult to tolerate, teachers may harbor negative attitudes toward parents who manifest *attributes* similar to those of children they dislike. For different reasons, teachers may have negative attitudes toward aggressive children and parents, where the common denominator is aggressiveness and not the fact that they belong to the group "children" or "exceptional parents." Other common denominators that cut across group identities include speech; sex; socioeconomic status; laziness (noncooperation); and cultural, national, or ethnic affiliation. Additionally, teachers' attitudes may be influenced by other characteristics regarded as deviations from the norm, e.g., emotionally disturbed or mentally retarded parents.

In a remarkably trenchant sociological analysis of the teacher in our society, Lortie (1975) uncovers the vulnerable position in which the teacher is often found. Teachers, Lortie asserts, have discernible reasons to distrust and even fear parents. In America, parents enjoy considerable rights in tending to the educational affairs of their children. Parents may and sometimes do complain to teachers or to administrative personnel about the teacher's performance. Repeated or serious complaints can have a deleterious effect on the teacher's standing within the school system. Lortie points out that teachers have the license to discipline children, but with conditions. Teachers who give vent to anger may fear parental sanctions, not the least of which is a lawsuit. Because of real or perceived threats, teachers do experience a sense of vulnerability which has its roots in reality.

Teachers are required to maintain a social order of democracy and fairness as well as a viable instructional group, often under difficult circumstances. Lortie points out that a parent who asks for special treatment for his child places the teacher in conflict, which is compounded when several parents make contradictory requests. The teacher is forced to choose between a philosophically democratic and fair social order and parental wishes for special attention. A barrage of parental requests make the teacher fear that her social order is beginning to unravel. To make matters worse, teachers are trying to sustain a social order with pupils over whom they have only limited authority.

Teachers are also dependent on parents in that they must rely on them to influence their children in ways the teacher values, namely, to infuse a positive attitude toward schoolwork. Fears are generated by the teacher's awareness that parental influence can range across sentiments of strong help and support to indifference or open hostility (Lortie 1975). How parents choose to influence their children can have an important effect on the students' behavior in the classroom (Luszki and Schmuck 1965), and according to Fox *et al.* (1966), studies have shown repeatedly that when the values of the family and the school are contradictory, the pupil's schoolwork suffers.

In a study reported in 1975, Lortie asked teachers about what they see as ideal parent-teacher relationships. In the study, teachers often depicted parent-teacher conferences as "a waste of time" or as interpersonally awkward. Respondents wanted more contact with parents, but only when their children were having trouble in school. Eighty-eight percent of the teachers in the lower-status elementary schools wanted more contacts with parents, compared with 23 percent of teachers employed in higher-status schools. Parents in lower-status schools often failed to respond to teacher requests for a conference, whereas parents in the higher-status schools often showed up without invitation, a situation not to the liking of teachers.

Lortie's analysis suggests that the desired relationship places the teacher in the superordinate role, where the teacher defines occasions that justify parental involvement. Chronic, spontaneous visitors were characterized by teachers as "academic hypochondriacs worrying and fussing without cause." In other words, teacher-initiated conferences were looked upon favorably, but other parent visits were considered "interruptions."

Teachers' dependence on parents to properly motivate their child clashes with their wish to control the parent-teacher relationship. Even though teachers want to control the relationship, they do not have the status to make parents comply, making their vulnerability genuine.

> The wish to control the workplace is combined with the wish for support from influential others—independence and dependence are contained in a formula based on boundedness and teacher initiation. The teacher's concerns are placed at the center of the ideal relationship; parents should comply with arrangements which meet teacher needs. [Lortie 1975, p. 191]

From Lortie's research and analysis we begin to gain some insight into the underlying causes of tension between parent and teacher. An added confounding influence is the principal. The teacher wants to achieve autonomy from her superior yet requires the principal's protection from overly intrusive parents. This situation throws the parent-teacher-principal triad into a remarkably interlocking and potentially difficult system, with the teacher assuming the pivotal role—a role infused with contradictory needs and desires which require the teacher to choose between alternative resolutions of what must be a perplexing and tension-producing enigma.

In asking teachers to describe the "good parent," Lortie reported that two central themes were reflected in the responses, namely, that parents should not intervene and parents should support the teacher's efforts. "Good parents" were characterized as "distant assistants," by imbuing the child with a positive attitude toward school, cooperating with the teacher yet not interfering, and taking the lead (direction) from the teacher.

Barsch (1969) makes the observation that parents of exceptional children accord the teacher a significantly more positive status than teachers accord parents: ". . . Clinical experience with over 12,000 sets of parents and wide professional experience with many teachers confirm a belief that the parent is more favorable to the teacher than the teacher is to the parent" (p. 8). Bailard and Strang (1964) add that parents are appreciative of the genuine concern teachers show for their children. Shapiro (1975) reports that good teachers are mentioned more often than any other factor when parents explain why their schools are good. He drew the following conclusions from his national survey examining parents' attitudes toward teachers:

> The lesson to be learned from the national survey data is that, when people scan the universe to identify what is helping children's chances for a good life, they are more likely to identify schools than any other agent. Further, when asked to scan the universe to identify what might be hurting their children's chances for a good life, they are quite unlikely to identify schools. . . . [p. 270]
>
> If we can transmit [the public's] faith to beginning teachers, I believe they will feel free to function happily in their professional role, secure in their knowledge of the unique value that society accords them. [p. 273]

This paradox—where the teacher is negatively predisposed toward the parent and the parent is positively predisposed toward the teacher—is, according to Barsch, at the root of many of the problems reflected in negative school-parent encounters.

Moreover, Waller (1961) pointed out that parents and teachers differ in their perception of the child. To the teacher he is one member of the category "student," and to the parent he is a special, prized person. Special considerations for a child, which are sometimes asked of the teacher and emerge from the parents' vantage point that their child is unique and deserving of special attention, run counter to the teacher's perception that he is just another pupil.

Adding to the growth of unfortunate stereotypes is the belief that parents fall into the same general categories as their children; that is, parents of physically handicapped children are somehow different than parents of mentally retarded children, etc. Barsch's (1968) study of child-rearing practices among parents of five different disability populations failed to substantiate the belief that there are significant differences among parents that could be attributed simply to the exceptionality of their children.

Along the same line Bissell (1976) argues that parents are dehumanized by categorical references and generalizations. Parents tend to be cast into two discrete groups: those with normal children and those with handicapped children. Bissell finds these stereotypes of parents to be quite prevalent and surprising at a time when educators are endorsing prescriptive, individualized, noncategorical approaches to education, especially in the education of exceptional children. In referring to his own experiences, he comments:

> [My] initial high levels of anxiety related to a perception of these parents as pathological [which] did not enhance the probability of establishing a climate of positive mutual regard and effective communication. Only through experience was [I] able to learn that each parent is a unique developing individual, and [my] helping efforts were maximized as [I] became able to discard negative perceptions. The cliché's and myths about exceptional parents and techniques for *handling* them were minimized by real experiences with parents as persons. [p. 219]

Teachers may generally feel threatened by professionals, who are perceived as better educated or more intelligent, a problem that often reflects a more generalized sense of inadequacy. Being somewhat in awe of famous or highly educated exceptional parents is not uncommon, but the teacher should keep in mind that these people have the same repertory of coping mechanisms and have similar vulnerabilities as other parents and at times require a teacher's expert counsel about their child and themselves.

Bissell (1976) argues that parents are frequently viewed by teachers from a pathological perspective, i.e., in terms of maladaptive adjustments to their handicapped children, a reality that I attribute in part to the remarkably pathological way parents are characterized in the professional literature. (This topic will be discussed in further detail in Chapter 3.) Further, Bissell observes that parents are seldom viewed as desirable or competent full-fledged members of the interdisciplinary team because their perceptions of their own child are regarded as negligible, or even more negative, are seen as a distortion of reality.

The emergence of parent groups has come to be viewed as a threat to the teacher; they are seen as enemies having tremendous resources and presenting realistic dangers. According to Carberry (1975) and Losen and Diament (1978), parents have traditionally been viewed as adversaries rather than allies.

It is true that parent groups have grown in popularity, and it is a fact that some of these groups have acted assertively in causing positive changes in school programs, and hence, opportunities for exceptional children. Parent groups have been a major force in influencing legislative efforts in the interest of their handicapped children. Most groups have been formed for mutual self-help and are not designed to threaten or cajole anyone, much less the teachers whom parents admire and rely upon.

However, I am also aware of teachers who apparently do not feel threatened by such groups, who show a sincere desire to work cooperatively with parents and voluntarily attend their meetings. The interchange that takes place allows the parent to ask educationally relevant questions of the teacher and enables the teacher to learn about the mechanisms of peer self-help groups and gain a more intimate understanding of the problems exceptional parents experience. Perhaps the most important gain is the parents' perception that teachers care and that parents can be their allies.

A publication by the Council for Exceptional Children notes that it is little wonder why some teachers are afraid to talk to parents (CEC undated). A handicapped child's parents tend to be thought of as "problems" with which the teacher must contend. Some teachers believe that others who have worked with the child and/or the parents contribute to their current problems. Unconsciously, or consciously, teachers may blame parents for causing a child's problems, or at least for not having prevented them.

Just like counselors who, on occasion, are assigned clients they simply do not like, teachers may find themselves in a similar position with parents. Unlike many social service agencies, however, where a transfer can be made to another counselor or social worker, the teacher finds herself in a less flexible position. In such instances, the teacher might try to examine what she and the parents each contribute to evoke her negative feelings. She can be introspective about the relationship or discuss it with a supervisor or colleague.

While recognizing that there are attributes of parents that are difficult to accept, a teacher may wish to consider some of their positive characteristics and try to respond to and reinforce these in parent-teacher meetings, while ignoring their negative characteristics to the extent possible. The opportunity to confer with a colleague or supervisor should always be available to teachers faced with a difficult situation or when a third-party objectivity may be necessary. Intractable negative feelings toward another is somewhat rare, but they do arise and should be considered normal. Instead of dealing with the parent in a hostile, negative fashion, and/or allowing herself to develop excessive guilt feelings about her negative reactions, the teacher might consider these alternatives in taking an active role toward resolving an uncomfortable situation.

Reynolds and Birch (1977) note that teachers are often asked to assume several different roles in relation to parents. These roles, which are in addition to and augment the pedagogical role they have traditionally held, include supervising parent aides, evaluating student progress and conveying the information to parents, working with parents on school policy and in developing community activities, and acting as the child's "parent" during the school day. Whether teachers assume all these roles or take on other responsibilities, it is obvious that additional pressures have been placed on them in recent years. In authoritarian, nonsupportive climates, in particular, teachers may react strongly against assuming added responsibility—an attitude that ultimately affects their relationships with students and parents. In more supportive settings, people tend to work cooperatively toward productive ends. In any case, overwhelming burdens and pressures may be an important cause of negative reactions to parents. In such instances, parents may be seen as an added pressure, consuming inordinate amounts of time and energy, resources that the teacher feels she can ill afford. (Hetznecker *et al.* 1978):

> Educators find themselves in a psychological squeeze. They are required to be more "accountable" for the effectiveness of programs; they are subject to pressures by local communities and by state and federal attempts to establish standards of quality and equality. At the same time, they find themselves increasingly burdened with responsibility for basic socialization for children, and experience frustration, discouragement and anger over what they view as an abdication of responsibility by parents. [p. 364]

Parents have a mix of positive and negative emotions toward their handicapped child, and the teacher should be accepting of these contradictory, yet normal, human feelings. Although teachers may find burdensome a parents' gloomy outlook, ambivalent feelings, or occasional acute bouts of depression, it is important for them to recognize and allow for contradictory feelings and actions and not regard them as "bad" or abnormal. Our culture guards well the reality that *all* parents harbor mixed feelings about their children, fostering the myth that our feelings are only positive.

Clearly, teachers' attitudes toward parents are unhealthy. The combined factors of working with genuinely difficult parents; added roles, pressures, and responsibilities teachers have been asked to assume; and negative stereotypes which have developed over the years result in attitudes that impede rather than facilitate rapport between parents and teachers. I believe that concerted efforts must be made by school personnel to recognize this situation, and supervisors and educators must develop (in college and university teacher-training programs and in in-service meetings) strategies that will change it.

The first step, then, is accepting the existence of these attitudes; recognition of a problem generally provides the impetus or motivation for subsequent change. The second step is the implementation of strategies designed to modify attitudes—admittedly not an easy task but one that must be undertaken. The exercises included in this text should prove helpful.

Teachers' Attitudes Toward Change

In recent years the field of education has embarked on a new venture, namely, the appropriate education of exceptional children in regular public school classrooms. This trend has implications for special as well as regular schoolteachers—a trend that is being met with a mixed response. As with other innovations in education, the teacher is rarely consulted or considered but is merely informed of anticipated changes and required to attend brief workshops in which the new ideology or methodology is expounded (Stern and Keislar 1977). The general disregard for the feelings of the teacher, combined with a tendency for people in general to resist major changes in their personal or professional lives, has major implications for how current mandated changes will be carried out.

Teachers' attitudes toward new programs tend to be well received when certain conditions are met. Attitudes toward such relatively recent innovations as open education (based on the British primary schools), voucher systems, performance contracting, and individualized instruction were more positive than expected, although variations in receptivity were noted (Stern and Keislar 1977).

The resistance and trauma connected with the mainstreaming of exceptional children in our public schools require immediate and intensive study. This problem has become particularly acute since the passage of Public Law 94–142 (The Education for All Handicapped Children Act), which reinforces our national commitment to a free and appropriate education for every handicapped child. Attitudes toward new ideologies and programs have a direct bearing on their effectiveness when they are implemented. Thus, how regular schoolteachers feel about having exceptional children in their classrooms, and how special-education teachers feel about their changing roles, are areas that should be subject to investigation now and in the coming years.

In realizing constructive attitudinal change toward new programs, it is imperative that we do not follow the same unproductive practices used in attempts to change teachers' attitudes toward student characteristics. The brief workshop falls far short of achieving fundamental changes in ideology and behavior (McCauley 1972). Successful implementation of organizational changes is a gradual, long-term process in which the new ideology and its accompanying strategies are the subject of ongoing interaction. Equally important in this process is the opportunity for teachers to express their feelings, without threat, and be given the chance to provide input into new and developing programs. The likelihood of success of new programs and positive teachers' attitudes are immeasurably greater if the principal is supportive and provides a positive model for staff and faculty (Stern and Keislar 1977). Administrative support of parent involvement in the schools is so important that it bears repeating. Glass (1969), psychiatric consultant to the schools in Baltimore, Maryland, advises,

> One of the important factors of getting parents into the school is to develop a climate within the school—that is, within the faculty—that will be favorable towards the parents, an atmosphere

that will encourage parents to participate. The development of this climate is the responsibility of the administrator and his representatives. [p. 167]

It is essential to recognize that beliefs developed over many years do not dissipate by mandate but may be subtly altered over time and under conducive circumstances. Attitudinal changes toward changes in organizations or programs appear more likely and easier to accomplish than firmly held attitudes toward other people.

> With reference to the general issue of effecting teacher attitude change, it should be pointed out that even in the most strongly held beliefs about organization, methods, and content of instruction, there is far less resistance to modification than when deep-seated emotional feelings are tapped. Attitudes toward children from different religious and racial groups, from different cultures and environments, are based on the teachers' own lifetime history of conditioning and are far more impervious to short-term, superficial training models. [Stern and Keislar 1977, p. 73]

Parents' Attitudes Toward Teachers

We will recall Barsch's (1969) observation that teachers view parents much more negatively than parents view teachers. Although parents have made complaints about and widely hold negative attitudes toward professionals in general, teachers tend to be spared (see Chapter 3). This is not to say that parents' attitudes toward teachers are uniformly positive, as the following discussion will reveal.

Rowe (1978) hypothesizes that unconscious transference * occurs in the parent's relationships to the professional. For example, the parent may transfer feelings he still has for important figures in his childhood. Some parents, seeing the teacher as a parent, may try to take the role of the dependent child by trying to please or placate her. Parents may present themselves to teachers with an unconsciously rebellious or hostile attitude that is really an expression of unresolved feelings for their own parents.

---

* Transference is the reenactment of previous relationships with other people, principally of the parent-child relationship (Shertzer and Stone 1974, p. 213).

Also, parents may view teachers as solely imparters of information to children and may, therefore, balk at scheduled parent-teacher conferences. If teachers are seen only in this role, parents could well be puzzled by comments they make about the child's emotional responses and classroom behavior. Such narrow perceptions of a teacher's role generally diminishes as the parent gains a clearer perception of his multifaceted responsibilities; most parents probably would find considerable comfort in knowing that the teacher is keenly aware of their child's development from more than just an academic point of view.

Some parents' perceptions are colored by unfortunate professional encounters in the past. These parents will approach the teacher with caution to see if prior experiences will be repeated. Such parents will be relieved and able to change their preconceived attitudes in the company of a facilitative ally.

Lortie (1975) notes that teachers may be seen by parents as competitors if the values they emphasize do not coincide with the parents' own. In such an instance, parents may feel undercut in their efforts to raise their child, and they envy the teacher who excites the child's affection and respect. This reaction may be particularly true of parents whose sole source of emotional gratification is their exceptional child. If the teacher senses competition for the child's attention from the parents, the issue should be addressed as soon as possible. The teacher might mention the child's comments about his parents or objects he made for them (birthday or Christmas gifts) to reinforce the critical role they play in his life. It might be well to point out that children tend to talk about their teachers in their parents' presence, and that it is not uncommon for the child to speak proudly of his parents in the classroom. Another possibility is the involvement of the parents in the child's education, thereby decreasing their feelings of competition.

As mentioned earlier, the parent-teacher relationship as well as student learning is greatly enhanced when parents convey to their children positive attitudes toward school. Conversely, parents who have bitter memories of school and communicate their unsympathetic attitudes to their children can have an adverse effect (Rainwater et al. 1959).

Another source of parents' negative or cautious attitudes toward teachers was noted by Naegle (1956), who observed that students reveal much of the inner life of families, both in their behavior and in conversation. Parents may wonder about and be threatened by the revelation of family secrets, especially in this era of open communication and affective education.

An inflated view of the teacher's ability could result in parental demands and expectations the teacher is unprepared and unable to fulfill. Teachers may be perceived as counselors and psychotherapists, capable of dispensing advice about significant psychological problems (Meadow and Meadow 1971), or as clergymen or attorneys of sorts, qualified to advise about religious or legal matters. There will be times when a teacher is in a position to provide support and comfort, and occasions will arise when direct advice is appropriate, but a teacher should be careful to stay within the boundaries of her competency.

Barsch (1969) believes that parents of handicapped children tend to view their child's teacher as well trained and assign her the prestige of a "specialist." Barsch finds this an interesting paradox, as teachers generally view the parents they work with negatively.

Age-old concerns about proper child-rearing practices may emerge as parents come to know the teacher's style of interaction with children. Methods of discipline that the parent practices at home will probably be the ones the parent wishes to see the teacher use in school. Permissive parents may be appalled by the teacher's use of what they consider to be harsh disciplinary methods, whereas strict parents will be puzzled by the permissiveness with which their child is treated at school. In either case, the teacher should be prepared to explain to the parent the potential benefit of her approach. This effort should lessen the parents' concern, as they will then view the teacher as one who has a well-thought out strategy and is willing to share it, thereby opening the channels of communication and forming the basis for a feeling of mutual respect. Teachers should be careful of believing that withholding information from parents is a sign of professionalism.

In their sincere desire to motivate parents to help their child, teachers may make impossible demands, which can cause discouragement and despair and lead to what Meadow and Meadow (1971) refer to as "parental paralysis." Insensitivity to the resources of the parent is counterproductive.

The teacher should maintain continuous awareness of how he or she may be perceived by the parents. Parents may, for example, react with anxiety and begin to develop negative attitudes toward the teacher as a result of a previous meeting. It is difficult for a teacher to know how a particular comment will be received, although sensitive teachers with good interpersonal skills rarely make potentially destructive comments. Nevertheless, a teacher may have inadvertently and without malice touched upon a particularly sensitive area or made a comment that was misconstrued. In either event, a change in the parents' typical way of interacting may signal that something has gone amiss. The teacher should make an inquiry at this point instead of waiting until negative attitudes or feelings become more intransigent and it becomes increasingly difficult for either teacher or parent to broach the issue.

Barsch (1969) makes the important distinction between parents who knew early of the child's exceptionality and have become accommodated to the situation as opposed to parents who are just beginning to realize their child's limitations. Such dawning awareness is not necessarily a reflection of denial now giving way to reality but of the emergence of more obvious manifestations of impaired development not apparent during earlier years.

Although professional helpers must allow for individualized expression of stress, the teacher might expect the "accommodated" parent to be less questioning, less fearful, less confused, and probably more confident than the newly aware parent. The latter may require more support from the teacher as well as honest and understanding responses to his questions.

Being aware of the parents' position in the denial-acceptance continuum (discussed in Chapter 3) should help the teacher anticipate feelings and behaviors that correspond to a particular stage and respond to them accordingly. This behavior should predispose parents to view the teacher in a more positive fashion. By the same token, the teacher must be aware that her best predictions may turn out to be wrong and that she must remain open to unanticipated experiences.

Negative parental attitudes may not be directed toward the teacher but reflect what *the conference* may mean to the parent. As mentioned previously, negative meetings with other professionals predispose parents to view subsequent conferences with apprehension. Parents may feel concerned that the conference will deal only with the child's weaknesses—deficiencies that are painfully apparent and that the parent does not wish to have validated by still another professional. There will probably be more cooperation from parents and better attendance at conferences if they are balanced to reflect both strengths and deficiencies. The teacher should try not to barrage parents of significantly impaired children with a laundry list of their problems. Such conferences can have a devastating effect on the parent psychologically and can destroy whatever rapport the parent and teacher may have developed.

In team meetings where other professionals may be present (e.g., school psychologist, social worker, occupational therapist, speech therapist), special efforts must be made to keep the conference in perspective. Because hearing about the child's limitations from each of the professionals represented at the meeting may be more than a parent can endure, the meetings must be conducted with sensitivity and good judgment. The communication of negative or delicate material should be done on a one-to-one basis, allowing parents to meet with someone with whom rapport has been established.

Parents who have had life-long problems with authority figures may have negative attitudes toward the teacher before they ever meet. The anxiety generated by conferring with yet another authority (in this case the teacher) could result in one of two contradictory reactions: taking the offensive (directing angry remarks to the teacher) or withdrawing (not attending scheduled parent-teacher conferences). In the first instance, the parents' anxiety and anger should diminish in the presence of a professional who does not reciprocate in kind. In the second, the parents' courage may be summoned by a teacher who, perhaps more than once, warmly invites them to meet with her.

Reynolds and Birch (1977) and Duncan (1977) believe that the parent-teacher relationship is greatly improved when both parents are present at the conference. In this way both mother and father are involved, and the chances for distortion of what occurred are minimized. Granted, sex roles are less rigid now than in the past; however, in many families the mother is still considered the one who is responsible for the basic needs of the children—which includes schooling. Therefore, the teacher should not be surprised if only the mother attends the conference.

It should be noted that a spouse's reluctance to attend a conference may be more related to anxieties about the child than a reflection of sex-typed behavior.

Gently urging the parent to bring her spouse to a subsequent conference is to be encouraged. But if the teacher senses that there is considerable resistance, the matter should be dropped, at least temporarily. Although some liberated teachers may rail at the rather stereotyped and rigid role behavior manifested in some families, it is essential that the parents' life style and role structure be respected.

Special consideration should be given to the single parent exceptional family. Reliance on the teacher for support and help may be heavy because single parents must necessarily assume greater responsibility for themselves and their offspring. Also, as Schlesinger (1969) points out, the single parent structure is a minority one with which our society is ill equipped to deal effectively. The minority status of being a single parent is compounded by that of being a parent of a handicapped child—a dual burden that may be overwhelming psychologically.

Foster parents and adoptive parents would hold attitudes toward the teacher similar to those discussed in this chapter, but their special relationship to their children may generate problems of a slightly different nature. For example, foster parents generally keep the child for a particular period of time; thus, the parents' involvement may be more marginal. On the whole, foster parents genuinely care for the children they accept into their family. However, the teacher should be watchful of neglectful foster parents whose motive is to provide a home for the child is more closely related to monetary gain than genuine affection. Although it is not always the case, often parents who voluntarily accept a handicapped child into the family unit do so with considerable knowledge of the problems that lie ahead. Such parents should prove to be cooperative and helpful and generally to harbor few negative attitudes.

Some negative attitudes seemingly directed toward teachers have little to do with either the teacher or the conference per se. Parents may feel intimidated by the educational discrepancy between them and the teacher, and as a result, they may approach the conference with a feeling of inferiority. Barsch (1969) asserts that this factor may cause the parent to be less open during conferences. However, as the parent-teacher relationship evolves, parents should feel more comfortable in the teacher's presence as they sense her nonjudgmental attitude. Skillful teachers who can communicate a feeling of positive regard irrespective of the parents' personal qualities eventually gain the trust of the people with whom they work. It should be noted that positive regard which is expressed unconditionally (that is, no matter what the person's attributes) is an important characteristic for helping professionals to have. It may be learned over time, but it is used more easily if a person has internalized early the philosophy that people who are different in a variety of ways have worth (Rogers 1942). In this sense, unconditional positive regard is more a component of one's personality than an easily acquired skill.

Age differences initially may be viewed by parents in a negative manner. A recently graduated young teacher conferring with older parents may cause them some consternation during the first few sessions. However, the teacher's rapport with the parents as well as the demonstration of her expertise will reduce their preoccupation with age differences. In rare instances, parents may continue to regard a young or young-appearing teacher as a "learned daughter." Actually, this perception is not at all negative, as long as the parent remains cooperative and the primary focus is on the child's development.

Interestingly enough, age differences can constitute more of a problem for the teacher than the parents. Perceiving the parent as his older and more knowledgeable mother can be a source of difficulty to the teacher. In countertransference * terms, some teachers may view and react to the parent as they responded to their harsh and demanding mothers or fathers, especially if the parent possesses some similar characteristics and mannerisms. A helpful strategy for teachers is to continually separate, at a cognitive level, the exceptional parent from their own parents. The teacher might say something like, "Although they are older and have some similar characteristics [to my parents], they are, after all, *not* my parents but people who have come to me as a professional." Because such countertransference is sometimes resistant to change, professional psychotherapists are required during their training programs to engage in personal therapy so that previous reactions to significant others do not interfere with their efforts to help their clients.

Not only can parents and teachers differ in their perceptions of proper disciplinary strategies, but also each party may experience different "truths" about a particular child. (Hetznecker *et al.*

---

* Not only do parents transfer conflicts with past figures onto their relationships with the teacher, but also the teacher does likewise with the parent. These feelings of the teacher for the parent are called countertransference. Ideally, the teacher should be totally aware of them so that they do not interfere with the relationship. The negative aspect of countertransference is that the teacher is not able to understand the parent objectively because of his own conflicts and needs. But by monitoring the feelings the parent elicits in him, the teacher can often gain an understanding of the conflicts facing the parent and thus can better appreciate how the parent affects other people.

1978). Chances are, parent and teacher are both right, and wrong. Ritualized, time-limited conferences do not allow for the interchange leading to perceptual modifications, compromise, and a more accurate and comprehensive picture of the child. A richer perspective can be obtained if the teacher learns more about the child at home and the parent learns more about the child in the classroom. Different perceptions of the child need not end in controversy but should culminate in a better understanding of the child's world, which encompasses more than just school or home.

In their efforts to get parents more interested and involved, teachers and principals may launch an aggressive program to achieve better home-school relationships. Such an attitude and enthusiasm can hardly be criticized, yet a few precautions are necesary. Overeager teachers may actually generate negative attitudes if parents feel pressured into greater school involvement or more frequent parent-teacher conferences. Such feelings generally stem from the way in which parents are approached. Frequent notices brought home by the child, "reminder" phone calls, or letters mailed to the parent should be avoided. Notes or letters should only be sent occasionally and be written in a way that would allow parents to feel invited but not coerced or made to feel guilty. The same is true of phone calls.

Conversely, school personnel may become disheartened if they perceive that their enthusiastic effort born of genuine concern has seemingly reaped few benefits. Too often, excessive enthusiasm leads to rather grandiose expectations and then discouragement. Too much is anticipated too soon. As Glass (1969) suggests, school personnel should savor the gains they have made, whether large or small, and build on what has been accomplished. A lesson that has been poorly learned by many professional helpers is that change in the attitudes and behaviors of human beings is often painfully slow.

Parents' perception of teachers, the school, or schooling constitute a varied tapestry of attitudes and expectations. On the whole, parents tend to value their child's teacher as one who is generally knowledgeable, a specialist in working with children, and a source of encouragement and support. With the exception of a minority of exceptional parents considered to be difficult to work with, they constitute a formidable ally for the teacher in the teaching-learning enterprise.

CHAPTER 3

Understanding the Dynamics of Families with an Exceptional Child

Insights into family dynamics help the teacher make a more realistic appraisal of the exceptional child and his family, their enormous burdens, their coping mechanisms, and the strengths that sustain them through crises. Also, such knowledge helps the teacher understand parental reactions that might otherwise appear to be strange, unreasonable, and at times, incomprehensible.

Some Basic Principles of Family Dynamics

Just as a physical insult to the body or a severe psychological shock can impede an individual's development, an event of major proportions can have a similar effect on a family. Families, like individuals, progress through various stages, and many interacting factors help fashion a family's response to events—a response that may interfere with normal family development. Also, the family unit is not a singular entity reacting as one to external stimuli but an interacting, interdependent group of individuals. An event that affects one member also either directly or indirectly affects the others. Moreover, the family is not a closed group, existing in isolation, but an open system relating to other such systems in the total transactional field (Bell and Vogel 1960).

Role changes may affect a family unit. Consider how social roles may be altered as a consequence of the following events:

1. the first baby born to a man and wife
2. father laid off from work and mother forced to secure job for financial reasons
3. coddled daughter greeted by demanding newborn sibling (Alfred Adler referred to this phenomenon as the "dethroning" of the first born.)
4. divorce—impact on both parents and children
5. death of a father or mother
6. grandparent joining (living with) the family

Other important aspects of family dynamics are decision-making processes, dominance behavior, conflict resolution, social behavior, social status, and need for upward mobility (discussed in detail in Turner 1970). In complex ways, these aspects influence how a significant event will be perceived and dealt with, or conversely, how the event will contribute to the modification of certain family processes.

An important aspect of family dynamics is the notion of social roles, defined as a goal-directed pattern or sequence of acts tailored by the cultural process for the transactions a person may carry out in his social group or situation (Spiegel 1957). Each position involves roles relative to other positions in the network as determined by cultural expectations and values. For example, a mother enacts certain roles and holds certain role expectations from her children and husband. The fluidity of roles that increasingly characterizes society today makes role expectations more difficult to predict.

Social roles do not exist in isolation but tend to compliment the role of someone else or fit into the role structure of a group (or family).

As long as the role each family member occupies is complementary with and conforms to the role expectations other members have for him, the family lives in dynamic equilibrium. As soon as a discrepancy occurs, however—that is, when two or more family members have conflicting or incompatible notions on how to play their reciprocal roles—complimentarity fails and the role system moves toward disequilibrium. Such disequilibrium is experienced by the family members in the form of tension, anxiety, hostility, or self-consciousness and individuals will try to deal with these reactions in a variety of ways. [Ross 1964, p. 7]

Defense Mechanisms

An understanding of how human beings cope with stressful situations represents an important dimension for understanding families with an exceptional child. In this overview of defense mechanisms, reference will be made as to how they relate to problems faced by exceptional parents.

The Psychiatric Dictionary defines defense mechanisms as "the means by which the organism protects itself against impulses and threats" (Hensie and Campbell 1970, p. 182). To put it another way, defense mechaisms help one to cope with excessive anxiety. Anna Freud (1948) discussed in some detail the defense mechanisms in common use today. It is of some importance to note that these mechanisms sometimes serve in a positive way to lessen anxiety; at other times, they interfere with an objective appraisal of a situation or event and, therefore, hamper its resolution. The double-edged nature of man's defenses (or coping mechanisms) against anxiety will become clearer in the following discussion.

Situations that generate unacceptable impulses or anxiety are sometimes perceived as if they have their source outside the self. The defense mechanism that projects blame to an external source is called *projection*, where an action or behavior is attributed to another person, group, or institution. Ross (1964) explains that the use of projection by parents of exceptional children, by thrusting blame for the child's condition onto sources outside the self, is a defense against unconscious guilt. The unconscious guilt may be related to realistic or less realistic factors that the parent believes are related to the child's handicap. The physician may be the object of the projection, or the source of blame may be something less tangible, like heredity or poverty. The ambiguity of not being able to pin a child's exceptionality on a particular cause allows it to be ascribed to a host of causes and results in fantasies about the probable cause or whether it could have been prevented (Hollings-worth and Pasnaw 1977).

It has been suggested that in looking for someone to blame, parents may blame each other, a grandparent, the school, or the teacher (CEC undated), although doctors make convenient scape-goats during the infant years. Unconscious guilt at not spending more time with a child or not helping with academic subjects may be converted into blaming the teacher for a child's slow progress. In such an instance, denial (another defense mechanism, to be discussed below) may be operating in conjunction with projection. In sensing that parents may be projecting blame on the teacher or the school, the teacher might try to help them understand that her main interest is not in *why* the child is not learning but in how to help them overcome the handicap to the extent possible.

Bibring *et al.* (1961) define *denial* as "Literally seeing but re-fusing to acknowledge what one sees, or hearing and negating what is actually heard . . ." (p. 65). Ross (1964) adds:

> Denial is one of the more primitive defenses against the threat-ening recognition of the discrepancy between the hoped-for healthy baby and the reality of the defective child. Parents will try to establish the myth that there is nothing wrong with the child and since this pretense serves to protect them from anxiety, they must try to maintain the myth against great odds. [p. 62–63]

Parents are often reinforced in denying their child's handicap by professionals. Because of the professionals' own anxieties against which they must defend, they may hedge on accurately communi-cating the severity of the problem, be unrealistically hopeful, or promise unattainable cures. Parents, aided by well-meaning but misguided professionals, secretly hold on to the magical belief that the problem will somehow go away or that the child will grow out of it. Shopping around for a favorable diagnosis is caused by parent denial, which is often reinforced by the professional's in-ability to deal honestly with parents of exceptional children.

Gorham *et al.* (1975) point out that a physician's training in the care of exceptional children and their parents is minimal. They assert that the physician is a professional, but also human, and un-derstandably uncomfortable with the situation. The physician often seeks refuge from his anxiety by pronouncing his diagnosis and terminating his responsibility for and involvement with the parents, often by referring the child and parents elsewhere. This is often the parents' first exposure to rejection, a harsh reality to confront, especially from one perceived to be intimately involved with human problems.

From the perspective of the child's development, denial has two counterproductive consequences: On the one hand, parents may overprotect their child, keeping him out of situations that would help in the normalization process. For the parents, such exposure poses the threat that their child's defect will become glaringly obvious to others and, of course, to themselves. On the other hand, denial may lead the parents to exert tremendous pressures for achievement on the child, leading to frustration for both child and parents. Such pressure may lead to subsequent emotional problems, which further complicate the child's condition.

The Council for Exceptional Children cautions teachers that what sometimes appears to be denial may in fact reflect the parents' accurate perception. Because of their closeness to their children and their opportunities to observe them, their perception of what might be contributing to their child's problem may be accurate. Therefore, careful, nondefensive listening by the teacher is essential. By the same token, if the teacher is convinced that it is important that parents be more aware of an aspect of their child's exceptionality, she might consider inviting them to visit the classroom to observe. Concerning denial, the teacher should remember the following:

> They [parents] do this, not because they are mean or unfeeling, but because they have no way of dealing with the hurt and hopelessness they feel when they think of their child. If you think the parents are rejecting their child—if they are too busy to talk about his problems or seem unconcerned about his progress—try to remember they may be unhappy people. Sometimes it is a stage parents go through when they learn of a child's disability, but if it continues, they will need more help than you can give. [CEC undated, pp. 4–5]

Rationalization is a word often used (at times beaten to death) by professionals and the public. It "means justification, or making a thing appear reasonable, when otherwise its irrationality would be evident. It is said that a person "covers up," justifies, rationalizes an act or an idea that is unreasonable and illogical" (Hensie and Campbell 1970, p. 645). Tied into the mechanisms of denial and projection, rationalization provides the "solution" for an undesirable situation; for example, a parent may inform the teacher that his son is behind in his classwork because he is going though a developmental stage, when the evidence clearly points to mental retardation. Or in scoring significantly below what he expected on an examination, a college student may rationalize as follows:

> I didn't do well on the examination because I didn't hit the sack until 2 o'clock last night. Also, the examination room was so hot that I had trouble concentrating.

This rationalization may have a grain of truth in it. Nevertheless, one can see how it helps the individual avoid the possibility (and concomitant anxiety) that the low examination score may reflect his lack of preparation or, even more devastating, that the material was too difficult for him to grasp.

Bibring *et al.* (1961) define *intellectualization* as "a systematic overdoing of thinking, deprived of its affect, in order to defend against anxiety attributable to an unacceptable impulse" (p. 68). That is, anxiety is warded off by verbal excesses, especially in situations where strong emotions (affect) are aroused. There is a qualitative difference between intellectualization and being intelligent, with the former referring to a coping mechanism and the latter being an indication of one's potential.

Strong impulses, generally of an aggressive or sexual nature and considered to be unacceptable to society, are, at an unconscious level, deflected into socially acceptable, constructive activities. Gratification of a socially objectionable impulse in a socially valued outlet characterizes the defense mechanism of *sublimation.* For example, having the impulse to aggressively strike back at the perceived sources of a child's lack of academic or therapeutic alternatives in the community, a parent of an exceptional child may help form a citizens group dedicated to the orderly and legal pursuit of expanded opportunities for exceptional children.

Ross (1964) defines *repression* as

> . . . the mechanism through which unacceptable and threatening psychological content is kept from conscious awareness. Repressed activities, impulses, and conflicts which are thus excluded from consciousness are not eliminated and they continue to cause stress which may become expressed in various indirect symptoms. Because of the continuing threat posed by repressed material, other defense mechanisms are called into play, making repression the mechanism which is central to many other psychic operations. [p. 53]

Thus, repression keeps impulses and events that cause excessive anxiety essentially hidden (unconscious); and yet, according to psychoanalytic theory, content that falls into the unconscious is manifested in some way, e.g., through denial, projection, or sublimation.

"Repression" and "suppression" are often used interchangeably, even though they are significantly different. *Suppression* is the act of *consciously* inhibiting an impulse, idea, or emotion—a *deliberate* attempt to forget something. In talking with a parent who wishes to suppress an uncomfortable thought, one might hear something like the following: "I realize that Tommy won't ever be able to walk like other children. I find this so upsetting that I don't want to think or talk about it."

Kicking the family dog after an unnerving day at the office is the popular characterization of *displacement,* the shifting of an impulse from one source to another in order to "solve" a conflict and avoid anxiety. The impulse (e.g., feeling angry and acting aggressively) does not change, but the direction of the impulse is deflected (e.g., kicking the dog instead of asserting oneself with one's boss, the real source of anger).

Deflected impulses are not always directed to an external source but are sometimes turned against oneself. Ross (1964) notes that impulses turned inward find expression through bodily symptoms, a mechanism called *somatization,* and sometimes take the form of excessive self-blame. For example, after an emotionally laden meeting with the principal, a teacher may incorrectly assume the blame and responsibility for a situation that objectively is not her fault. This teacher may be particularly susceptible to guilt and self-blame and often feels at fault for situations not of her doing.

A response, albeit generally a temporary one, to an uncomfortable situation is to withdraw. *Withdrawal,* a fairly common and normal reaction to a threatening situation, can become a characteristic way of responding, a signal that professional help is needed. In order not to face a painful evaluation of their child, for example, parents may absent themselves from parent-teacher conferences. More often than not, however, parents will summon the needed courage to attend scheduled meetings, believing that no matter how uncomfortable, it is a situation that must be faced in the interest of their child. Chronic withdrawal, however, indicates that excessive anxiety may be present.

A Handicapped Child in the Family:
Expectation, Reality, and Reaction

It is inevitable that a parent about to give birth has a host of expectations, not the least of which is the anticipation of a child with all the attributes of normality which will enable him to assume the roles generally ascribed by society. Although expectations vary, deepnding on a multiplicity of factors, parents tend to expect that their child will achieve at least as much as they have been able to accomplish in their lifetime. Writing of parental reactions to children born with severe brain defects, Baum (1962) cites Kozier in observing that

> In many ways, a child represents to the parent an extension of his own self. . . . When the baby is born the mother's wish to be loved is partially transferred from her own person to that of the baby. To the father, a normal child is often an affirmation, at least in part, of his sense of success. The capacity to produce unimpaired offspring is psychologically and culturally important for the parents' sense of personal adequacy. [p. 385]

The ritual performed shortly after birth of counting fingers and toes reflects an underlying fear of most parents that the infant may have been born defective. Although this fear is expressed in subtle and camouflaged ways, the counterbelief that "It can't happen to me" is also present. When the parents' expectations of a healthy, normal child are contradicted by the birth of a handicapped one, their coping mechanisms are severely put to the test. Coping tends to be a complicated process in that the developmental sequence of stressful events is cyclical, but the effect on the parents may be both cyclical and cumulative.

The more immediate biological role of the mother in the birth process may endow the discrepancy between expectation and reality with greater psychological meaning for her than for her husband. After all, it is the mother who "produced" the infant, and therefore, it is the mother who may experience severe feelings of guilt, remorse, and lowered self-esteem.

Although it is not clear whether or how the birth of a handicapped infant affects mothers and fathers differently, the shock renders both parents physically and psychologically vulnerable.

During this period, their ability to recognize, evaluate, and adapt to reality is often significantly impaired. Of course, some handicaps are not detectable at birth but may become manifest as a child fails to complete developmental tasks. In retrospect, after discovering their child's exceptionality months or even years after birth, mothers often admit that they suspected rather early that their child was "different."

Although mothers seem to be involved more deeply with the child at the time of birth, we should not ignore the feelings and reactions of the father. Unfortunately, research on early child development and investigations of families with handicapped children have focused upon, and to a certain extent, placed the joy or burden of the child on the mother. The research related to the feelings and reactions of fathers is regrettably in short supply, a fact that perpetuates an injustice to fathers and mothers alike. Nevertheless, educated speculations of the fathers' contributions may at least serve as a point of departure for this discussion and for future research.

Because of his secondary role in the birth process, the father is or feels more removed, less emotionally involved. In this regard, Wunderlich (1977) notes that the father's reactions are more reserved initially. He inclines toward such coping mechanisms as intellectualization, withdrawal, or sublimation. It is only when his ideas and plans for the future cannot be realized that his emotions will be strongly aroused. By the same token, males have often been characterized as less expressive, making it difficult to assess their reactions. This phenomenon is often perceived as a reflection of a need to project a masculine image, an image of the all-powerful male, undaunted by the vicissitudes of life. Since the father is a partner in the conception and subsequent development of a child, there is little reason to assume that he experiences significantly dissimilar feelings of guilt, remorse, and loss of self-esteem often attributed to the mother, yet our understanding of the father's reactions are limited.

We can, however, hypothesize that the father's fantasies of a normal baby are crushed as feelings of disappointment and confusion grow, accompanied by anxiety over the tremendous psychological, physical, and financial burden he must bear. The pipe dream of playing games with a strong, physically agile child is snuffed out, and instead he sees years of hardship ahead.

As suggested above, a father's feelings may roughly coincide with those of the mother. We must say "roughly coincide" because of the reality that the mother, and not the father, experiences the first important intimate relationship with the child as reflected in early maternal-infant bonding mechanisms (Klaus and Kennell 1976). Levine's (1966) study should alert professionals to the forgotten role the father appears to play in the family. His investigation indicated that fathers are more affected by a mentally retarded son than daughter, a factor perhaps attributable to the different expectations fathers have of sons and daughters. Levine supports the active involvement of fathers in counseling, especially if the child is male. The findings of the study point to the necessity for studying fathers as well as mothers, especially as parental sex roles may interact with the sex of the child. Peck and Stephens (1960) showed a high correlation (.83) between a father's acceptance or rejection of his mentally retarded child and the amount of acceptance or rejection in the home, indicating that the father's feelings are related to (or set) the general tone in the family.

As noted previously, a handicapped child may be perceived as a reflection of the mother's inadequacy. Also, Ross (1975) asserts that a baby may be viewed as a gift, a present the mother has "produced" for her husband or her own mother. Should the birth reveal that the infant is impaired, the value of the gift is reduced, if not destroyed, and the mother may be fearful of the husband's disappointment in her. In situations where a child is viewed as salvaging an unstable marriage, the birth of a handicapped infant may be another "sign" that the marriage is doomed to failure.

From another perspective, the baby may be seen as a divine gift, a sign of grace (Ross 1975). Generally, when the expectation for a perfect baby is dashed by the birth of a handicapped child, disgrace has fallen on the parents. In contrast, an exceptional child born to parents of staunch faith may be viewed as a sign of special grace because only the most worthy would be entrusted with his care.

> You were born one pain-filled day.
>   In love you'd been conceived.
> Despair is in the words we pray;
>   God knows we feel bereaved.
>
> The Doctors say you'll never be
>   as other children are,
> thus shattered were the dreams and hopes
>   that you would reach your star.

He hears our prayers; He'll calm our fears,
  He'll lead us by the hand
and gently wipe the healing tears,
  He'll always understand.

They tell us you're a "special child."
  Our love is special too.
We hold you in our arms and know
  that God chose us for you.

                              —Vera Robb Whitmer *

In addressing the issue of belief in a well-meaning deity, Ross (1964) observes:

> If the child is seen as a divine gift and a defective child an expression of divine will, the unexpressed question, "Why did this happen to *me?*" has the correlary "Why did He do this to me?" and raises the age-old philosophical question "If God is good He would not have done this." [p. 62]

MacKeith (1973) believes that the reactions of parents to children with different handicaps will not be identical but will resemble each other to a considerable extent. Although commonalities exist, MacKeith also contends that reactions do differ as a consequence of whether the handicap is evident at birth or shows up later (after the parents have grown to love the child), whether it is severe or mild, whether it is obvious to other people, and the perceived attitudes of other people.

From Shock to Acceptance: The Psychological Process of Adjustment

The title of this section may be somewhat misleading in implying that full acceptance is necessarily the end stage of the adjustment process. Although many people who experience a traumatic event tend to follow a shock–acceptance continuum, this is not

---

* This award-winning poem, written for friends to whom was born a brain-damaged child, has appeared in several publications. The child, Christopher, who was not expected to be able to walk, talk, or see, now (though he cannot talk, suffers seizures, and has limited vision and coordination) walks and plays happily. The poem is reprinted by permission of Mrs. Whitmer, who may be contacted at 550 Courtland Avenue, Marion, Ohio 43302.

always true. In some instances, a handicapped infant is never accepted by the parents, a reaction that may be attributable to a variety of causes, not the least of which include the reactions of those personnel attending the mother shortly after birth (Solnit and Stark 1961).

There is hardly a paucity of contributions to the literature about parents' reactions (especially the mother's) to the birth of a handicapped child and the subsequent psychological stages generally traveled. To make existing observations even more meaningful is the consistency with which social scientists, educators, and parents view the process of adjustment. This uniformity of observation allows for needed consistency so that theories can be put forth, but on a negative note, it has also contributed to a rather narrow view of exceptional families. For example, Searl (1978), a father of a mentally retarded child, takes issue with the so called "stages" parents are thought to experience. The reactions to his child is reflected in the following passage: ". . . the shock, the guilt and the bitterness . . . never disappear but stay on as a part of the parents' emotional life (p. 27)." Given these divergent views the stages of parental adjustment described in this chapter and elsewhere must be flexibly and cautiously applied.

With few exceptions, the literature reveals that the emotional assault experienced by parents after having produced a handicapped child somehow falls outside a more generalized conception of reactions to trauma. The periodical literature strongly implies that exceptional parents are the victims of an event so devastating that no other experience could match it in shock, intensity, destructiveness, and permanence. The birth of a handicapped child bears meager resemblance to other acute or chronic experiences, such as being raised by a violent, alcoholic father; experiencing the death of a loved one; being abandoned, raped, or forced to engage in an incestuous relationship. However, to their credit, Medinnus and Johnson (1969) have put the birth of a handicapped child in perspective by placing it in the context of how families cope with unexpected disappointment and trauma.

This discussion is not meant to deny the often devastating impact a handicapped child may have on the family unit, but it is offered to suggest that traumatic experiences *of almost any kind* push to the limit one's capacity to cope. Of equal and related importance is the notion put forth by phenomonologically oriented philosophers and psychologists that the same event is perceived differently by different people. The discovery that one has an ulcer may be taken in stride by one person and may throw another into a chronic state of depression. In this regard, it is interesting to note that contributors to the literature, who engage in either research or clinical practice, invariably investigate or comment on parents whose child exhibits gross abnormalities. According to the phenomonological point of view, it is possible that parents with a severely retarded child may be considerably more accepting than another set of parents who have a mildly disabled child. Although many factors contribute to highly individualized reactions to stress, the sum and substance of our accumulated experiences predispose us to respond in certain ways to specific events. Schild (1976) concurs with the notion that parental reactions to a handicapped child differ dramatically.

The heavy-heartedness with which authors have written about handicapped children and their parents may have the unfortunate and unintended consequences of persuading less sophisticated readers to view parents negatively or with sympathy, as people whose supports have been kicked out from under them. Sympathy and pity are commodities least needed by exceptional parents—commodities that reinforce self-pity and block constructive impulses enabling them to deal effectively with their circumstances.

In contrast to the doomsdayers, the pollyannas reflect a point of view equally distasteful. The constituents of this philosophy include professionals *and* parents, writing in books, journals, and magazines, who construe coping with a handicapped child a blessing, a joyous romp through the world of the martyred underdog. Minute achievements are met with excessive praise, and problems are dealt with as if they did not exist.

Exceptional parents and the professionals who work with them need to acquire an optimistic, growth-oriented, yet *realistic* view of handicapped children and their families. It is only through the adoption of such a philosophy that distortions of reality are kept to a minimum.

The Stages of Mourning

Duncan (1977), an educator of teachers who work with exceptional children and their parents, observes that teachers who do not have handicapped children cannot really know how it feels. Even so, she urges teachers to try to understand some of the implications of an exceptional child in the family, especially as they become manifested through fairly predictable stages. Duncan equates the evolving adjustment process in exceptional families to Kübler-Ross's (1969) stages characterizing one's reaction to dying. These stages are

> denial
> bargaining
> anger
> depression
> acceptance

Similarly, Solnit and Stark (1961) view the birth of a handicapped infant as the loss of the baby that was expected. The mother's reactions are an expression of the lost (dead) child, which is characterized by a mourning process extending over a long period of time: "Feelings of loss [and] intense longings for the desired child; resentment of the cruel blow that life's experience has dealt; and the guilt that the dead or defective child may evoke by representing the consequence of unacceptable feelings or thought" (p. 14).

After the birth and initial adjustment to their handicapped infant, parents (roughly) follow the developmental sequence suggested by Kübler-Ross (1969) and adapted by Duncan (1977). These stages are essential knowledge for teachers, who might otherwise become unnecessarily puzzled, confused, anxious, or angry at the parents' feelings and behavior.

STAGE I—DENIAL

Again, denial is a defense mechanism that operates on an unconscious level to ward off excessive anxiety (in this case the frightening reality that one's child is abnormal). Kamer (1953) felt that some parents disguise their child's condition rather than either deny or accept it. In disguising, a causal factor is put forth as the reason for the child's problems, such as being lazy or uncooperative. Kamer's disguising parent seems to suggest a stage (or type of behavior) characteristic of a point somewhat beyond the denial stage.

Baum (1962) notes that reality may serve the cause of denial to some extent. For example, a mildly handicapped child may be an only child, making the opportunities for comparison of development limited. In addition, accurate intellectual evaluation of children with severe motor and sensory deficits is admittedly difficult, enabling parents and even teachers to believe whatever they need to believe about the child's true ability. In searching for a more favorable diagnosis and prognosis, parents may hop from one professional to another, often wasting time, energy, and money. Although such behavior is characteristic during this stage, it seems to have taken on a clearly negative connotation. Casting about for more positive news is sometimes considered a waste of time, culminating sometimes by the professional telling the parent to stop such unproductive behavior.

For some parents this activity is essential during this phase, and unless it reaches the point of absurdity, teachers should be cautious about dissuading parents. Such behavior is not always caused by denial but may reflect a realistic appraisal and necessary behavior due to the nature of the disability or the quality of professional assistance available. As Hollingsworth and Pasnaw (1977) assert, parents sometimes have good reasons to request additional evaluations if they are dissatisfied with previous ones.

Teachers sometimes aid and abet the parents' denial by using ambiguous terminology.

> I have found that teachers tend to avoid absolutes. Therefore, they use a lot of phrases such as "maybe," "it is possible," etc. While the teacher may really mean "no" by the use of these statements, the parent hears it as "yes." As this statement gets repeated by the parent to whom you made it, to the child's significant others, it seems to get more and more positive. Therefore, false hopes may be built [Duncan 1977, p. 3]

In helping the parent move out of the denial phase, Duncan urges teachers to create situations where the parents (if they are willing) can see their child involved with normal children of the same chronological age and with children having the same handicaps. A general rule is never to try to force a parent to cast aside a defense mechanism; the abrupt unveiling of what is being kept from conscious awareness can have a devastating effect. The strategy of encouraging parents to become aware of their child's handicap is a necessary but painful insight; however, *this step is never*

*to be attempted when the teacher senses that the parents are tena-
ciously holding onto their unrealistic view of the child.*

Denial is a process that diminishes over time as the parent's
rejection continually flies in the face of reality. However, chronic
denial, according to Baum (1962) and Ross (1964), can have
severe consequences if parents do not seek out needed assistance
and/or make unrealistic demands of their child.

Duncan (1977) warns against having only one parent involved
in the process of overcoming denial. Additional strain is placed
on the family when one parent begins to realize a child's serious
handicap and the other continues firmly to deny it.

Because grandparents may contribute to the parents' denial,
Duncan suggests that they become involved at this stage if feasible.
Telford and Sawrey (1977) contend that sympathetic friends, relatives, and professionals unintentionally support the parents' denial
of their child's shortcomings by stressing assets and minimizing
limitations. Also, some parents never completely go beyond the
denial stage. They may accept the diagnosis but reject its prog-
nostic implications by holding out the possibility of a miracle drug
cure, a new operation, or a radically new diet. Solnit and Stark
(1961) observe that parents may become fixated between the recognition of their child's deviation and the denial of its implications.
For example, the parents may steadfastly deny the child's handicap
but continue to seek special help to enable him to overcome his
difficulties.

Parents' denial of their child's exceptionality is a popular concept and one that is accepted rather broadly. A study conducted
by Schulman and Stern (1959), however, challenges the assump-
tion that denial is as pervasive as some would believe. The investigators asked fifty parents to estimate the developmental age of their
retarded children before intelligence tests were given. Parents' esti-
mates were then compared with the obtained intelligence test
scores. Schulman and Stern found that the mean obtained IQ was
55.5 compared to the estimated IQ of 57.2—a difference in mean
score that was not statistically significant. The results of this study
jeopardize the rather firmly held generalization that parents are
unaware of their child's limitations. The denial stage is generally
seen as a parental reaction to a handicapped child *shortly after birth*
and is thought to give way to more realistic appraisals as the child
grows older. Even so, Schulman and Stern's study sow a seed of

doubt about cherished beliefs related to an accepted psychological phenomenon.

Denial that is chronic and tenacious requires professional attention. In such instances teachers should not assume the role of a psychotherapist but, as gently and as honestly as possible, urge the parents to seek professional assistance. Because denial is at work, such a recommendation from the teacher may be met with protestations or hostility. Nevertheless, the teacher owes it to the parents, their child, and her own professional integrity to make the referral.

STAGE II—BARGAINING

The length of time spent in any particular stage is highly individual. After a period of time, as reality continues to bombard the parents, the child's exceptionality begins to break through the initial layer of protective denial. A dim awareness of their child as he is intrudes on the parents' conscious thought, but full awareness remains unachievable. Instead, a type of magical or fantasy thinking replaces denial; the belief is fostered that their child will improve significantly as they engage in certain activities (Duncan 1977).

In their attempt to help their child, parents tend to become immersed in activities involving organizations for the handicapped. The underlying theme—that if the parent works extra hard the child will improve—is a mistaken motivating factor. The bargain or trade-off is: "If I work hard, somehow my child will get better." This, in effect, is one's compensation for hard work, being useful to others, and contributing to a worthy cause. During the bargaining stage, parents may join local groups in activities for the benefit of a particular handicapping condition or volunteer to help the teacher. According to Duncan (1977), teachers should beware of encouraging unwarranted optimism when they accept parents as volunteer aides and begin to work cooperatively with them in the classroom.

Some parents may for the first time in their lives turn to religion, or it suddenly may play a larger role. They may look for a miracle or for support and inspiration needed during this time of crisis. In this regard, Telford and Sawrey (1977) refer to studies that find Catholic mothers, who are generally more religious than Protestants, more accepting of their handicapped children than comparable non-Catholic mothers. Additional research is needed to study the relationship between religion and acceptance since some contradictions in findings have been noted.

STAGE III—ANGER

In trying to cope with the emerging reality of their situation, coupled with feelings of ambivalence and guilt toward their child, parents often find themselves striking out at something or someone other than the source of their anger. These feelings are often as puzzling to the parents as they are to the object of their reactions:

> . . . Feelings of hostility, surprising and quite inexplicable to the [parents], which appeared sometimes to be spread out over all relationships and, at others to be channeled into "furious hostility" against specific persons . . . the bereaved either makes unreasonable demands or else hardly seems to know what he wants, and often becomes irritable and ungrateful to those who try to respond. [Bowlby 1960, pp. 18, 19]

Baum (1962) and Duncan (1977) agree that if angry reactions are regarded as occasional and temporary stages of the mourning process, the teacher's personal sense of threat will be kept in check and he will be less likely to respond defensively. Baum (1962) reminds us that although the climate has improved significantly over the years, we must not forget that reality often contributes to hostile feelings, e.g., living with a frustrating child, living in a rejecting community, dealing with well-intentioned professionals who hold different views. Baum along with Sarason (1959) make the cogent point that the effect of the handicapped child on the family can be somewhat less damaging if professionals make every effort to remove any real basis for these hostile feelings, including their own unwittingly hostile responses.

The defense mechanisms of projection and/or displacement are operating when angry feelings are deflected or projected from the child to another source, although angry responses may be directed to the child himself. Often the direct expression of anger is reflected in needlessly harsh treatment of a child. Child-battering is caused by the direct expression of hostile feelings, or as in displaced anger, it may represent hostile reactions to another source. A more subtle manifestation of anger coupled with rejection is neglect, a prospect the teacher should be aware of.

Projected anger generally takes the form of blaming others for the child's conditions. Teachers, doctors, counselors, social workers, or society at large may be the scapegoats. Pertinent to teachers working with angry parents, Duncan (1977) related the following incident:

> I have known a parent to come to school very angry at me because her teenaged profoundly handicapped son had come home with a wet diaper. As we began to talk, she confided that her real anger was that her friends were now enjoying their children's dates and parties and she was still changing diapers. This incident re-emphasized to me the need to let parents know it is okay to occasionally be angry at their handicapped children, as it is to occasionally be angry with their normal children. However, if we as teachers become involved in their misplaced anger, we may become defensive and lose this opportunity to allow the parent to come to the realization that it is okay to be angry. . . .
>
> Telling the parent that his anger is unjust or unfounded does not change his feelings. When the teacher becomes defensive she causes the parent to feel that he should discontinue the expression. As a result, the parent often feels only more strongly that his impressions are valid. . . . [pp. 5, 6]

A third form of anger is turning guilty feelings inward. The parent assumes full responsibility for producing or contributing to the child's handicap, and as a consequence, blames and becomes angry at himself. This type of anger, which is related to excessive guilt feelings and shame, may ultimately lead to depression. Parents who consider themselves to blame for a handicapped offspring can find the burden so great that suicide is seen as an escape or, in anger, a way of getting back at the world for dealing her such a blow. Guilt and shame are the precursors to the next stage, depression.

STAGE IV—DEPRESSION

Guilt refers to the parents' feelings of self-reproach or self-condemnation. Hostility toward the handicapped child evokes guilt, which clashes with what is thought to be a feeling that is socially unacceptable. That is, feelings of anger toward one's offspring are considered "bad" and are not condoned by our society. Adults who are aware of their feelings know that from time to time, negative feelings surface about their normal children. As Baum (1962) states, "Normal parental ambivalence, the love-hate conflict, is as unavoidable in parents as it is in children" (p. 400). Nevertheless, parents of exceptional children may be excessively burdened by guilt, as feelings of anger (or even rejection) are considered much less acceptable than similar feelings toward a normal child, given the "unfortunate" status of the handicapped.

Society often emits double messages regarding the handicapped. Subtle and overt forms of distancing are practiced, and yet, in a variety of ways, we are told to act sympathetically and in an understanding way toward handicapped citizens. A prime example of the latter is the telethon, designed to collect money for a handicapping condition by promoting feelings of sympathy and caring by the creative selling of people variously afflicted.

Guilt refers to the individual's feelings of self-reproach, feelings based upon the internalization of (usually one's parents') values. Guilt, then, comes from within. Shame refers to what other people think and say and evokes the expectation of ridicule or criticism. (Because of their own sensitivity to the reactions of others, shame may be apparent in siblings of exceptional children.) According to Telford and Sawrey 1977), feelings of guilt (self-blame), with their concomitant anxiety and lowered self-esteem, result in depression. On the other hand, shame, with its accompanying anxiety, may result in the following actions:

> When the parental reaction is dominantly that of shame, the threat to one's personal prestige and the family's social status looms, often realistically, like an ever present shadow. The anticipation of social rejection, ridicule and loss of prestige, when extreme, may result in an immediate and drastic solution to the problem. To avoid social rebuffs, some parents try to withdraw from social participation. Attempts at immediate foster-home or institutional placement of the defective child may be the parental reaction to the threat of social ostracism. The defective child . . . becomes the traditional skeleton in the closet, the forgotten child. [p. 139]

In contrast to parents of normal children, parents of an exceptional child may have little to look forward to; that is, they will always be burdened by the child's unrelenting demands and unabated dependency. Instead of depression, a temporary stage moving toward acceptance, Olshansky (1962) speaks of "chronic sorrow," a state experienced by parents of exceptional children. Olshansky's point is that these parents, because of their perception of a bleak future, experience sorrow on a chronic basis. However, he makes it clear that feelings of satisfaction and joy from a child's achievements are not precluded. In writing about parents of mentally retarded children, Olshansky finds little wrong with parental sorrow, but he considers a professional's reactions to this phenomenon a source of significant concern:

> The reality faced by the parent of a severely retarded child is such as to justify his chronic sorrow. When the parent is asked to "accept" mental deficiency, it is not clear just what he is being asked to do. The great stress professional workers tend to place on "acceptance" may suggest to the parent that he is expected to perceive his child from the point of view of the professional helper. This expectation may make him both resentful and resistent. Why does the professional worker become so impatient with the parents' slowness or occasional regression and why does he feel such a great sense of urgency to do something about it? After all, the parent has a lifetime in which to learn to deal with the needs and problems of a mentally defective child. In most cases one can ask what will be lost if the parent is unable for several years to view his child as mentally defective? [p. 191]

It is important to reiterate that ambivalent feelings such as love and hate toward others who are not handicapped are infrequently the source of excessive guilt and depression. Because of the double messages conveyed by society, that the handicapped are different (deviant) in some significant way and yet should be protected and loved, guilt generated by angry feelings may be so intense that they naturally lead to depression. Other factors mentioned earlier contribute in a cumulative way to the feeling of despair. Whenever anxiety mounts and the stresses of life seem overwhelming, despondency and depression are likely to ensue.

Because of their low energy level, depressed parents may be more difficult to work with (Duncan 1977). Plans are rarely carried out during this stage, according to Duncan, even though the parent tends to agree with the teacher's recommendation. The most useful action teachers can take when faced with a depressed parent is to play down the weaknesses of the child and point out strengths, as long as the teacher remains realistic and doesn't build up false hopes. Also, the teacher should sense when the depression is so significant or chronic that professional counseling is required.

As is the case for most people, depression runs in cycles, although not predictable ones. Unless the depression appears intractable, it is a normal phenomenon. Even when depression is severe, it is a form of mood disorder that is responsive to treatment, e.g., counseling, antidepressive drugs, and in many cases, just plain activity.

Since activity often helps depressed people, the teacher might wish to consider ways to motivate a dispirited parent to become involved in school activities, such as helping the teacher in the classroom, assisting with party preparations, driving a small group of children to a special event, and so on. Finally, if parents seem willing, the teacher might initiate a limited discussion around their feelings (e.g., angry feelings toward their child), which might forestall a subsequent visit to a professional in mental health.

STAGE V—ACCEPTANCE

From the teacher's point of view, her major contribution in helping parents accept themselves and their child is communicating a sense of caring and concern for the parent. Of equal benefit is the parents' perception that the teacher likes and accepts their child. Professional reactions, whether negative or positive, have a potent effect on parents. A teacher can judge the parents' acceptance of their child by observing the following:

1. are willing to attend parent-teacher conferences
2. are able to discuss the child's shortcomings with relative ease
3. can abandon overprotective or unduly harsh behavioral patterns toward their child
4. are able to collaborate with the teacher to make realistic short- and long-term plans
5. become involved in advocacy functions and parent groups but not at the expense of interaction with the child
6. pursue own interests unrelated to child, again not to the exclusion of the child
7. can discipline appropriately without undue guilt feelings.

Acceptance, like depression, may not be a one-time event; that is, acceptance varies with the existence of other anxiety-producing factors. However, the acceptance that waxes and wanes (assuming that basic caring and love are present) is not to be confused with the acceptance that, at an earlier stage, represents the opposite of rejection. At this point we would do well to review Olshansky's (1962) question: "Why does the professional worker become so impatient with the parents' slowness or *occasional regression* and why does he feel such a great sense of urgency to do something about it?" (p. 191).

Toward Understanding Parents of Exceptional Children: Other Issues

A number of issues were alluded to in previous sections that require further exploration. Also, some factors were not touched upon but have a direct bearing on exceptional parents and their children.

THE LITERATURE

The periodical literature is weighted toward reports on the parents of *severely* handicapped children. There is a definite lack of clinical observation and research about parents whose children fall into the mild or marginal categories. For example, authors report extensively on the severely retarded child and family to the exclusion of children considered to be educable or learning disabled. There are articles and books that address mildly handicapping conditions in terms of assessment and teaching strategies developed *for children,* but significant gaps exist in the literature on a variety of unique problems faced by the parents of mildly handicapped children.

For example, disabled people who do not neatly fall into either the normal or handicapped group may have problems not heretofore considered, not the least of which is the exclusionary aspect of not belonging to *any* group. According to Sonstegard and Dreikurs (1975), writing about Alfred Adler's theory of personality, man is viewed as a social being motivated by a strong desire to belong. It is only within the group that man can fulfill his potential. As a result of inferiority feelings, man may doubt his place in the group, culminating in his discouragement, maladjustment, and ultimately lack of adequate functioning. This conception may or may not apply to mildly handicapped children and their parents, but clinical observation must be reported and empirical data gathered and interpreted so that a better understanding of the marginal conditions will ensue.

One can understand the concerted focus on the severely handicapped, assuming, as we do, that severe disabilities are the most disturbing and the most disruptive to the family unit. Nevertheless, an uneasy sense of having only partial answers exists. Some clinical observations already indicate that a child with a mild handicap may have more severe adjustment problems stemming from disturbed parent-child relationships than does the child with a severe handicap (Miller 1958). In this regard Ross (1964) states:

> When a child has a severe handicap the obvious and concrete nature of his disability leaves less room for questions about the presence, permanence, and consequences of the handicap, thereby reducing the likelihood for unrealistic expectations, ambivalence about getting help, and disagreements between parents regarding the child's condition. It also appears that some parents are more comfortable with a concrete defect whose basis is readily communicated to relatives and neighbors than they are with a vague and intermittently noticeable defect which leaves people to wonder what might be wrong with the child. [p. 124]

In what might appear as a contradiction, there is at the same time a lack of published literature on parents of *multiply handicapped children*. A favorite focus appears to be the severely *mentally retarded* child and family. A better understanding of families of other exceptional children is lacking, especially those who are impaired in hearing and vision; however, the reason for this lack may be reflected in Barsch's (1968) research, which indicated that parents of deaf and blind children showed the greatest extent of general ease in child rearing compared to parents with children of other handicaps. This finding is corroborated in part by Hollingsworth and Pasnaw (1977), who claim that children with physical handicaps can often learn ways to compensate; but the mentally retarded children cannot compensate and may therefore require more care and supervision. However, Barnebey and Ruppert (1978), do not differentiate the mourning process experienced by parents of severely retarded children and those whose children are chronically ill or physically handicapped.

Although there have been several significant attempts to study exceptional families from the empirical point of view, much of the research is observational and anecdotal—a valuable *adjunct* to more objective investigations, but in the absence of empirical support, little more than an accumulation of subjective views. A contributing factor are the enormous difficulties in doing research in this area (Medinnus and Johnson 1969). The tools of data collection are severely restricted: self-reports via surveys and interviews and observation, which generally take the form of insights gleaned from clincial practice.

With few exceptions the literature in this area is grim. In an attempt to highlight and to some extent dramatize the plight of the exceptional parent, writers tend to focus more on family problems than on assets and coping ability. Parents are rarely portrayed as adjusted and realistically optimistic, but tend to be projected as poor souls beset by frustration, anger, and depression, hardly in a position to interact comfortably and constructively with professionals and friends, much less with each other. The focus of the published literature is on pathology (what is wrong) to the virtual exclusion of ego (coping) mechanisms. A recent publication (Bernstein 1978) dramatizes this point:

> Some parents overprotect and do not stimulate the child to use the abilities he has. Others are so depressed that they cannot do much for the child. In still others, the sadness is interwoven with a kind of impotent rage toward the world. Many parents are angry at the retarded child, though they try to cover this up, hating to admit feelings of anger toward a helpless child. Most try to do their best in spite of their personal sense of loss and sadness, but some become cool and distant and withdraw from the retardate the sustained warmth and stimulation that he requires even more than other children. Some parents try to quash their own sadness and embark on brisk programs, pushing the children relentlessly toward speech training, toilet training, nursery school, exercises, and a host of other "stimulating" activities. If they push too hard, they overwhelm a vulnerable child and tend to make him withdraw even further. [pp. 558–59]

One cannot deny that exceptional parents have significant problems in dealing with the educational, psychological, financial, and social ramifications of their child's handicap. By the same token, without turning to an unrealistically optimistic philosophy, the literature might well reflect a more balanced view of parents and their problems, weaknesses, *and strengths*. The danger with the pathology model is that teachers, as well as parents, may as a result perceive all or most exceptional parents as unstable, hostile, or both—a belief of such a jaundiced nature that it serves as a wedge between necessary parent-teacher cooperation and collaboration. Commentary like the following by Wunderlich (1977) is all too rare:

> There is no doubt that the birth of a [handicapped] child confronts the parents and the entire family with serious psychic, physical, and material handicaps. On the other hand, such a misfortune mobilizes positive forces which often would not have been awakened without such an event, and which result in astonishing positive transformations in personality. This is a fact which we are able to observe daily, and which impresses us again and again with its frequency and magnitude. [p. 84]

The teacher would do well to keep in mind that much of what one reads here and elsewhere represents the current state of the art, a state that leaves considerable room for improvement. The plight of the exceptional family is a recently discovered one, and thus existing knowledge reflects an early stage of development.

PERIODS OF CHANGE DURING THE GROWTH OF THE EXCEPTIONAL CHILD

Parents can usually anticipate the termination of child-rearing responsibility when their children are between eighteen and twenty-five years of age. This point in a family's development is looked upon ambivalently: on the one hand the child advances to a stage of independence where college, marriage, and vocational success are anticipated and viewed with a sense of satisfaction; on the other hand, a degree of sorrow is felt when the family's patterns of gratifying mutual interdependence is changed.

It is within this cultural backdrop of expectancy that exceptional parents must view the future of their child (Barsch 1968). Parents of normal children experience a series of developmental crises (e.g., the terrible two's, and the teen-age years), but because of the arrest or slowness of growth characteristic of handicapped children, these parents may be considerably more apprehensive about whether their child will be able to attain normal levels of development. Our sense of security is determined not only by our past but also our current realities, *and our conception of what the future holds.*

Knowledge of periods of change for the family of a handicapped child is essential for teachers working with parents. The teacher is then in a better position to be of help to parents when changes occur. At the least, she will be better prepared to understand what the parent is experiencing. A brief discussion of four major turning points in the developmental cycle of exceptional families follows:

1. *When parents first learn about or suspect a handicap in their child.* Parental reaction to this stage, discussed in a previous section, remains one of the liveliest topics in the literature. Support, assessment or diagnosis, and honest feedback are the responsibility of the physician and other health-related professionals at this point.

2. *At about age five or six, when a decision has to be reached regarding the child's education.* Unless some type of early childhood education was instituted, this is the parents' first encounter with the educational system. Parents, educators, psychologists, and doctors are very much involved at this stage, which Hollingsworth and Pasnaw (1977) refer to as "going public."

3. *When the time has arrived for the handicapped person to leave school.* Concerns about independence, work, marriage, or additional education become particularly acute. Depending on the magnitude of the problems experienced, a number of professionals, including educators, may be consulted at or somewhat before this time. During this period, when the handicapped person reaches adolescence, Kershaw (1973) cautions that handicapping disabilities can become intensified. The disabling condition may exacerbate the turmoil adolescents normally experience. Hollingsworth and Pasnaw (1977) consider adolescence crucial when the handicapped child develops sexually.

4. *When the parents become older and may be unable to care for their handicapped child.* Parents look ahead with considerable apprehension to their child's future as they find themselves less able to care for him. This is a period during which concerns about care after the parents have died are evident. Social service workers are indispensable at this point to counsel the parents, provide realistic courses of action, and inform parents of the available alternatives.

The American Medical Association lists ten periods of change experienced by exceptional families: suspicion of handicap, final diagnosis, entering school, rejection by peers and siblings, acute diseases, general family crises, sex problems, professional adaptability, marriage, decision to institutionalize, and the separation connected with it (Gur 1976). Should any of these stages become crisis-laden instead of temporarily problematic, counseling may be required—a fact professionals, especially teachers during the school years, need to keep in mind. Gur urges professionals to work toward preventing crises and not only to deal with their aftermath.

FAMILY INTEGRATION

The effect of a handicapped child on the stability of the family unit has been the subject of considerable comment and some research. A few large-scale studies have been reported on parents of severely retarded children. Farber's classic studies conducted in the late 1950s and early 1960s are the most frequently cited and will be one of the two major investigations considered here. Although Farber's studies were conducted in a sophisticated manner and his subsequent findings have not been contradicted, the reader should bear in mind that they were made a number of years ago, the population studied was parents of retarded children, and the children were severely retarded. Therefore, generalizations to other populations should be made with caution.

Farber (1959) conceived of long-term changes in the family unit as the life cycle of the family, and the relations among family members as an interacting system of roles. As family members interact over time, the life cycle proceeds from one stage to the next in roughly the following sequence: the married couple, the family whose youngest child is of preschool age, the family with a preadolescent youngest child, the family with an adolescent youngest child, the family in which all children are adults, and the family in which all children are married.

The life cycle is arrested when one of the children in the family is severely retarded, and the retarded child assumes the social position of the youngest regardless of birth order. Because of the severely retarded child, Farber theorized, the family does not emerge from the preadolescent stage of its life cycle, resulting in disruption of family integration because each individual is frustrated in his anticipated roles.

Farber studied 240 families with severely retarded children (IQ of 50 or below) who were sixteen years of age or under. One hundred and seventy-five families of the 240 had a retarded child at home, and sixty-five had placed their child in an institution. A two and one-half hour interview of the parents was conducted in the home. In addition, parents were asked to complete a series of scales and questionnaires, and the family's marital integration was measured by still another instrument. Thus, the subjects were scrutinized rather intensively, which makes Farber's research one of the most important in this area. However, Ross (1964) points out that data were not based on comparisons between family integration before and after placement of the child in an institution, which constitutes a weakness in the study and leaves unresolved the question of whether better marital integration is achieved as a result of the decision to institutionalize or whether other factors are operating.

The results of Farber's studies showed the following:

1. Marriages were more adversely affected when the retarded child was kept at home only if the child was a boy. This finding was more pronounced in lower- than in middle-class families.

2. Normal brothers were adversely affected by the institutionalization of the retarded sibling.

3. Normal sisters showed more personality problems when the retarded sibling was in the home than when he was in an institution whether the institutionalized child was a boy or girl.

4. Emotional support available to the mother outside the immediate family appears to have a positive effect on marital integration, especially when the wife had frequent interaction with her own mother.

5. Beneficial effects of placing the retarded son in an institution were found among non-Catholics but not among Catholic families. Non-Catholics sufferered more marital discord when the retarded boy was at home.

Farber (1959) concluded:

> . . . the parent can expect that a retarded boy, especially after the age of nine, will probably have a disruptive effect on marital relations; he can anticipate personality problems for the sister, who is given many responsibilities for the child; the parent must be aware of the degree to which the family has its own resources and supportive interaction in facing crisis situations; and he can expect the degree of helplessness of the retarded to affect the personality of his normal children adversely. [p. 80]

Subsequent studies by Farber (1962) revealed that

1. Normal brothers and sisters who had sustained interaction with their retarded siblings professed such life goals as, (a) de-

votion to a worthwhile cause and (b) making a contribution to mankind. On the other hand, they placed less emphasis than infrequent interactors upon having many close friends, on focusing life around marriage and the family, and on being a respected community leader. Normal siblings come to regard sustained interaction with retarded siblings as a duty and in turn seemed to select life careers which require dedication and sacrifice in the service of mankind.

2. Families with a child-oriented, home-oriented, or parent-oriented philosophy were more integrated than those lacking a consistent orientation whether the child was at home or in an institution.

Farber's studies reinforce the notion that parents of handicapped children must be viewed in the context of a variety of interacting factors. Exceptional families are not homogeneous groups, and such factors as sex, age, psychological support systems, religion, social class, and institutionalization need to be considered.

Although a variety of factors were examined in Farber's research, families were primarily analyzed according to whether their child was institutionalized or lived at home. In an era where the concept of community living is gaining momentum, research should be directed toward situations and events that exist in noninstitutionalized milieus. Investigations should be focused on options available to parents *in the community*, even though for the severely handicapped, with minimal family and community support, institutions continue to be a viable alternative.

A less extensive yet major study of more recent vintage was carried out in Toronto by Fotheringham *et al.* (1971). The investigators hypothesized that living with a severely retarded child would be difficult to endure and, therefore, the family would be subject to stress, the degree of which would be influenced by the characteristics of the child, the family's capacity for coping, and the available community support. The study examined the consequences on the family of severely retarded children who were either institutionalized or remained at home. One hundred and sixteen institutionalized subjects were compared to thirty-eight community subjects. An important aspect of this study is that subjects were identified before institutional placement. Informaion on the children in both groups was collected through parent interviews, agency reports, and testing—which took place one to three months before institutionalization and again one year after admission. A previously validated scale was used as the main measure of family functioning. Average IQ of the institutionalized and community children was 37 and 44 respectively.

The general results of the Toronto study did not indicate significantly different changes in the functioning levels of the retarded children in the two different living situations (home and institution) over the one-year period. The proportion of institution families showing improvement was greater than that of community families, and the greatest decrease in functioning in the latter was observed in the siblings and parents' adequacy in caring for the retarded child.

These two studies, taken together, strongly suggest that the severely retarded child's presence impedes the family's development and places significant stress on the family unit. Farber reflects on the sociological and psychological ramifications, and Fotheringham *et al.* speak to the issue of alternatives to either home or institutional care. The interested reader would find their discussion most informative.

SIBLINGS

There is a pervasive belief that a handicapped child "contaminates" the family and generates great psychological burdens, especially on normal siblings. A handicapped child does have an effect on normal siblings, but its nature is mediated by such factors as the sex of the normal sibling and institutionalization.

According to Klein (1972), Love (1973), and Telford and Sawrey (1977), negative influences are particularly felt when normal siblings are required to supervise, care for, defend, and protect the handicapped child. In addition, when the handicapped child receives attention and affection and the normal sibling is neglected and deprived of educational and recreational opportunities, resentment is significantly magnified. On the positive side, Klein (1972) and Grossman (1972) provide initial evidence that normal siblings tend to adopt the parents' attitudes toward the handicapped child. In an optimistic note Grossman concludes:

> It is the family's definition of the problem that most directly affects the ability of individual members of the family to adjust to a retarded child. The presence of a retarded child can enhance a family's normal development, or at least not hinder it. [p. 104]

In her study, Grossman collected data on eighty-three college students, each of whom had a retarded brother or sister. A matched control sample of students with normal brothers and sisters was used for comparison. Each student was interviewed individually about his experiences, and tests were given to obtain additional information. Retarded siblings ranged from mild to severe retardation with about 25 percent mongoloid. Grossman's data revealed the following:

1. A number of subjects appeared to have benefited from the experience of growing up with a handicapped sibling. These students appeared to be more tolerant about prejudice and its consequences and more certain about their own futures and about personal and vocational goals than comparable young adults who had not had such experiences.

2. There were clear indications that some normal siblings were harmed by the experience; they showed bitter resentment of their family's situation, guilt about the rage they felt at their parents and at the retarded sibling and fear that they themselves might be defective.

3. As in studies cited earlier, families tend to exempt their sons from the demanding duty of caring for their retarded sibling, whereas daughters were more actively involved in their brother or sister's care.

4. The strongest single factor affecting the normal sibling's acceptance of his retarded brother or sister is parental feelings and reactions, especially those of the mother.

5. Upper-income families, because of their resources, had more opportunity to relieve their normal children of the burdensome care of the handicapped child, but not without some negative yet manageable consequences, e.g., guilt feelings.

6. Lower-income families experienced more hardship as a consequence of the retarded child, especially as the young normal women were expected to assume a major share of responsibility for their handicapped siblings. Young women from larger families fared better, probably because they had normal sisters and brothers who shared responsibility.

Grossman's research indicates the differential impact of sociocultural status as it affects the family's ability to secure relief from the chronic burden of caring for a handicapped child. Lower socioeconomic families already tied up in a day-to-day struggle to survive were in a poor position, either psychologically or financially, to take on the additional responsibilities of a significantly impaired child. The major outcome of this investigation is that brothers and sisters of handicapped siblings responded in significantly different ways, negative for some and surprisingly positive for others.

For teachers working with exceptional parents, it is useful to be cognizant of the impact a handicapped child may have on normal siblings. Depending on the parental attitudes toward the handicapped child and the amount of responsibility assigned to normal siblings, it should not come as a surprise when parents appear more concerned about the psychological adjustment of normal offspring than their handicapped ones.

COMMUNITY AND FAMILY SUPPORT

Psychological support for exceptional families includes immediate and extended family relationships (siblings, spouse, grandparents, and other relatives) as well as that found in the community through the availability of services and prevailing attitudes. From the studies cited earlier preliminary information indicates that positive, optimistic, and realistic attitudes within exceptional families bear a relationship to the positive feelings and enhanced self-esteem of the mother, resulting in a healthy climate for the handicapped child. Some sketchy data suggest that support from other family members also adds to a more favorable family atmosphere. It would appear that accepting and realistic grndparents, in-laws, and other close relatives could add immeasurable positive support to parents and their handicapped child.

Professionals have not taken seriously the potential benefit emanating from extended family members, an added dimension in their arsenal. Teachers, in assessing the family's circumstances, should take other family members into account as they contribute or detract from healthy family relations and may consider recommending their increased involvement. It has also been noted, however, that close relatives may aid in the parents' denial of their child's handicap.

Not infrequently parents are faced with few or inadequate services for their handicapped child. At other times, services may be available but their existence is not known to the parents. Teachers should consider involving themselves in the community's efforts to secure appropriate services. Also, they should keep abreast of available services in the community so that referrals can be made when appropriate (see Appendix for referral sources).

There is little a professional can do in a direct sense for a parent who has the misfortune to reside in an unfriendly, unaccepting community. Perhaps the most useful activity is to counteract unfriendly community attitudes by relating to the parents in a warm, accepting manner. When appropriate, referral to community-based self-help groups can be made when parents need support not available in their immediate surroundings from others in similar circumstances. In general parents should be informed of all available support systems, such as ministers, charitable organizations, preschool nurseries, day-care centers, special education classes, relatives, sheltered workshops, and parent organizations. The teacher should be wary when he senses that parents are withdrawing from normal social contacts—an indication of self-imposed isolation, which will increase their problems. If the teacher is certain that parents are moving toward such isolation, a referral to a psychologist may be necessary.

As suggested earlier and further supported by Farber (1959) and Zuk (1959), religion may constitute an important source of support. Thus, parents who were previously unaffiliated may become, for the first time, religiously involved and others may increase their commitment.

Finally, support from the professionals who come in contact with exceptional parents is essential. For some parents, professional encouragement may represent the last bastion of hope; for others it affirms the manner in which they are coping and gives them additional security. In this regard, Clements (1963) (Mark Twain) once wrote:

> . . . there is something that he [man] loves more than he loves peace—the approval of his neighbors and the public. And perhaps there is something which he dreads more than he dreads pain—the disapproval of his neighbors and the public. [p. 344]

Between a Rock and a Hard Place

This phrase refers to one's sense of being threatened, coerced, or suppressed through remarkably sophisticated and subtle forms of manipulation. Sentiments of indignation and outrage for parents of exceptional childen and their sometimes remarkable experiences with public and private institutions have not as yet been made public; but these experiences leave in its wake victims as helpless as those subjected to more publicized acts against innocent people. The subtle abuse perpetrated against exceptional families is of a nature that is difficult to detect and almost impossible to prove. To some parents it may be experienced as a vague feeling of pressure or coercion. To others, the name of the game, how it is played, and the consequences of not playing it correctly are painfully known. The game is called something like "How to conform and have your child accepted for needed services." The "rock" is the unavailability of appropriate alternate services, and the "hard place" is the pressure to conform with agency and school wishes so that one's child will remain eligible.

This game is very carefully played by agency and school personnel so that parents cannot point to obvious verbal threats demanding parental conformity and/or significant growth from the child. Schleifer (1971) offers the following illustration of how a child's lack of "progress" affects his eligibility:

> Failing to find an appropriate public school placement the family finds a special program for their child. The child has just finished his third year. The family has been called in by the school director to discuss their child's progress. The director tells the family that the child cannot return in the fall. There has been so little progress during the course of the past year that it is not worth the family's money or the school's time to continue the child in this program. The parent is asked to accept the twofold assumption that continuous progress in necessary every year and the lack of it is part of their child's disability. [p. 4]

Another ploy is to empathize with the parents' sense of frustration and feelings of anger while placing constraints on free expression. The ensuing message may be more complicated than it first appears because the parents are encouraged to express angry feelings *as long as the representative agency is not the target*. Parents keep comments about perceived deficiencies in the institution or school to themselves to avoid the risk of being labeled troublemakers. The risk is that if the parents are seen as troublemakers, their child's eligibility might be in jeopardy. It appears that much more (often negative) attention is given to the vocal parent or the parent who is truly unreasonable than to the cooperative parent deeply concerned about his child. Some professionals appear to have given little thought to what Gorham (1975) refers to as a "lost generation of parents," who live lives of enforced silence and acquiescence.

Facilities are expanding, but not fast enough to accommodate all the people who need them. The resulting competitive atmosphere, played to the hilt by some agencies and schools, force exceptional families to examine what they must do to make themselves acceptable for services.

> They often find themselves trying new things, whether they are suitable or not, in order to cross the agency threshold. Trapped in this fruitless, and often painful, mutual encounter, family and agency unnecessarily expend a great deal of energy criticizing each other. [Schleifer 1971, p. 4]

Because they want to be accepted, primarily for their child's welfare but also for their own sense of self-esteem, parents are often at a loss as to how they should behave. Like taking certain psychological tests, where it is impossible to escape some stigmatizing label or diagnosis, there is simply no way to avoid falling victim to some (usually derogatory or "sick") label or category.

> If the parent is militantly aggressive in seeking to obtain therapeutic services for his child he may be accused of not realistically accepting the child's limitations. If he does not concern himself with efforts to improve or obtain services he may be accused of apathetic rejection of this child. If he questions too much he has a "reaction formation" and may be overprotective and oversolicitous. If he questions too little he is branded as disinterested and insensitive. (In short, parents tend to be classified if they . . . failed to match up to the expectation of the school or clinic.) [Barsch 1968, pp. 8–9]

In addition to verbal limitations that the parent senses, other barriers stand in the way of their child's acceptance. He might be too young, too old, too bright, too retarded; or the parent might have too high or too low an income or live in the wrong geographical area.

Gorham et al. (1975) believe that parents are unduly grateful to principals or school directors for merely accepting their children in their programs: "The spectre of 24 hours a day, 7 days a week care at home, with the state institution as an alternative, has made us too humbly thankful" (p. 552). Children are often referred elsewhere because school personnel want only those children who will make their program succeed. To parents, another referral can be a devastating blow. Ironically, the assistance provided by social service delivery systems works in inverse ratio to the help needed by parents; the more crisis-laden the child and the family, the less likely they are to find help (Gorham *et al.* 1975).

It is hoped that in future years professionals will vigorously oppose these practices. The disturbing trend noted by Feldman *et al.* (1975), that parents have learned that minimal contact with their child's school is best, especially needs to be reversed.

Professional Helpers

Telford and Sawrey (1977) report their impression that parents of handicapped children are almost universally dissatisfied with their experiences with professionals. The authors quote a mother who characterized her conferences as ". . . a masterful combination of dishonesty, condescension, misinformation and bad manners" (p. 143).

Fox (1975) found that parents believed that professionals didn't want to become involved with them or their difficulties in dealing with their child. Not unlike parents, professionals may resort to defense mechanisms which reduce anxiety by avoiding its source. It is not implausible that physicians consider the birth of a handicapped child as a reflection of their adequacy, as if they are in some way responsible for the child. Even so, as Wunderlich (1977), a physician, points out, the activity of the doctor must never be allowed to end with the disclosure of the diagnosis. He believes that the physician's task only begins at this point, since with the disclosure he should take on the responsibility of providing meaningful care for the exceptional child and his family. If the physician fails to take advantage of this opportunity, valuable time is lost which cannot be recovered.

According to Fox (1975), parents noted the lack of counseling about the nature of the child's handicap and what can reasonably be expected of him socially and educationally. They also mentioned the need for practical help, such as a list of good residential care facilities and the like. In this regard, Gorham *et al.* (1975) believe that professionals are ill informed about referral services, pointing out that schools do not generally assume responsibility for finding programs for children whom they cannot serve.

A frequent complaint is the lack of a central coordinator, a major problem for parents who may need numerous services and find themselves balancing the contradictory advice from various specialists. This can be an enormously confusing situation for parents and may account for some of the negative feelings often expressed toward professionals. In addition, as they are confronted by the panoply of services ad specialists, parents may become convinced of the enormity, complexity, and hopelessness of their child's problem.

Among six problems faced by exceptional parents, Murray (undated) lists that of receiving inept, inaccurate, and ill-timed professional advice. She further notes that parents' reactions to their child depend to a large degree on the maturity of the professional with whom they consult. According to Anderson and Garner (1973), parents complain about professionals who provide information in highly technical jargon or convey their impressions in purely pejorative terms.

Perhaps related to the distancing phenomenon reported by Fox is the contention that many professionals hold negative views regarding certain handicapping conditions and tend to see parents as "disturbed" Gur (1976). Roos (1977) points out that professionals view exceptional parents as having such problems as (1) the inability to accept the fact that their child is handicapped; (2) manifest pathological depression; (3) expressive overprotection of their child; (4) irrational hostility, which is usually focused on the professional; and (5) tenuous marital relationships (p. 97). According to Roos, destructive stereotypes and a general lack of understanding of handicapping conditions result in much professional mishandling of parents.

A source of considerable consternation is the frequency with which professionals (physicians for the most part) urge parents to institutionalize their handicapped child before adequate information is attained about the handicap and without full knowledge of the parents' psychological resources. An astonishing example of the negative attitude professionals harbor toward the people they serve can be seen in the position specialists in alcoholism show toward alcoholics (Connor 1974), a position that may contribute to their poor record of success in treating this population.

Gorham *et al.* (1975) and Hobbs (1975) vigorously attack the negative effect *labels* have on children and their parents. The professionals' propensity to rely on labels in lieu of descriptive statements of strengths and weaknesses must be abandoned. In their attempt to adjust to the system, some parents learn to manipulate their child's diagnosis to get the best program available (Gorham *et al.* 1975).

There is a tendency for professionals to discount whatever parents say about their child, as professionals believe that their perceptions are the only valid ones and that parents' observations are colored by subjectivity, denial, or distortions of reality. At times this belief might be true, but often there is more than a kernel of truth in what parents report.

It makes sense to urge professionals to treat parents as intelligent, and their observations and child-rearing practices as worthy of consideration and not a reflection of their neurotic behavior. "Again and again we have heard the plea from parents that the diagnostician respect the occupation of parenting, that he not only listen to the parent but *hear* what he or she says" (Gorham *et al.* 1975, p. 163). Baxter (1977) puts it clearly:

> The next time you are faced with a handicapped child and his or her family, don't be so ready to make judgments. If the child has only one visible handicap, don't automatically assume that that is all you have to deal with. If a parent comes across as very verbal and competent, don't assume that they have everything under control, or that they are cold and unfeeling. Listen for the little clues that tell you that the intellectualizing is their way of handling feelings that are too painful to surface easily. Don't be easily misled if the child is pretty and has a winning smile and seems very docile in your presence. Listen, really listen, to what the parents tell you about the child at home. And, perhaps most importantly of all, help parents to admit to feelings of grief, and shame, and anger, and tiredness, and despair. If you do that, you will not only help parents to seek the fulfillment of their own personal lives, but you will have helped immeasurably to make the child's personal burden much lighter. [pp. 7–8]

Parents find disturbing the practice of hiding confidential information from them. Confidentiality refers to keeping information about clients or patients from people who are not professionally involved in a particular case; it does not mean keeping such information from parents, a practice that adds to their sense of distrust and contributes to poor rapport. Also, some information is recorded in such highly technical terms that only other professionals can decipher it; or a form of professional shorthand is used so that only the person making the entry is able to interpret it. Confidential records must remain available to *involved* professionals (e.g., consultants) but also to parents, who have the right to see what others have recorded about them and their children.

Anxiety on the part of the professional accounts for some of the discomfort and hostile reactions parents experience. Another contributing factor is the lack of adequate training in interpersonal skills as well as the lack of knowledge about the potential social and psychological impact a handicapped child may have on the family.

Murray (undated), president of the Virginia Association for Retarded Citizens and a parent of a handicapped child, believes that parents should not be excessively harsh on professionals; they do not know how to handle parents wisely, she hypothesizes, because of ignorance and inexperience, but they are genuinely concerned and want to help. Implied in Murray's comments is the plea that professionals are human too and as such are subject to human foibles.

Much of the criticism leveled at incomplete and inadequate professional training is aimed at physicians, although educators and social service workers are not exempt (Fox 1975; Gur 1976). As a consequence of this criticism, attempts have been made to list the characteristics of professionals that lead to successful helping. The one that tops the list of informed and perceptive professionals and exceptional parents alike is *honesty*. Open, candid responses within the context of a caring relationship is essential. Parents find little value in abrupt or evasive answers to their questions.

Ross (1964) also regards as essential the human qualities of acceptance, understanding, and warmth, as well as the professional attributes of objectivity, confidence, and knowledge. Familiarity with available community resources, the sensitivity to know when and how to obtain consultation, and a realistic appraisal of the limits of one's competence are additional but necessary components. Finally, professionals working with parents of exceptional children should be expert in the technical skill of interviewing.

These attributes and skills may seem impossible to achieve, but professionals who do not in some degree possess them should consider other work. Ross (1964) makes this point without equivocation in the following quotation aimed at professionals who wish to work with exceptional parents:

A student may be able to develop these in the course of closely supervised experience but some people lack these qualities in sufficient measure and these should probably not enter a profession whose central task is helping other people. No amount of exhortation can make a rejecting person accepting, a frigid person warm, or a narrow-minded person understanding. Those charged with the selection, education, and training of new members of the helping professions will need to keep in mind that the presence or absence of certain personality characteristics make the difference between a truly helpful professional and one who leaves a trace of misery and confusion in the wake of his activities. [pp. 75–76]

CHAPTER 4

Basic Principles of Interviewing

By now the reader knows why parent-teacher conferences are necessary and why they often go beyond the communication of a child's academic progress. We know also that conferences are often initiated by teachers, but parents, the school social worker, school nurse, counselor, or school psychologist may also request them. The notion that teachers may be considerably less effective conducting parent conferences than they are in teaching children is a very real possibility and one that must be faced by practicing professionals as well as the training institutions responsible for their education.

We are now ready to consider building relationships and developing facilitative interpersonal skills. It is important to remember that the attitudes and actual interpersonal dimensions included in this chapter are designed to increase one's facilitative skills and not to prepare one to become a psychotherapist. In other words, such attitudes as being nonjudgmental and accepting as well as such skills as listening attentively, using questions appropriately, being supportive, and the like are to be emphasized as opposed to the acquisition of in-depth psychotherapeutic skills.

Personality Characteristics and Interpersonal Style

Even though this Chapter 4 and Chapter 5 will focus on skills that may seem somewhat foreign and strange, it is generally a good idea to practice them and try to assess the degree of "fit" between that behavior and one's personality. One may wish to monitor how comfortable the new behavior or skill appears to be. Before discarding a behavior that seems unnatural, one should try to integrate it into one's natural style of response. It would be unusual if the new behavior did not feel somewhat awkward; most new experiences do.

A word of caution is in order. I agree with the point of view expressed some time ago by McGowan (1956), who felt that new behaviors or orientations should be compatible with one's natural style of response. In other words, new behaviors or skills should be incorporated into one's natural way of interacting with others. The newly learned behavior is subject to modification, not one's characteristic style of response. For example, one is often encouraged to engage others with a considerable amount of eye contact; but if one happens to be a sensitive and perceptive listener with minimal eye contact, it would be contraindicated to insist on a change in this behavior. In such an instance, other assurance that the person is interested and attentive should be given.

Values and the Parent–Teacher Conference

Having lived for a particular span of time during which we have encountered many people, experiences, and beliefs, we inevitably develop values about every aspect of our lives. Some values involve preferences in food, automobiles, clothes, schools, flowers, movies, music and so on. Differences of opinion between individuals over these preferences (or values) might take the form of a friendly argument about the virtues of Beethoven's music over Mozart's.

Other values lead to powerful emotions, to strong and sometimes inflexible convictions, which often cause strained interpersonal communication and under certain circumstances may even polarize large groups of people. Such values, for example, are concerned with religion, politics, abortion, integration, and sexual behavior and orientation.

Of course, all of us have values. One might consider parent-teacher conferences as encounters of two unique sets of values. Strong feelings about religion or politics, for example, are generally not discussed in a parent-teacher conference, yet they are not *always* absent. Perhaps related to their child's handicap, parents may communicate strong convictions about abortion, convictions that run counter to those of the teacher. Or a parent may openly support a candidate for election who is opposed to pay raises and better working conditions for teachers and has generally denigrated the profession. In such instances the teacher must remember the purpose of the conference, namely, to help the parent, to communicate observations of his child, and so on. A heated discussion over religious or political views has no place in a helping interview.

In a sense what is being suggested is that the teacher adopt a philosophy of neutrality. She may respond with anger or resentment, and her stomach may feel knotted or her palms may be perspiring, but the awareness of what is happening internally *and why* is important. The notion that parents (or anyone else for that matter) have as much right to their point of view as does the teacher is a reality that requires a considerable degree of acceptance.

The more we know about our own values and how they are developed, the more accepting we can be of the values of others. Such self-enlightenment helps set the stage for a productive, tension-free meeting.

Platitude or not, I believe the more we know about ourselves, the better we can understand, evaluate, and control our behavior and the better we can understand and appreciate the behavior of others. As we become more familiar with ourselves, we may feel less threatened by what we find. We may even get to the point that we genuinely like some of the things about us and, therefore, become more tolerant of the things we like less or do not like at all. And, then, as long as we continue to examine, discover, and explore, it is possible for us to grow and change. Oriented to ourselves, we may become comfortable with ourselves and thus be able to help others become comfortable with themselves and with us. In addition, because we are at ease with our own self, there will be less of a tendency for it to get in the way of our understanding another self during the interview. [Benjamin 1974, p. 6]

Basically, to me acceptance means treating the interviewee as an equal and regarding his thoughts and feelings with sincere respect. It does not mean agreeing; it does not mean thinking or feeling the way he does; it does not mean valuing what he values. It is, rather the attitude that the interviewee has as much right to his ideas, feelings, and values as I have to mine and that I want to do my utmost to understand his life space in terms of his ideas, feelings, and values rather than in terms of my own. Such an attitude is difficult to maintain and even more difficult to communicate to the interviewee. At times it may be misunderstood and interpreted as agreement, consent, or reassurance. And yet we have no choice but to attempt to be accepting. Otherwise, the interviewee will suspect that we are judging him, asking him to feel and think as we do or, even worse, to think and feel as we believe he ought to be thinking and feeling. [p. 39]

An exercise developed by Schulman (1974, pp. 53–54) will help readers be aware of their values: Make a list of the behavioral traits in people that annoy you. Then rate all the items on a scale from 1 to 5 (rate the most bothersome items 5, the least 1). Gather all your 5 ratings and all your 1 ratings and study them carefully. What do these lists tell you about yourself?

Now we will turn to an examination of values held by the teacher. It is not unusual to find ourselves in a position of dissuading a friend or relative of a particular point of view—and this is to be anticipated and accepted in a nonprofessional encounter where there is little or no disparity in status. Even so, the point is well taken when Samler (1962) notes, "We know that in their behavior, defenses, and values, human beings change least of all by exhortation" (p. 135).

In a conference with a parent the imposition of a teacher's values should be most assiduously avoided:

The hazard lies in an imposition of values by the counselor [teacher]. The danger is great because the counselor may not consciously intend for this to happen. But when it does happen, the counselee [parent] feels somewhat pushed down as a person. An implied denial of the worth of his own views and experiences is given to him, and he senses the disapproval and rejection of himself as he is at the moment. [Johnson and Vestermark 1970, p. 78]

To as full an extend as possible, the counselor should be aware of his own biases, attitudes, and prejudices. He needs to understand what prompts his own motivations during the counseling interview. If some of these emotional value orientations were unwittingly to be expressed, the disclosure could present hazards for the counselee, for it is likely he would react in some way. He could be attracted or repelled, feel resentment or resistance or a lowered respect for the counselor. Or some of the counselor's same bias or prejudice could germinate within him. As we have stated earlier, when values in any form are expressed by the counselor, the counselee should be helped to realize that these are expressions of how the counselor feels and a counselor needs to recognize the hazards of subtle encroachment upon counselees. These hazards can be largely avoided when the counselor does understand his biases and so, in fairness, does not want to inflict them unconsciously upon the counselee. [pp. 82 and 83]

Ross (1964), who wrote the classic *The Exceptional Child in the Family,* is adamant about the view that "The professional must . . . attempt an honest examination of his own feelings and attitudes before he can expect to be helpful and if he is unable to do so, he will need a consultant, supervisor, or therapist who can help him with this examination" (p. 73).

Finally, Shields (1974) supplies evidence that professionals are often less objective about families whose backgrounds are either greatly different from their own or so similar as to recall attitudes and feelings from which they may wish to disassociate. Should such unconsciously (or perhaps even consciously) held beliefs exist, the professional may categorize parents inaccurately, be unable to surmount communication barriers imposed by differing social histories, or make inappropriate or poor judgments about parental strengths or weaknesses. Thus, teachers must be aware of their prejudices and blind spots and work hard at overcoming them, or at the very least, keep them in their proper perspective during conferences.

The Setting of the Conference

Garrett (1972) asserts that "The physical setting of the interview may determine its entire potentiality" (p. 72). Benjamin (1974) takes a more conservative position in suggesting that the physical setting of the interview is largely a matter of personal preference. If possible the conference should be held in a small room where there are no external distractions and where one may not be overheard. Most teachers do not have an office available to them, so the use of their classrooms should suffice if these conditions are met.

Sitting behind a large desk is often viewed negatively since physical objects of any size are felt to represent barriers to a comfortable interpersonal exchange. To some extent this is a matter of choice and comfort. Some teachers, especially when they are novices, feel more comfortable having a physical object between themselves and the parent. In this case sitting in one's chair behind a desk in the following fashion

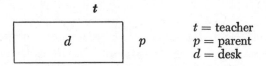

is considerably more desirable than the alternative below:

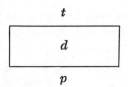

The most desirable seating arrangement for an interview is to place two comfortable chairs reasonably close to each other, at a 90 degree angle, with a small table nearby.

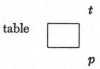

This arrangement allows parents to look at the teacher or straight ahead, whichever makes them feel more comfortable at any particular point in the conference. It also allows the teacher to vary his gaze, depending on his comfort or that of the parent. An ashtray may be on the small table for the convenience of either party.

It is unwise to have parents wait much beyond their scheduled appointment, an action that implicitly conveys a lack of interest and concern. In addition to being an inconvenience, a protracted wait may be considered rude and generate feelings of frustration and anger.

Noise and distractions of any sort should be avoided. Those who wish to discuss important matters with a professional want that person's undivided attention. Interruptions such as the following can only hinder the conference: phone calls, people who want "just a word with you," secretaries who must have something signed immediately, etc. Arrangements should be made to complete any administrative details prior to the conference, and secretaries and others who might inadvertently "pop in" should be advised that you will be occupied for a specified period of time. Some enterprising teachers hang "do not disturb" signs on their doors.

The room in which the conference is held should be free of external noises which tend to disrupt the interview. Conferences are best held when all or most children and other school personnel have left for the day. Insuring that the conversation between the teacher and parent is held in privacy is important in developing trust and good feeling.

It is sometimes helpful to make a few notes about certain parental concerns or to jot down some information or data about the child. However, continuous or even frequent note taking *during* a conference is to be avoided unless it is *essential*. This necessity is most unlikely to occur. Not only is continuous note taking rude, but it also conveys a sense of disinterest and overconcern with cold facts. To keep brief records of parent conferences the teacher, at her leisure, can jot down the gist of the conference for future reference after the parent leaves. Continuous note taking during a conference may be indicative of the teacher's attempt to maintain distance.

Finally, the possibility of having a conference at the parents' home should not be ruled out, especially when meetings at the school may be a hardship for them. Such a conference can give the teacher a more complete picture of the child's environment. It also reinforces the positive perception of the teacher's interest and concern in that she may be seen as extending herself beyond the call of duty. Home visits are also desirable because they allow working parents and/or both parents the opportunity to confer with the teacher. In considering a conference in the parents' home, the teacher should be sensitive to the parent who might feel that such a visit would be an imposition or an indication of the teacher's "nosiness."

Whether at school or at home, early meetings (either before the school year begins or shortly thereafter) with parents tend to diminish problems of attendance, discipline, and dropouts and have a favorable effect on grades and subsequent home and school contacts (Duncan and Fitzgerald 1969).

The Establishment of Goals

In most scheduled conferences or interviews one can ferret out the purpose of the meeting. Thus, the teacher may wish to consider how she might facilitate movement toward shared goals. Conferences normally begin with a certain amount of small talk about the weather, inflation, or an event in the news. This conversation is to be expected and serves the function of warming-up or settling in before more serious business is pursued. Abrupt, discourteous interruptions of this kind of talk are to be discouraged. For example, it would be inappropriate, after a short period of time, for the teacher to comment, "I know you didn't come here to talk about the kidnapping of Karen Green so let's get down to business." Sooner or later, one of the two will gradually begin to discuss the (usually) anticipated content of the meeting. People tend to sense when the time has arrived to begin to address more serious concerns. An abrupt response generally signals feelings of nervousness or impatience or, more seriously, indicates a most insensitive teacher.

Whatever the objectives of a conference are, Losen and Diament (1978, p. 61) believe it is important to keep the following principles in mind:

1. Working objectives should be clear.
2. Objectives should be mutually agreed upon.
3. There should be a specific timetable established for their accomplishment.

When unanticipated topics arise, the most productive posture is to remain calm, expect surprises, and try not to explain away or become defensive about them. The conference goal may shift from what the teacher had set initially to one of thoughtful listening, understanding, and responding. Interpersonal interactions are not programmed mechanical meetings, where the content and outcome is always predictable. As Lisbe (1978) notes,

> The realities of "people work" require a presence unlike other fields where processes are replicable. Carpenters follow blueprints, automobile manufacturers use molds, accountants work from forms, and pilots read instrument panels. There are no such guidelines when one human being faces another, where the uniqueness of each encounter requires uncompromising intensity. [p. 242]

During the course of a conference with a general goal (for example, the quarterly parent-teacher conference about a child's performance at school), the parents may mention, for example, that they are in the midst of divorce proceedings, which may have serious implications for the child's future. Generally, when such an event is communicated, it is done to alert the teacher to anticipated changes in the child's environment which may affect his schoolwork and behavior. Possibly the disclosure also serves a carthartic purpose; that is, it provides the parents with a chance to talk about an impending and emotionally filled event. In either case, empathic and supportive listening is all that is called for in most instances of this nature. Teachers should know that parents in difficult situations are often bombarded with well-intentioned but mostly unnecessary advice from a variety of sources and welcome the presence of an interested listener.

Another example is when a parent calls in an obvious state of distress and requests a conference without disclosing the problem. This type of a call would be disquieting to a teacher, who begins to search for the possible cause of the parent's concern, more often than not ascribing blame to himself. However, clear-cut, anticipated goals must be abandoned, except for one: careful, sensitive, attentive listening and appropriate responding.

Schulman (1974) discusses three general types of goal-oriented interviews, two of which will be examined here.

THE INFORMATION–ORIENTED INTERVIEW

The information-oriented interview is not supposed to deepen the contact between people but instead focuses on the collection of information or data. Some examples are public opinion polls, personnel interviews, or journalistic interviews.

Both the parent and teacher may, at different times during their relationship, need to seek information from the other. For example, the teacher may wish to gently probe into the various facets of the child's home environment. Generally, questions about a child's family situation need not be asked directly. Over a period of time the teacher gradually becomes aware of the family configuration, the feelings the parent as well as the siblings have toward the handicapped child, the support system (friends, relatives or professional help) available, and the like. The gathering of information is a gradual and ongoing process which generally takes place over time.

Parents may also need information, which often may be asked for quite directly. In responding to questions the teacher should try to be open; when asked a personal question or one she does not wish to answer for some reason, she should politely decline to give a full response. It is unlikely that a teacher will be asked a very personal question. More likely, information-seeking questions like the following may be anticipated: "How long have you been teaching at this school?" "Have you worked with retarded children long?" "Can you tell me how Adam is doing in his arithmetic?" "How have the other children been interacting with Adam?" "Have you lived in this town for many years or are you a newcomer?" "From which college did you get your education?"

Sometimes questions like these are asked just to make small talk; sometimes, so that the parent will feel on an equal footing with the teacher. Other parents may ask somewhat personal question to form an impression of the teacher. During initial meetings, human beings collect data on new acquaintances so that they can decide about developing potential friendships based on similarities in values and interests.

Variables in interpersonal attraction play an important role in the maintenance of friendships. Social psychologists have been particularly interested in and have written extensively on this subject (Berscheid and Walster 1969; Rubin 1973). Although the parent-teacher encounter resembles a professional rather than a personal relationship, and therefore some of the variables in interpersonal attraction are less salient than other factors in determining the course of the relationship, nevertheless, some sizing up of one another does take place.

During professional meetings—and to some extent in more personal encounters also—initial impressions are either reinforced, modified, or completely discarded as the relationship continues. The teacher may feel that some evaluative processes are in motion during initial conferences. In fact, it is not unusual for initial meetings between two people to be exploratory and to some extent superficial. Information-oriented interviews, then, serve a definite and important socializing purpose.

THE EXPERIENTIAL INTERVIEW

The experiential interview *focuses on the relationship* between the parties. The sharing of thoughts and feelings within an accepting atmosphere is the hallmark of this interview, and judgmental attitudes have no place. "This kind of interview becomes a microunit of life in which two people, the interviewer and interviewee, share feelings, understandings and behavior—a small unit of life experience in which the individuals involved share themselves" (Schulman 1974, p. 78). An illustration of an experiential interview follows (Johnny's mother is distressed over his lack of progress and has called on his teacher to discuss her concerns):

Teacher: Hello, Mrs. Wright. I'm glad we have a chance to get together. Would you care to sit down?

Mrs. Wright: Thank you. I feel foolish coming here to talk to you about this when I know you have other things to do.

Teacher: It sounds as if you do not wish to intrude on my time and that your concerns about Johnny seem minor compared to my other activities. I can understand how you feel, but I believe it is important to meet with the parents of the children I teach. The fact that *you* feel that a discussion is necessary tells me that our meeting is important. [The teacher is reflecting what she believes the parent is feeling, empathizing with her and assuaging her feelings of guilt and insignificance.]

Mrs. Wright: Well, I do feel somewhat better about taking up your time. I've come to talk to you about what my husband and I see as a lack of progress on Johnny's part. [Feeling less of an intruder now and sensing that the teacher is indeed with her, she proceeds.]

Teacher: I wonder if you could be a bit more specific. Are you referring to his progress academically or are you referring to his behavior? [To be able to respond adequately, the teacher requests additional information.]

Mrs. Wright: I am referring to his schoolwork. As a matter of fact, Johnny has become much more manageable at home than he has been. In contrast to the past, he is actually a pleasure to live with. That is one of the reasons why we don't want to say too much about the drop in his academic subjects.

Teacher: It sounds as if you are pleased with the progress Johnny is making in his behavior but are concerned that if you mention his schoolwork he may not be as pleasant to live with. [The teacher is correctly *ferreting out and communicating* the crux of the problem.]

Mrs. Wright: That's exactly right. My husband and I are afraid that he may become uncontrollable again if we push his schoolwork. We are very much concerned about this and are not quite sure whether we should leave him alone or push his schoolwork. [Implictly asking for advice from the teacher.]

Teacher: I can see the position you're in. You want Johnny to continue his social progress but you also don't want him to ignore his schoolwork. Let me describe what has been happening with Johnny at school and perhaps some way of dealing with the situation will become clear. I agree with your observations that Johnny is paying less attention to schoolwork. But I've noticed that he has been making a strong effort to develop friendships with others in class. As a matter of fact, his efforts are beginning to pay off. He has developed a relationship with two people in class—relationships that I see becoming stronger over time. Along with these friendships has come a greater acceptance of Johnny on the part of others in the class. My guess is that Johnny is learning that when he gives others a chance, he can develop friendships and that he really is a likeable person. He seems to be getting positive attention from others by being kind and reaching out rather than by being mean and abusive. It seems that his newly discovered social life is so demanding that he puts all his effort into his relationships at school *and* at home and that his schoolwork is slipping. I can't say for sure, but my guess is that as less energy is concentrated in becoming an acceptable friend and a welcome family member, he will begin to consider more seriously his academic status. [Provides observations and *ventures* an hypothesis that may lead the parent to a course of action.]

Mrs. Wright: What you are saying is that making friends with others seems to be very important to him now and that when he feels more comfortable with others his attention will hopefully shift to his schoolwork. If that's so, I think that it might be a good idea to continue to work on *our* relationship with him at home and lay off the academics for the time being. (The parent is led to a conclusion with the guidance of the teacher, who quickly comprehended her concern, empathized with her feelings, provided her with data from observations at school, and presented a way, without lecturing or giving direct advice, in which she could deal with the child. This method allows the parent to arrive at her own conclusions, based on a better understanding of the problem and by possessing the data required to take action.)

Teacher: What you are saying makes a lot of sense to me. I'll try to do the same at school. Why don't we talk again in another three months to see how things are going? [The teacher reinforces the idea that the parent made the decision about how to proceed, and she offers to meet again to re-evaluate the situation.]

In contrast to the information-oriented interview, the experiential interview may include information or data but stress is placed on the following: the feelings behind expressed verbalizations, accurately comprehending the problem by reflecting the content of the interview, sharing perceptions with the interviewee, being supportive, and facilitating the decision- or resolution-making process for the interviewee.

Listening

The reader may question the propriety of including a section on listening. Most of us assume that we all listen and that we listen well. Take a few moments to reflect on situations where someone else was physically present, ostensibly hearing what you were saying and yet not really *listening* to what you are trying to convey. All of us have encountered parents, friends, teachers, supervisors who heard but did not listen. More often than not our reaction to this inattention is to feel hurt, ignored, or possibly even angry. Frequently, the reaction to a non-listener is to change the subject, physically remove oneself from the situation or uncomfortably continue on with the fragmented and superficial chatter. When sufficiently angered we sometimes "return the favor" by in turn becoming inattentive ourselves.

What are some of the characteristics of good listeners? What behaviors are involved? What are some of the indicators of a poor listener? What specific skills can one develop to become a better listener? These are some of the questions to be addressed in this section.

Listening is not a mechanical activity. It is hard work and requires deep concentration, patience, and practice. It involves hearing the way things are being said, the tone used, while observing the speaker's gestures. In listening attentively, one must hear what is not said, what is hinted at, what may be held back, or what lies beneath the surface. We must learn to listen with our third ear (Reik 1972); or to put it more concretely, we hear with our ears, but we listen with our eyes and mind and heart and skin and guts as well (Ekman 1964).

Benjamin (1974) proposes a simple test to determine whether one is learning to listen:

> If during the interview you can state in your own words what the interviewee has said and also convey to him in your own words the feelings he has expressed and he then accepts all this as emanating from him, there is an excellent chance that you have listened and understood him. [p. 45]

There is no need to wait for a parent meeting to practice Benjamin's suggestion. It can be tried with friends, relatives, or colleagues.

The interviewer should become as physically relaxed as possible so that careful listening is accomplished more easily. Schulman (1974) believes this step is so critical to good listening that she proposes a set of relaxation exercises for interviewers who find it difficult to feel physically at ease.

Kroth (1975) presents an interesting conceptualization of the phenomenon of listening by constructing the following model:*

Figure 1
A Listening Paradigm

Listening

	A	B	
Passive			Active
	C	D	

Nonlistening

1. QUADRANT A—PASSIVE LISTENER

The passive listener is "there." She is with the parent in the present. In effect she thinks out loud with the parent, conveying

* From *Communicating with Parents of Exceptional Children*, p. 29. Adapted by permission of Love Publishing Co., Denver, Colo.

the feeling that what is being said is indeed understood. Nonverbal signs of acceptance—leaning forward, slight head nods, a smile— assures the parent that it is all right to continue to talk. Another term used to describe the passive listener, and one that to some has a more positive connotation, is "supportive listener." Often the parent is surprised that he could talk so much in the teacher's presence or that so much time could have passed.

A person who is not naturally a passive listener may find the role uncomfortable at first, but practice tends to decrease the initial uneasiness.

2. QUADRANT B—ACTIVE LISTENER

Kroth characterizes the active listener as one who will probably lean forward and maintain more than the usual amount of eye contact during a meeting. Verbally important and complex statements will be reflected back to the parent. However, the teacher must not dominate the interview by talking more than the parent nor should he engage in moralizing. His basic goal is to listen carefully and then respond appropriately by clarifying the problem and helping the parent to put it in perspective.

3. QUADRANT C—PASSIVE NONLISTENER

This type of listener simply does not concentrate on what is being said. Not only is content ignored or misunderstood but also underlying feelings are bypassed. To the parent this is probably the most frustrating interpersonal encounter, barring verbal or physical abuse. Passive nonlisteners who are being partially attentive may pick up some content, miss the rest, and be completely ignorant of affect.

A teacher may be particularly liable to passive nonlistening when a number of parent-teacher conferences have been held in succession. In such instances the teacher must make a concerted effort to block out previous conferences and overcome fatigue to listen attentively to the parent in front of her. Perhaps a more sensible plan would be to space conferences over several days, or at least to build in some breathing time by taking breaks between them.

As one approaches the end of a difficult day and begins to reflect on what has occurred, it is very easy to slip into a passive nonlistening role. We should all be allowed these temporary regressions. Only if passive nonlistening begins to become a pattern does the matter become serious.

4. QUADRANT D–ACTIVE NONLISTENER

Social chatter at a party is an example of active nonlistening. In such instances people talk to or *at* each other but seldom *with* each other. Neither party is particularly interested in what the other has to say, and their conversations are fragmented; that is, what person A says is not picked up by person B, who will normally introduce another topic. In conferences where both the parent and teacher have separate agendas, the possibility of such a fragmented exchange is greatly increased:

Teacher: I'm so glad you could come. I've been wanting to talk with you about Billy.

Parent: I'm having trouble getting Billy to do his homework. He always wants to put it off, and we have frightful arguments around the home.

Teacher: He's been fighting on the playground. I've had to keep him in from recess twice this week.

Parent: I don't think he understands the new math. That's probably why he doesn't do his homework. I wish you could do something about it.

Teacher: Do you have any idea why he's started fighting so much? Does he ever talk about it at home? We just don't know what to do with him. It's getting to be a real problem.

Parent: We're having a real problem, too. We're open for any suggestions. This arguing that Billy does is getting both of us upset.

Teacher: We at school want to cooperate in any way that we can. If you have any ideas about his fighting, call me, will you? It's sure been nice taking to you, and I'm so glad you could come. You're always welcome at school.

Parent: I'm happy to have met you. If you have any ideas how we can help at home, just call. We want to work closely with the school.

Kroth believes that this type of conferring happens quite often. Both parent and teacher are trying to communicate and cooperate, but they are not taking the time to listen to what the other has to say. In such instances both parties leave the conference feeling uneasy and frustrated. From the teacher's perspective, it is best to allow parents as much freedom to air their concerns as possible. After the teacher has responded to these concerns, the conference can shift to matters that she wishes to discuss.

Often the teacher's concern correspond to those of the parent, so that topics need not shift aimlessly. Should this give-and-take interchange not materialize and the parent talks for most of the session, a subsequent meeting might be scheduled where *the teacher* has an opportunity to discuss matters of importance. In such an instance a teacher may say, "I'm pleased that we had this talk about Audrey today. Unfortunately, time will not permit me to bring up a few thoughts that I wanted to share with you. I wonder if we could set up another meeting in about two or three weeks." Such a response tells parents that the teacher is willing to listen to their concerns, that she has certain time constraints, and that she has something to contribute which will serve as the structure for the next meeting.

Barriers to Effective Listening

Even though we cannot draw on research to substantiate any of the following hypotheses, there may be value in speculating on what factors constitute barriers to effective interpersonal communication.

Graduate training programs in education, and surprisingly even in counseling, put little value on the development of facilitative skills. In teacher education such training is of mild interest and therefore is relegated to a position of low priority. However, teachers are, whether they know it or not, also cast into the role of helper, facilitator—one who has a significant psychological affect on others. The acquisition of facilitative interpersonal skills, therefore, must be given higher priority in the curriculum. Teachers should read about interviewing skills, and then actually *practice* them under expert supervision.

In counseling, the acquisition of counseling skills is given much lip service, and in fact a considerable amount of theoretical material is mandatory reading for graduate counselors in training. But although it seems that counseling programs are becoming more experiential in nature, they are still imbalanced toward a *cognitive* understanding of theories and methods.

Another block to the development of facilitative interpersonal skills is related to the personality and skills of those supervisors and professors who educate teachers. It is not unusual for matriculated students to emulate the practices and behaviors of their mentors. Yalom (1975) observed that "Pipe-smoking therapists often beget pipe-smoking patients. Patients during psychotherapy may sit, walk, talk, and even think like their therapists" (p. 17). This behavior is as true in teacher education as it is in psychotherapy.

Write down those former or current supervisors, professors, or colleagues whom you emulate to some degree. Then try to identify those characteristics, behaviors, and attitudes that you have integrated into your personality or behavior, for example:

Person	*Characteristics, Behavior, Attitudes*
Ms. Swanson, teacher, supervisor	Impressed by and try to emulate the easy-going and relaxed way she has in relating to students
Professor Grant	Had an honest, effective, and nondefensive way of responding to questions he could not answer

Teacher educators and supervisors are not always the most effective social models for their charges. Teaching, whether in college, in elementary school, or in the field, is an *influencing* process; and we are often remarkably naive about the impact our social-interpersonal conduct has on those we teach and train. In discussing the effects of social modeling in counselor education, Jakubowski-Spector *et al.* (1971) observed the following:

What a counselor educator *does* may be more influential than what he *says;* our role as a model may be more important than our role as an instructor. If a counselor educator is trying to teach genuine communication, the educator's interpersonal dealings with his students should reflect or model the kind of behavior he endorses. Through our dealings with students, we show them what we are and what we expect from people. Too often, a counselor educator verbalizes the importance of genuineness and self-disclosure while his students do not find these behaviors in their interaction with him as an advisor, practicum instructor, or professor. As models, counselor educators could more effectively facilitate learning through striving to consistently act out the behaviors they are trying to teach. This may lead to a more consistent behavior in counseling students. [pp. 248–49]

Teachers should be aware of the learning objectives they have formulated and how their interpersonal behavior either reinforces these objectives or detracts from them. The discussion now turns to several barriers to effective interviewing *during* parent-teacher conferences.

Dealing with children for several hours a day is work, hard work, and fatigue at the end of a typical day is not uncommon. When psychologically or physically tired it is most difficult to be an attentive listener, but inattention due to fatigue conveys a lack of interest and concern. Teachers should be aware of their tolerance levels and regulate their working day to insure that they are alert when conferring with parents.

A factor often difficult to distinguish from physical fatigue is boredom. It is not an easy task to uncover the reason for one's boredom, but one might consider the following possibilities: disinterest in listening to the problems of others, hearing essentially the same story for the sixth time, preoccupation. Different action is required depending on the causal factor(s) operating.

Preoccupation with personal circumstances can be a barrier to effective interviewing. Also, novice interviewers may be thinking ahead, that is, thinking about their responses while the parent is talking. Transitory preoccupation is common and is to be expected, but chronic preoccupation necessitates some introspection.

Strong feelings about the parent is another barrier to effective listening. Being angry with or anxious about someone we are conversing with cannot help but interfere with the interview. Here again it is helpful to be aware of the source of the anger or anxiety before taking action. Often such awareness defuses the situation to such an extent that little else is required; the negative emotions decline in intensity and attentive listening can resume.

It is difficult to attend to another person if there is a great deal of *distraction*, either visual or auditory. The physical comfort of the teacher and parent can have an effect on the interaction, and there is some evidence that the interviewing environment is a factor (Sachs 1966).

Professional roles can be inhibiting, although how they interfere is unclear. Johnson and Vestermark (1970), who believe that some distancing is necessary, allow for the required sense of objectivity or perspective; others contend that professional roles, with their inevitable distancing, account for much of the ineffective interpersonal skills of people in the helping professions. Carkhuff (1968) marshalls a considerable amount of evidence in concluding that paraprofessionals (peers with some training in human relations) perform considerably better than professionals. Paraprofessionals, he argues, are perceived as friends who understand and genuinely care, as opposed to authority figures (professionals), who are removed from a clients' environment and presumably pretend to care because they receive remuneration for doing so.

Other possible barriers during conferences are differences in age, sex, race, or culture, as well as pacing and defensive behavior on the part of the interviewer. These variables require further attention and therefore will be discussed in subsequent sections.

Before continuing, consider the following questions:

1. In my experiences with others, which of the factors mentioned above have been interpersonal barriers for me? If I have overcome them, what process or technique has been helpful? If I haven't overcome them, perhaps someone else in the group has—but how?

2. In working with parents, which barriers may be the most difficult for me to deal with?

3. Are some of these barriers inevitable, and is there little hope that they can be changed successfully?

Other Negative Responses from Teachers

Benjamin (1974) discusses a variety of responses considered to be *nonfacilitative*. *Agreement and disagreement* can be used to indicate that in the teacher's opinion, the parent is right or wrong. Often these opinions are stated before adequate information is gotten from the parent, or the information is misinterpreted by the teacher.

> Example: *I can't agree with you. If I were you I'd place Robbie in a school for the deaf.*

A stronger sense of good or bad is involved in *approval–disapproval* responses. The teacher is expressing a value judgment from her frame of reference. Approval can be as dangerous as disapproval; if used too much it can shift the focus of the conference from helping the child to achieving approval for the parents. A real tug-of-war may ensue when the parent reacts to the teacher's disapproval.

> Example: *Your suggestion of encouraging David to read more in his areas of interest is a poor one. He should be reading in a variety of different areas.*

In using *ridicule or sarcasm,* the teacher condescendingly instructs the parent to demonstrate how absurd the parent's feelings or perceptions are.

> *Parent:* I'm sorry I couldn't make our last conference. You probably remember that day—it was raining so hard.
> *Teacher:* I can understand that. You probably would have gotten wet and melted on your way over.

In *threatening* a parent, the teacher makes it clear what steps will be taken should the parent continue on the same path. In short, the parent is warned about the consequences awaiting him should he persist in his erring ways. Of all the negative responses, implicit or explicit threats are the most deplorable.

> *(implicit)* Example: *I've told you before that it is essential that you keep me informed about David. You haven't been doing that so we will have to see what we are going to do about it.*

Defensive Behavior

Defensive behavior may be shown by either the parent or the teacher, and defensiveness by one party probably will result in some type of reciprocal defensive communication. An example of defensive communication is illustrated by the following remarks made by two teachers:

> *First Teacher:* I've been observing your method of trying to get kids interested and motivated in science. Your method is a flop. The kids you work with are actually more turned off now than they were before.
> *Second Teacher:* Maybe so but I've watched you trying to keep your kids under control. In watching you with your class I've often wondered whether they have a teacher at all.

The first teacher's comments contributed to the second teacher's feelings of inadequacy and subsequent hostility. The problem(s) they have with each other cannot be resolved as long as one or the other is made to feel inadequate and therefore defensive. The example illustrates rather overt hostility and defensiveness, but often the expression of these feelings is much more subtle.

It is a basic rule that whenever discernible resistance disrupts or impedes parent-teacher conferences, the exploration of such roadblocks must take precedence over other content. When a parent appears uncharacteristically quiet (or closed), the teacher should inquire about this behavior before going to an unrelated topic. Sensitivity and appropriate pacing are necessary for appropriate intervention.

Silence is one of the most common manifestations of resistance, especially when it is preceded or followed by other cues of avoidance. Superficial talk (or intellectualization) lasting over a considerable period is another indication that a parent may feel resistant, as is changing the subject, ignoring the teacher's comments, arriving late for appointments, or forgetting them altogether. Filibustering, excessive questioning, challenging the teacher about her shortcomings or flaws are other ways defensiveness is shown.

It is imperative that teachers understand what lies behind defensive behavior. Parents may, for example, be fearful of becoming involved in conferences, which they feel highlight their child's shortcomings and, by association, their own inadequacies. Parents who have attended several conferences liberally laced with their child's problems develop a generalized dread of all conferences, whether or not their fears are justified. Misconceptions of what parent-teacher conferences are about could result in negative attitudes; a parent may see them, for example, as a time to exchange social amenities. Also, parents may fear that heavy demands will be placed on them—demands that will be overwhelming. Anger at the school, the school system, or perhaps even at the teacher may account for resistance, as may fear that involvement with the teacher will require some sort of change in the relationship between parent and child. Finally, a parent's defensiveness during conferences may actually be a reflection of ambivalent feelings toward or rejection of the child.

Defensive behavior by the parent is to be expected at times, and it is the teacher's task to deal with it effectively. Conversely, defensive behavior by the teacher can be a serious matter and is not subject to modification by parents. The teacher is the professional helper and the parent is the recipient of a service. Should the teacher find herself feeling and/or acting defensively toward a parent, he would be well advised to think about the underlying reasons. Discussing the situation with an understanding friend, colleague, or supervisor often can provide fresh insights.

Interventions not necessarily defensive on the part of a teacher but capable of generating defensive behavior in parents are related to *pacing* or *timing*. For example, personal inquiries concerning parents' feelings about their exceptional child are most inappropriate during the first few conferences, and in general, ought not to be asked directly. Only after meeting with the parents several times and only when sensing that they want to discuss their innermost feelings about their child should the teacher broach the topic.

Moving too quickly can provoke anxiety; subsequent meetings will be fearful ones, if the parent shows up at all. By the same token, if parents disclose their feelings of shame and guilt, the teacher should be careful not to introduce disruptive and irrelevant remarks, such as "Joey was so excited last week when Santa visited the class." This type of response conveys to parents that the teacher is insensitive, feels awkward or uncomfortable by the parents' disclosure, or, even more serious, isn't interested in the parents' feelings.

There is nothing wrong with being professional in one's work. It implies exercising good judgment and conducting oneself in a responsible and ethical manner. Unfortunately, some professional helpers equate the word professional with being aloof, distant, and even arrogant. This is a form of defensiveness that allows one to maintain psychological distance. However, such behavior seems to reflect a cold and uncaring person. Feelings of dislike, anger, or fear can lead to defensive or protective maneuvers by the teacher. Sometimes the teacher's feelings are submerged (unconscious) and not readily accessible to herself; at other times she is aware of her feelings (e.g., anger), but not of the manifestation of related defensive behaviors (e.g., stern look).

Before proceeding, take twenty minutes to discuss the following issues in your groups:

1. Can you think of parent-teacher situations that might make you feel or act defensively?

2. Under what other circumstances do you tend to feel threatened and become defensive?

3. When you feel threatened how do you show it?

4. When you behave defensively how do you think others react to you?

5. How do you characteristically respond to someone else who is being defensive with you?

6. Between the present group meeting and the next one, be alert to obvious and subtle examples of defensive behavior you observe others use. Also, remain aware of your own defensive feeling and behavior and be prepared to discuss your observations.

Specific interviewing skills detailed in Chapter 5 should provide a sound basis for coping with defensive behavior. Two major considerations, however, ought to be mentioned at this point:

1. Obviously, before teachers can deal with the parents' or their own defensive behavior they must be aware of its existence. Also, teachers must be continually alert to signs of resistance in themselves and the parents.

2. Defensive behavior should never be ignored. A teacher's defensive feelings and behavior ought to be subject to active introspection or she may wish to discuss them with a colleague or supervisor. However, the teacher should sensitively probe into the nature of a parent's resistance before moving on to other content. Ignoring interpersonal impasses generally leads to deepening feelings of distrust.

Lecturing and Moralizing: Barriers to Effective Communication

Lecturing or moralizing has no place in helping relationships, and it is of questionable value in other interpersonal situations as well. Some may even doubt its positive value in the classroom or in church when it becomes strongly moralistic or repressive.

Lecturing and moralizing share some common properties. They both imply condescension and judgment. Although teachers are generally viewed as knowledgeable and helpful people, those who lecture or moralize may be seen as intellectual or moral superiors, not to be questioned, at best, *and not caring*, at worst. Parents who are recipients of such behavior will act with surprise or even shock. They will feel and act defensively (revolt and argue) or feel guilty and ashamed (become passive). The result is contradictory to healthy and productive interpersonal relationships, positive self-concepts, and personal growth.

Because lecturing and moralizing have so much in common it is difficult to point out distinguishing characteristics. Both suggest judgment and may imply that the teacher is disapproving.

> Example 1: *You know that the doctor told you that George had to have a new pair of shoes every two months. Not buying the shoes when he needs them can lead to permanent damage.* [In this comment the doctor is used as the authority, and guilt is generated by alluding to "permanent damage" as a consequence of the parents' negligence.]

> Example 2: *We discussed working with Lucy at home at other conferences. I am disappointed that you didn't take my advise seriously. It is absolutely essential that you put aside thirty minutes each day to work with her. There are several studies that show that parents who help their children at home are able to improve their IQ score by 10 points. I know you'll want to do what is best for your child.* [This lecture includes a variety of goodies: The parent is made to feel stupid because precious advice given at previous sessions had not been followed. The teacher registers his own sense of disapproval, thereby making the parent feel like a bad child. Authority is marshalled by citing studies indicating the parent has erred badly by acts of omission, e.g., not working with the child. Finally, a parting shot from the teacher injects a dose of guilt by implying that the parent hasn't been acting in the best interest of her child and that she had better change.]

Communications that imply "You shouldn't have done that," "That's a stupid thing to do," "You should respect me [the teacher] more," etc., leave the parent resentful and alienated, hardly in a mood to be accessible and cooperative.

In lecturing and moralizing, sophisticated weapons are brought to bear on the parent. Research studies, school authorities, doctors, or the teacher may be called upon to motivate or to change the parents' behavior. Moralizing can be made even more potent, and is thereby distinguishable from lecturing, by using religious tenets. Teachers with strong religious convictions must be careful not subtly or otherwise to use personal beliefs to manipulate parents, as illustrated in this somewhat extreme example:

> *We know that in God's eyes some people are born inferior and because of that I can see why you find it hard to accept Sam the way he is.*

On rare occasions personal religious beliefs are used in grossly misguided efforts to be helpful. Infrequently a small minority of those in the helping professions are so caught up by their missionary zeal, combined with a genuine desire to be helpful, that they try to proselytize others into the service of their particular sect.

> *I know how anxious and depressed you are about your child's handicap and your home situation that keeps getting worse. It seems like there is little hope—a very bleak future ahead. By the way, a religious organization that I belong to has been of help to others who are in despair. Our next meeting is Thursday. Why don't you come along with me and see what you think.*

Although these remarks cannot be classified as moralizing in the strict sense because they do not imply a judgment, personal religious beliefs—as well as personal beliefs about such issues as abortion, women's rights, busing, etc.—have no place in parent-teacher conferences. There is a significant difference between trying to coax a personal friend to a meeting of a religious group and a parent of an exceptional child. When referrals are required, teachers should make them to other *professional* services and agencies, not to religious or quasireligious sects, faith healers, and the like.

Moralizing or lecturing represents the antithesis of effective interpersonal communications, as illustrated by the following poignant remarks by Benjamin (1974):

> The interviewee is trapped. To surrender is to admit defeat. To resist is to declare himself an outlaw. Shall he bend the knee or raise his head in challenge? Thus beleaguered, he may act in a number of ways, but the chances are it will be acting, pretense. What is really happening within himself he is sure to keep well hidden. The foe is too formidable, the pressure too great, for anything but playacting or evasion. True, it may not always be playacting; the "culprit" may genuinely feel guilty and be shocked by his own behavior. Moralizing has been known to work. [p. 139]

Silences

Schulman (1974) points out that Western cultures, in contrast to Eastern ones, find silence between people barely tolerable. Because silence is viewed as an empty situation without meaning, when it does occur between two people or in a small group those involved often feel uncomfortable. However, people engaged in helping others must have an understanding of and be able to use and tolerate silences. Before continuing, take fifteen to twenty minutes to discuss the following related issues:

1. How you *feel* when there are periods of silence with one other person.

2. How you *feel* when there are periods of silence in a small group.

3. What your *feelings* would be if the discussion at this moment fell silent. (Should silences occur while doing this exercise, reflect upon and then discuss your interpretation of them.)

4. Situations in which you have been keenly aware of silences and how you (internally) responded to them (e.g., in a doctor's waiting room, in the teacher's lunch room, on elevators, sitting next to a stranger on a plane).

For people who conduct interviews, silences should be considered a positive form of communication. Beginning interviewers feel they must talk when pauses or silences occur, and an uneasy sense of wasting time or not doing a good job causes them to make inappropriate comments or ask unnecessary questions. Unfortunately, there are no rules about how long is too long for a period of silence. Each situation has to be assessed on its own merit. Silence is worthwhile only as long as it is communicating something or is serving some function. It can best be understood if the meaning of the pause and the context in which it occurs are clear. A high degree of sensitivity is required for the teacher to know when to remain quiet and when to make an appropriate remark. Sensitivity is generally acquired as one gains experience, but a review of silent behavior and what it may mean may help one's awareness.

Strong emotions may emerge, temporarily interrupting the flow of a parent's verbalization. Hammond *et al.* (1977) believe such emotions may be the result of the discussion of painful events, the recall of emotionally laden situations, or sudden insights. According to Schulman (1974), silence during the early part of the interview may reflect embarrassment, resistance, or fear of what the interviewer is thinking. Generally, as the interview progresses, silences gradually take on a more supportive meaning and serve as a medium for emotional expression and thought. Schulman believes it is essential for clients or parents to discover that they can be quiet and still be liked. They may use periods of silence to delve deeply into their feelings, to struggle with alternative courses of action, or to weigh a decision.

Bernstein *et al.* (1974) contend that silence may be a consequence of an apparent search for words or an attempt to clarify thoughts and feelings. For a teacher to interrupt during a silent period would interfere with the parents' struggle to organize their thoughts. Teachers should anticipate silences after responding to a parent with reflections on content or feelings. This pause allows the parent to contemplate what has just been said. When a teacher senses that long silences with a particular parent is an expression of resistance or defensiveness, it is the teacher's responsibility to actively deal with the problem. If she believes that she understands the nature of the resistance, a response like the following may be appropriate:

> *I wonder if the long silences we have is because I suggested at our last meeting that you might want to consult a psychologist. If so, I would very much like to know what your thoughts are about my suggestion.*

Should she be quite sure of the resistance but not know its source, the teacher might say something like:

> *I'm sure that we are both aware of the times we sit here not saying anything to each other. I sense a feeling of tension between us but I don't know what is causing it. Do you have any idea?*

Except as a manifestation of defensive behavior, teachers should view silences in a much more positive fashion than is generally the case in our culture. Silences, more often than not, give a parent a chance to rest or to reflect and organize his thoughts. Also, since a teacher's primary professional activity is to teach—in which speaking is essential—teachers may not be inclined to value silences. Thus, they should consider the virtues of silence and its appropriate use.

Overtalk

Teachers are trained to convey information, to put across ideas, to answer questions and to ask them. To engage in such activities teachers must be verbal; therefore, they talk more, and appropriately so, than the children they teach, although good teachers also listen.

In conferring with parents, the pendulum should swing in the direction of increased listening, and talking becomes a secondary role. This shift may be a problem for some teachers, as it appears that students selecting teaching as a profession have a propensity for verbalization. In my experience, students in teacher training programs appear to be more verbal, for instance, than students in counselor training programs. If teachers are more accustomed to talking than listening, they must make a concerted effort during parent-teacher conferences to control their speech and concentrate on what is being said. Also, Langden and Stout (1954) urge teachers to abandon "teacherish" speech when conferring with parents. Hetznecker et al. (1978) believe that overtalk can best be unlearned in simulated conferences where role playing is emphasized. This change is critical, the authors feel, because both parent and teacher in their respective roles vis-à-vis the child are accustomed to talk more than to listen.

> Advice, correction, admonishment, persuasion, information giving, and questioning are the adult techniques both parent and teacher direct at children. When relating to parents, a teacher needs to shift to a more receptive, attentive mode which emphasizes listening. [p. 366]

In defense of excessively verbal teachers it should be said that professional helpers in other fields also talk more than listen, particularly during their initial stage of training. Overtalk tends to decrease with training, in which feedback from supervisors and peers highlight positive and negative aspects of an interviewing style.

Overtalk may be symptomatic of a teacher's nervousness or represent a characteristic most of us share, namely, the tendency to give advice prematurely. Unlike counselors and psychotherapists, teachers do not have opportunities to work on their interviewing style in their training programs, where interpersonal facilitative behavior is not the prime focus.

A way to ascertain one's talking-to-listening ratio * is to record role-played interviews. To add a realistic dimension to the self-

---

* "Ratio" here does not refer to a mathematical concept. It does refer to one's overall assessment—more of a "feel" or sense than actual data.

evaluation, one could record a few actual parent-teacher conferences, being sure to obtain the parents' permission first. Tell the parents why you intend to record the session and how the recording will be used.

Another method commonly used to train social workers requires the interviewer to write down as accurately as possible what each person in the interview said. This is called a process recording, of which the following is a brief illustration:

> *Mrs. Brown:* I feel awful about Terry's performance in school. He is falling farther and farther behind.
>
> *Teacher:* I can sense your concern about Terry's lack of progress. What makes the situation even worse is your feeling that your son is losing ground that he won't be able to make up.
>
> *Mrs. Brown* (moves uncomfortably in her chair): Yes, and the more he gets behind the more his father and I push him to work harder. But the more we push him the less he seems to do. I'm just at my wits' end with Terry—what do you think I ought to do?
>
> *Teacher* (feels uncomfortable, feels she must come up with a solution): Well, maybe what you can do is to tell him about his other friends who are doing well in school because they work hard on their subjects. You could also tell him about some famous people who were very poor but overcame their problems by hard work and concentration. Another possibility would be to have him evaluated by our psychological consultant. There may be a psychological reason for his lack of progress.
>
> *Mrs. Brown* (looks confused): Well we told him so many times about his friends Jerry and Roger and how well they do in school because of their hard work. I think it's a good idea to talk to Terry about some people who have made it and the hard work it took to get there but—do you think there is something psychologically wrong with our son?

and so on, and so on.

As you lisen to a tape recording, go over a process recording, or if you are simply reflecting on an earlier meeting, keep the following points in mind:

1. Did you find yourself giving advice inappropriately? That is, did you offer advice before you really understood what the parents were saying?

2. In your eagerness to respond, did you catch yourself interrupting the parents?

3. Do you detect indications that you repeated yourself unnecessarily?

4. Were there indications that you tended to overelaborate a point? Try to recall your feelings during the conference. Did you, for example, find yourself repeating statements during uncomfortable silences? Did you catch yourself interrupting a parent because you were afraid of forgetting the point you wanted to make? Did you have a tendency to overelaborate when you were fearful of the parent, thereby giving him less time to talk and thus reducing your anxiety?

Teachers' Self-Disclosure

An essential response of parents during conferences is the expression of their reactions to the teacher's observations about the child's progress, their perceptions of how the child relates to other family members at home, their own feelings and those of other family members toward the child and so on. These verbalizations characterize a level of self-disclosure (or personal sharing) that is critical to cooperative and helpful parent-teacher conferences. In a sense this is the parents' contribution to rapport.

Although self-disclosure by the parent is important, the same cannot without qualification be said of the teacher. This issue is somewhat more complex in that a teacher's limited comments about his social and professional life and his reactions to a parent or a child are appropriate and often turn out to be helpful. In contrast, self-disclosures that dwell at great length on his educational achievements, professional reputation, marital problems, or sexual indiscretions confuse and bewilder parents, who sense that the teacher is in need of help or finds it necessary to have others view her in a certain way. In either instance, the parent is placed in a position of counselor. Although there is merit to authenticity in parent-teacher conferences, a teacher's indiscriminate self-disclosure serves the need of the wrong person.

The following exercise will allow you to examine a teacher's self-disclosing responses and your perception of which are appropriate and which are not. Also, in your groups, give examples and discuss what you consider to be proper and improper self-disclosing comments in a parent-teacher conference.

1a. Inappropriate: *You know I can relate to what you just said. Sometimes my boy friend treats me as if I don't exist. It really bugs me but I'm afraid if I mention this to him he might leave me.*

1b. Appropriate: *Yes, I know what you mean. There was a time when I had to juggle a job, a growing family, and school at the same time. It must make you feel like you're pretty much under the gun.*

2a. Inappropriate: *Boy, I am really angry! Ms. Kern, who just left, called me an incompetent teacher when I try to spend extra time with her boy. Sometimes I just don't feel appreciated in this job.* [Not only is the self-disclosure in poor taste but the teacher's remarks raise an ethical issue; what is it?]

2b. Appropriate: *The pleasure you feel when you help David reminds me of how good I feel when I take the time to work with my son.*

3a. Inappropriate: *I know what you mean. Dealing with in-laws can be a real pain. My mother-in-law really makes me feel inadequate. If I let her she would mother my kids and husband to death. She kinda makes me feel left out.*

3b. Appropriate *(in response to a question): Yes, the teaching profession can be demanding. The pressures pay off though when you see kids improving and liking what they are doing.*

Termination

Ending a conference is generally not difficult although it can be a problem in some circumstances. A parent's behavior may reflect a defensive need to keep talking or perhaps a need to have someone to talk with, compensating for a loneliness. At other times, it may indicate a more generalized difficulty with termination, a holdover perhaps from an earlier experience when it was traumatic to end an important relationship. Also, parents may be reluctant to end a conference because opportunities to talk with their child's teacher are rare and they want to get in all the time they can. If this is the case the teacher may wish to consider scheduling more frequent meetings.

Parent-teacher conferences are often circumscribed by time. These time limits may be the result of realistic constraints, such as a teacher's other duties; a policy determined by the school; or a teacher's thoughts on what amount of time is adequate.

Whenever possible, rigid time constraints used under all conditions should be avoided. Semiannual or quarterly conferences designed to communicate a student's progress may be scheduled for a fifteen-to-twenty-minute time period. Conferences designed to discuss issues in more depth should run longer (perhaps thirty-to fifty minutes).

For some interviewers, beginners in particular, closing is not easy. The teacher may be fearful of giving the impression that the parent is being pushed out—and depending on how termination is handled, a parent may indeed have this feeling.

Benjamin (1974) believes that the closing phase of an interview is critical, and two basic factors should be kept in mind: (1) both people in the interview should be aware of the fact that closing is taking place and accept it, the interviewer in particular; (2) during termination no new material should be discussed because this phase should focus on that which has already taken place. If fresh information or concerns emerge during closing, another interview will have to be scheduled.

There are important reasons for deferring new material during the final minutes of a conference. The teacher may have to keep another appointment and therefore will find it difficult to be attentive. She may also become covertly angry at the parent for coming up with new material that could have been introduced earlier. New information may be introduced (in fact, there is no way to avoid its introduction), but it can be deferred to the next meeting: "What you just mentioned is certainly worth discussing. Unfortunately, our time has run out, but I think we might want to discuss it first thing at our next conference."

Unless parents are especially sensitive or experienced, they will not necessarily know how much time is at their disposal. In this instance, the teacher can help by indicating that time will be up shortly: "Well our time is just about up. Is there anything else you'd care to mention before we close?" A teacher may wish to restate the gist of the discussion and, if necessary, comment about the focus of the next meeting:

> *I'm glad we had a chance to go over Ray's academic work. We both seem to agree that his language development and reading are coming along. We also talked about his problems in math, a concern that we plan to watch. At our next meeting let's spend some time on how our plans to help Ray seem to affect his attitude and his ability to complete his math assignments. Does this make sense to you?*

The termination of a conference should not be taken lightly. What occurs during the closing stage is likely to determine the parents' experience of the interview as a whole. Teachers should leave enough time for closing so that they don't find themselves rushed, since this might create the impression that the parent is being evicted. In general, the task of ending an interview becomes easier as the teacher appreciates its importance and learns to feel comfortable with it.

CHAPTER 5

Specific Strategies Useful in Working with Parents of Exceptional Children

The preceding chapter examined some of the conceptual principles involved in conducting effective parent-teacher conferences, but the teacher must also be exposed to practical skills. This chapter explores a variety of strategies generally used in interviewing. Where appropriate, role-playing exercises are included which are designed to allow the reader to practice the skills discussed.

Because principles and skills are sometimes difficult to separate, the reader will encounter topics that could possibly have been placed in Chapter 4. The decision to include them in this chapter was not arbitrary, however, in that concepts easily translated into specific skills are more appropriately placed in a chapter on skill development.

Establishing Rapport

The word "rapport" is thrown around more often by professionals, educators, and students in the helping professions than a

114

basketball at a neighborhood pickup game. To put it succinctly, rapport in the interviewing process refers to a comfortable yet rewarding (productive) meeting between two or more people. It is enhanced by good listening and responding as well as the sense of acceptance resulting in a mutual feeling of respect. Intuitively, both parent and teacher generally sense when rapport between them is good and when it is not. This intuitive feeling exists in other interpersonal encounters as well, for example, between a teacher and his supervisor, colleagues, other students, and social friends. We tend to avoid acquaintances when we sense a lack of mutual caring and respect.

In working with parents it is essential to deal with the issue of rapport (if it is lacking) before proceeding to other concerns. The teacher might consider the following causative factors:

1. You have a strong dislike for the parents' child, who happens to be the most demanding and exasperating youngster you've worked with in years. Your sense of frustration with the child makes it difficult to be open in your relationship with the parents.

2. You sense that there is an adverse reaction to you but you are not sure why.

3. You know that the parents view their child's educational program with considerable skepticism.

4. Either you or the parents are preoccupied with events not related to the conference.

5. You sense that the parents are uncomfortable talking about their handicapped child.

6. You are threatened by the parents because their professional status equals or exceeds yours.

7. You are threatened by the parents because you know they are sophisticated in their child's exceptionality.

Sometimes just understanding why rapport is poor between the teacher and the parents is sufficient. For example, knowing that the parents are preoccupied with a personal crisis, the teacher may wish to acknowledge her understanding that the parents are experiencing a problem, give them an opportunity to discuss it if they wish, and reschedule another appointment at some future date. Understanding that parents are displeased with their child's educational program may be unsettling and pose a personal threat to the teacher. However, perhaps this dissatisfaction reflects the parents' excessive and/or compulsive concern about the education of their children (exceptional or not) or their tendency to be critical of most things, and is not a criticism of the teacher.

This awareness not only allows the teacher to feel less threatened but also provides cues about how she might work with this type of parent. For example, the teacher might keep excessively concerned and/or overly critical parents informed in detail of the educational program developed for their child. She may even wish to solicit their input, knowing they will be less critical of a program they helped develop. Parents' behavior is often a manifestation of anxiety. By intelligently and cooperatively working with the parents, the teacher can reduce their anxiety to the extent that at least a minimal level of rapport is possible.

When the teacher senses that anxiety arises when he begins to talk about the parents' child, he might consider a different strategy, for example, saying something like, "I'm not sure that I'm right but it seems that whenever we begin to talk about Judy you begin to tense up," or "You get an overly concerned look on your face whenever we begin to discuss Judy. Am I right or am I off the track?"

Such an inquiry can open the door to a frank discussion of the parents' feelings toward and perceptions of their child. It may be a relief for them to discuss secretly held concerns with an empathic listener. Should their concerns roughly correspond to those generally faced by parents of exceptional children, the teacher can, at least for a few meetings, help work through them. In this way the parent-teacher relationship can proceed, and with a feeling of enhanced rapport. However, if the problems are excessive, the teacher should listen attentively and, near the end of the conference, suggest that the parents consider discussing them with someone who is more qualified. It would be an injustice to the parents and ultimately to the child to ignore their discomfort and hope that rapport will magically develop. Indications of psychological problems that require attention by a mental health professional include the following:

1. when a parent feels compelled to psychologically or physically abuse her child
2. when a parent implies that the child's existence is the cause of considerable family discord
3. when a parent is unable to shake the feeling that the handicapped child is another indication of her inadequacy as a person
4. when a parent's guilt over bearing a handicapped child is unbearable to the extent that she has considered suicide

5. when a parent reports that since the birth of the child night-mares have become commonplace
6. when parents comment that the child is repulsive and an embarrassment to them and they cannot stand to be in her presence

Whenever the teacher is unsure of the magnitude of the parents' reaction, she should consider discussing her observations with the school psychologist or some other available psychological consultant.

It is difficult to be prescriptive when we consider human interactions. Some teachers would be comfortable if their responses to parents could be learned in a programmed fashion. In establishing rapport or confronting the lack of it, there simply is no substitute for a perceptive sensitive teacher with good judgment. There are times when confrontation will damage rapport even more, and times when it will help; but making believe that there is no lack of rapport or hoping that it will improve by itself is simply unproductive. A sensitive probe will more often than not lay the foundation for a more gratifying relationship between teacher and parent.

Nonverbal Behavior and Paralinguistics

Many authors who have written on counseling, interpersonal behavior, or interviewing eventually address the issue of nonverbal behavior. In relating to another person, we depend heavily, perhaps at a somewhat less than conscious level, on nonverbal or paralinguistic cues in our interpretation of verbal messages.

For purposes of definition nonverbal behavior includes general body movements, gestures, and facial expressions; paralinguistic behavior is manifested in tone of voice, inflection, spacing of words, emphasis, and pauses. Another dimension of nonverbal behavior is body language, which includes the distance between people and the orientation or direction of the body (proxemics) as well as its motion (kinesics). Schulman (1978) has developed a scale that can be used to tabulate the nonverbal behavior of people one is observing. In addition the scale also incorporates a unit on eye contact and one on attending behavior in general.*

* Reproduced by permission of the C. V. Mosby Co. (St. Louis) and the author from Eveline D. Schulman, *Intervention in Human Services*, 2nd ed., p. 48.

Measurement scale: listening and responding skills

Directions: Place a check (∨) next to the rating that most closely approximates your observation of the interviewer's behavior. Check under each behavioral characteristic.

Eye contact: Maintains appropriate gaze, which is not a stare, but does not look away.
  1. Gaze is persistent and comfortable. _____
  2. Gaze is appropriate most of the time. _____
  3. Shifts gaze a little too often. _____
  4. Frequently shifts gaze. _____
  5. Persistently shifts gaze or stares. _____

Attending: Maintains appropriate posture; bends slightly forward from waist; maintains comfortable distance from client.
  1. Persistently shifts position and moves about. _____
  2. Frequently shifts position and moves about. _____
  3. Shifts position a little too often. _____
  4. Most of the time maintains appropriate posture. _____
  5. Persistently maintains appropriate posture. _____

Hand gestures: Moves hands slowly and appropriately; gestures appear to be comfortable.
  1. Gestures are persistently comfortable and appropriate. _____
  2. Gestures are usually comfortable and appropriate. _____
  3. Some signs of "jerky" hand movements, which are disturbing. _____
  4. Tense, sudden movements frequently occur. _____
  5. Persistently uses inappropriate and annoying hand gestures. _____

Facial expression: Smiles or shows other expressions that are appropriate and pleasant.
  1. Persistently maintains unpleasant and inappropriate facial expression. _____
  2. Usually maintains unpleasant and inappropriate facial expression. _____
  3. Occasionally has unpleasant and inappropriate facial expression. _____
  4. Usually maintains pleasant and appropriate facial expression. _____
  5. Persistently maintains pleasant and appropriate facial expression. _____

Voice tone: Voice is pleasant, sounds relaxed, and has appropriate volume for hearing.
  1. Persistently has unpleasant tone that varies in loudness, either too loud or too low. _____
  2. Usually has unpleasant tone that varies in loudness. _____
  3. Occasionally has pleasant tone with appropriate volume. _____
  4. Usually has pleasant tone with appropriate volume. _____
  5. Persistently has pleasant tone with appropriate volume. _____

Comment: Write a brief comment about the interviewer that you think the supervisor should know.

The idea that speech is often intended to obscure a true feeling or a particular meaning has gone beyond hypothesis; that is, nonverbal cues do, in fact, more accurately reflect a person's inner life than what one says. Since this belief has been substantiated by a considerable amount of research (Knapp 1972), it is reasonable for those in the helping professions to become knowledgeable about and sensitive to nonverbal behavior.

For most of us the discrepancy between verbal and nonverbal behavior (e.g., someone tells you he fells perfectly comfortable in your presence while simultaneously he is sitting rigidly in a chair with his arms and legs crossed) by someone we are talking to is not traumatic, although it was maybe confusing and at times annoying. There is, however, some evidence that such double communication can have a devastating effect on children, who see their parents as communicating two contradictory messages (e.g., a mother telling her child she loves him while physically moving away).

An enormously useful skill for teachers, then, would be the ability to read nonverbal cues. These cues either augment what teachers are hearing or allow insight into a feeling or attitude that normally would be hidden.

However, teachers should be cautious in their interpretation of nonverbal cues. The same behavior manifested by two different people may have vastly different meanings. Interviewers often make a "perception check" on what they think they are perceiving. For example, a teacher may comment to a parent: "I hear you saying that you are pleased with George's progress but your facial expression leads me to believe that you are not entirely satisfied. Am I reading you right or am I off-base?" This type of check enables the parent to say what he is in fact feeling and to either agree with or refute the teacher's observation.

As she gains experience and becomes more aware of nonverbal behavior, the teacher's abilities to interpret and respond to these cues intelligently will grow. However, she should beware of such traps as that in which a misguided psychologist ascribed (in a Sunday-supplement) specific meanings to specific cues. This person undoubtedly wrote the article for its entertainment value and actually included a series of rather innocuous and amusing behaviors. Nevertheless, commentaries in which the behavior and interpretation appear to be inseparable should be taken cautiously.

Egan (1976) extends the concept of verbal listening to include nonverbal behavior. Below are three exercises he developed to help sharpen the reader's perceptual and communication skills:*

EXERCISE 1—BODY LANGUAGE

The purpose of this exercise is to provide several forms of nonverbal behaviors that carry messages. The behaviors listed below might accompany the words of a speaker, or they might be the behaviors of group members who are silent at the moment.

You are in a meeting, observing your fellow group members. You observe, at one time or another, the following nonverbal or paralinguistic (voice-related) behaviors. Without any further context, try to indicate what possible meanings each of these behaviors can have. Try to find more than one meaning for each behavior.

1. A person nods his head up and down.
2. A person turns her head rapidly in a certain direction.
3. A person smiles slightly.
4. A person's lower lip is quivering.
5. A person speaks in a high-pitched voice.
6. A person's voice is monotonous.
7. A person opens his eyes wide suddenly.
8. A person keeps her eyes lowered as she speaks to someone else.
9. A person's nostrils are flaring.
10. A person raises one eyebrow.
11. A person shrugs his shoulders.
12. A person has her shoulders forced back.
13. A person has his arms folded tightly across his chest.
14. A person is waving her arms.
15. A person is holding his chair tightly with his hands.
16. A person hides part of her body with her hands.
17. A person's breathing is quite irregular.
18. A person inhales quickly.
19. A person digs his heels into the floor.
20. A person continuously moves her legs back and forth.
21. A person sits with her arms and legs folded tightly.
22. A person is constantly squirming.

* Adapted from *Interpersonal Living: A Skills/Contract Approach to Human-Relations Training in Groups*, by G. Egan. Copyright © 1976 by Wadsworth, Inc. Reprinted by permission of the publisher, Brooks/Cole Publishing Co., Monterey, Calif.

23. A person holds her body bent to one side.
24. A person has a tic.
25. A person is getting pale. [pp. 100–101]

Compare your meanings with those of a partner or share them with all members of the group. How many different meanings are associated with each kind of behavior? What are the implications of this fact?

Notice that most of these behaviors have more than one possible interpretation. For this reason, both verbal and nonverbal behavior must be interpreted in the light of the total communication; the verbal and nonverbal behavior of the speaker and the context in which his communication is taking place.

EXERCISE 2—THE IMPORTANCE OF
NONVERBAL CUES FOR VERBAL
COMMUNICATION

The purpose of this exercise is to provide some idea of how much one depends on nonverbal cues in the interpretation of verbal messages.

Choose a partner from among your fellow group members. Sit facing your partner. *Close your eyes.* Have a two- or three-minute conversation on some topic you agreed to discuss earlier; remember to keep your eyes closed during the entire conversation.

Share your feelings during the conversation. What nonverbal cues did you miss the most? In what ways was the conversation stilted?

EXERCISE 3—LISTENING TO NONVERBAL
AND PARALINGUISTIC CUES

The purpose of this exercise is to become more sensitive to nonverbal and paralinguistic cues and messages, which may confirm, punctuate, emphasize, modulate, or otherwise modify the verbal messages of the speaker and thus contain the real message. For instance, if the speaker raises his voice (paralinguistic cue) and pounds on the table (nonverbal behavior) while delivering an angry message, then both cues underscore and emphasize his anger. However, if the speaker says in a very hesitating way (paralinguistic cue) while fidgeting with his hand (nonverbal cue) that yes, he would like to go out to dinner that night, these cues contain the real message—which contradicts the verbal one.

Divide into groups of four (Members A, B, C, and D). Members A and B should spend five or six minutes discussing what they like and don't like about their present interpersonal style (or any other topic relevant to the training). Members C and D act as observers. While A and B are speaking, C and D should take written notes of A and B's nonverbal and paralinguistic behavior, being careful not to overinterpret it. After five or six minutes, C and D should report to A and B the highlights of the observed behavior. Then roles are switched and the process repeated. Some examples of typical feedback are as follows:

> *Most of the time you spoke very quickly, in spurts. It gave me a feeling of tension or nervousness.*
>
> *You sat very still throughout the dialogue. Your hands remained folded in your lap the whole time, and there was almost no bodily movement. The position made you look very proper, and it gave me an impression of shyness or rigidity.*
>
> *When you talked about being a very sensitive person, one who is easily hurt, you began to stumble over your words a bit. The message seemed to be that you are sensitive about being so sensitive.*
>
> *You tapped your left foot almost constantly.*
>
> *You put your hand to your mouth a great deal. It gave me the impression of hesitance on your part.*
>
> *When B began to talk hesitantly about being shy, you leaned back and even moved your chair back a bit. I'm not sure whether you were showing him that he made you uncomfortable, or whether you were easing off, giving him room to speak.*
>
> *You broke eye contact a great deal when you were talking about yourself, but not when you were listening.*
>
> *You were so relaxed—at times you even slouched a bit—that you almost gave me the impression that you were uninterested in the whole task.*

Minimal Encourages To Talk

The interview may be thought of as a give-and-take meeting between two people, where one is generally (but not always) a professional helper of some kind and the other is in need of information or assistance. Before this mutual exchange, it is generally the responsibility of the interviewer (the teacher) to encourage the interviewee (the parent) to talk, to express as fully as possible the reasons for his visit or how he may be responding emotionally or behaviorally to a particular incident or event.

A teacher may impede the parent's full expression by saying too much or by intervening inappropriately. Particularly during initial meetings or during the first few minutes of a particular session, it is the teacher's task to stay out of the parent's way, and at the same time, to convey her attentiveness.

Minimal encourages to talk, by providing limited structure, will reinforce the parents' desire to communicate as well as convey the fact that the teacher is listening. Some kinds of minimal encourages follow:

> *"Could you tell me more?"*
> *"Where would you like to begin today?"*
> *"Oh?" "So?" "Then?"*
> *"And?"*
> *"Mm-hm." "Uh-huh."*
> *the repetition of one or two key words*
> *simple restatement of the parents' last comment*
> *silence (accompanied by nonverbal indicators of attentiveness, e.g., eye contact, forward lean)*

As an example, consider Benjamin's (1974) analysis of the utterance, "Mm-hm." By using "Mm-hm" the interviewer is saying, "Go on, I'm with you; I'm listening and following you," as well as indicating approval of what the interviewee is saying.

Of course we can communicate in a positive or negative vein by using paralinguistics (how words are expressed) or nonverbal behavior (like the raising of an eyebrow). As a general rule, minimal encourages (or invitation) to talk tends to convey, with the fewest words, the teacher's interest and reinforces the parent's communication. Of course, when a teacher wants to minimize a parent's chronic verbosity this strategy is contraindicated.

Other Helpful Leads

Below are some phrases teachers may wish to use when they feel fairly confident that their perceptions are accurate and that the parent is receptive:

You feel ———
It seems to you ———
From where you stand ———
As you see it ———
What you're saying is ———
I'm picking up that you ———
I really hear you saying that ———

When the teacher is uncertain about her perception or senses that the parent might not be open to her observations, she might consider using the following phrases, which are more tentative:

I'm not sure if I'm with you, but ———
What I guess I'm hearing is ———
Correct me if I'm wrong, but ———
This is what I think you are saying: ———
I'm not sure if I'm with you; do you mean ———
Let me see if I'm with you; you ———

Teachers should be cautious in apprasing what a parent may be communicating and consider most conclusions as tentative until they have been verified through the use of response leads, which enable the parent to confirm or deny stated observations. Although we see many people who seemingly behave the same way in comparable situations, share attitudes and beliefs that vary little from person to person, and appear predictable in a number of ways, we must remember the enormous complexity of human beings and how they are unique.

Microtraining

In 1967 Dwight Allen developed an innovative approach to teacher training which he called microteaching. Shortly thereafter a colleague of his at the University of Massachusetts adapted it to the training of counselors. Ivey's (1971) microcounseling model, which has had a dramatic effect on the training of counselors, has also been applied to teachers, paraprofessionals, children, teenagers and college students; in fact, it can appropriately and easily be administered to anyone interested in developing his interpersonal effectiveness.

According to Ivey, microtraining is based on several assumptions:

1. It is possible to lessen the complexity of the interviewing process by *focusing on single skills.* The objective of the interviewer is to master one skill at a time rather than becoming competent in all areas simultaneously. It is this aspect of acquiring single, isolated skills, each taught separately, that significantly distinguishes this approach from other models.

2. Microtraining techniques provide important opportunities for *self-observation and self-confrontation.* An interviewer's role playing should be subject to immediate examination and critical evaluation by a supervisor; by reviewing a videotape of the session with a supervisor, or by reviewing the videotape alone and conscientiously evaluating one's performance. What is critical is that the practice session is examined *immediately* and is subject to *evaluation.*

3. Interviewers can learn from watching *social modeling,* videotaped demonstrations of the skills they wish to learn. These sessions may be developed locally by participants knowledgeable in the microtraining technique. Also, Ivey has produced a series of microcounseling tapes that may be rented or purchased.

4. Ivey believes that the skills taught in microcounseling cut across theoretical lines because good initial interpersonal skills are basic to all communication and therapeutic approaches.

The implementation of the microtraining model corresponds to the following steps, which are applied in a sequential fashion (adapted from Ivey 1971):

1. The teacher receives instructions to enter a room where he will interview a parent. Depending on the situation, the topic may or may not be defined. Similar instructions are given to the volunteer parent, with the exception that he is told [that] he is about to be interviewed.

2. A five-minute diagnostic session (with the teacher interviewing the parent) is then videotaped.

3. The parent leaves the room and completes an evaluation form or [perhaps is] interviewed by a second supervisor. These data are then available for the supervisory session with the teacher.

4. The teacher reads a written manual describing the specific skill to be learned in this session. The supervisor talks with him about [relating it to the content discussed in the manual].

5. Video models of an expert demonstrating the specific skill

are shown. There may be a positive and a negative model of the skill.

6. The teacher is shown his initial interview and discusses it with his supervisor. He is asked to identify examples where he engaged in or failed to apply the specific skill in question.

7. The supervisor and teacher review the skill together and plan for the next counseling session.

8. The teacher reinterviews the same client for five minutes.

9. Feedback and evaluation on the final session are made available to the teacher. [the use of the words "teacher" and "parent" is mine]

To evaluate an interviewer's performance, Ivey (1971) has developed the following interviewing effectiveness scales:*

SCALE 1

insensitive	—	—	—	—	—	—	—	sensitive
irrelevant	—	—	—	—	—	—	—	relevant
nervous	—	—	—	—	—	—	—	calm
hesitant	—	—	—	—	—	—	—	confident
unskilled	—	—	—	—	—	—	—	skilled
unattentive	—	—	—	—	—	—	—	attentive
uncomfortable	—	—	—	—	—	—	—	comfortable
dull	—	—	—	—	—	—	—	interesting
confused	—	—	—	—	—	—	—	sensible
doubts his ability	—	—	—	—	—	—	—	confident
gloomy	—	—	—	—	—	—	—	cheerful
jittery	—	—	—	—	—	—	—	calm
unintelligent	—	—	—	—	—	—	—	intelligent
irresponsible	—	—	—	—	—	—	—	responsible
insincere	—	—	—	—	—	—	—	sincere
apathetic	—	—	—	—	—	—	—	enthusiastic
tense	—	—	—	—	—	—	—	relaxed
colorless	—	—	—	—	—	—	—	colorful
boring	—	—	—	—	—	—	—	interesting
formless	—	—	—	—	—	—	—	formed
unreal	—	—	—	—	—	—	—	real
unsociable	—	—	—	—	—	—	—	sociable
shallow	—	—	—	—	—	—	—	deep
careless	—	—	—	—	—	—	—	careful
rude	—	—	—	—	—	—	—	polite

Adapted from Allen E. Ivey, *Microcounseling: Innovations in Interviewing Training*, pp. 183–84. Reprinted courtesy of Charles C Thomas, Publisher (Springfield, Ill.).

SCALE 2

clumsy	—	—	—	—	—	—	—	skillful
incompetent	—	—	—	—	—	—	—	competent
confusing	—	—	—	—	—	—	—	clear
not meaningful	—	—	—	—	—	—	—	meaningful
shallow	—	—	—	—	—	—	—	deep
unsympathetic	—	—	—	—	—	—	—	sympathetic
distant	—	—	—	—	—	—	—	close
socially inept	—	—	—	—	—	—	—	socially adept
indecisive	—	—	—	—	—	—	—	decisive
hostile	—	—	—	—	—	—	—	friendly
unrealistic	—	—	—	—	—	—	—	realistic
irritable	—	—	—	—	—	—	—	pleasant
passive	—	—	—	—	—	—	—	active
insecure	—	—	—	—	—	—	—	secure
weak	—	—	—	—	—	—	—	strong
awful	—	—	—	—	—	—	—	nice
erratic	—	—	—	—	—	—	—	stable
inconsistent	—	—	—	—	—	—	—	consistent
indifferent	—	—	—	—	—	—	—	conscientious
lazy	—	—	—	—	—	—	—	industrious
immature	—	—	—	—	—	—	—	mature
inattentive	—	—	—	—	—	—	—	attentive
antisocial	—	—	—	—	—	—	—	social
inefficient	—	—	—	—	—	—	—	efficient

In a classroom or in a small group these scales may be completed by group members and given to the person who played the role of the teacher. The interviewer may look at the returned scales individually, or should one wish to quantify the data, compute a mean for each item. Such feedback should alert the teacher to areas of strengths and weaknesses. Of course, those areas of glaring deficiencies would be the ones to concentrate on in subsequent role playing.

To quantify data from the preceding scales it will be necessary to give each concept a numerical value, e.g.:

clumsy $\underline{\quad}\overset{1}{\quad}\underline{\quad}\overset{2}{\quad}\underline{\quad}\overset{3}{\quad}\underline{\quad}\overset{4}{\quad}\underline{\quad}\overset{5}{\quad}\underline{\quad}\overset{6}{\quad}\underline{\quad}\overset{7}{\quad}\underline{\quad}$ skillful

Each concept must be anchored with a negative word on the left (clumsy) and a positive one on the right (skillful). Positive and negative words are not alternated or mixed.

As a result of the insights derived from the microtraining model, virtually any counseling or teaching activity can be broken down into its component parts. Flanders (1970) has investigated the effect direct and indirect teaching has on the learning and attitudes of students. For example, indirect teaching includes such behaviors as minimal talk from the teacher and maximal talk from the students, minimal lecture and maximal discussion, stress on independent learning, frequent praise of students, etc.

Attending Behavior

Ivey broke down into teachable units what he considered to be the essence of good listening, which he called "Attending Behavior," and these units include eye contact, posture, and verbal following behavior. Ivey examines a number of studies supporting his contention that conscientious listening elicits uniformly positive feelings and behaviors on the part of others.

One approach to the teaching of attending behavior is to have the interviewer practice the direct *opposite* of the behavior to be learned. Then, to allow him to see the contrast between poorly and properly done behavior, he tries to do it correctly. The following model may be used:

1. Break up into pairs and decide (1) who will first play the role of the interviewer (teacher) and who will play the interviewee (parent); (2) the situation. You may refer to the critical incidents in Chapter 7 or make up other ones. It is generally helpful to give the teacher only a sketchy idea of the problem the parent intends to present.

2. For three to four minutes engage in the *opposite* of the behavior (say eye contact) that is under study.

3. After the three or four minutes, continue with the same topic but switch roles. Remember *lack of eye contact* is still to be practiced.

4. Reverse roles again and for about the same amount of time (three to four minutes) practice what you consider to be *appropriate* eye contact behavior.

5. Reverse roles again so that both people have had an opportunity to practice the behavior properly.

6. Begin a discussion of the two conditions. For example, what was your reaction toward the interviewer when she used comfortable eye contact as opposed to when she did not? What general *feelings* were you aware of under the two conditions? What *feelings about yourself* did you realize?

7. After practicing both proper and improper eye contact and after a debriefing session, move on to the next microunit and begin at number 1 again.

Below is a summary of Ivey's (1971) definitions of the three units that make up attending behavior. After reading the definitions you should be ready to begin role playing.

1. *Posture:* The teacher should be physically relaxed and seated with natural posture but with a slight forward lean. If the teacher is comfortable, he is better able to listen to the person with whom he is talking. Also, if the teacher is relaxed physically, his posture and movements will be natural, thus increasing his own sense of well-being. This sense of comfortableness better enables the teacher to attend to and to communicate with the parent.

2. *Eye contact:* The teacher should initiate and maintain eye contact with the parent. However, eye contact can be overdone. A varied use of eye contact is most effective, as staring fixedly or with undue intensity usually makes the parent uneasy. If you are going to listen to someone, look at him.

3. *Verbal following behavior:* The final characteristic of good attending behavior is the teacher's use of comments that follow directly from what the parent is saying. By directing his comments and questions to the topics, the teacher not only helps develop an area of discussion but also reinforces the parents' free expression, resulting in more spontaneity and animation in their talk. Paraphrasing, which is discussed later in this chapter, resembles verbal following behavior but is a somewhat more sophisticated response.

SUMMARY OF RULES

The teacher's goal is to listen attentively and to communicate this attentiveness through relaxed posture, varied eye contact, and appropriate verbal responses.

1. Relax physically; feel the presence of the chair as you are

sitting on it. Let your posture be comfortable and your movements natural; for example, if you usually move and gesture a good deal, feel free to do so at this time.

2. Look at the person with whom you are talking.

3. Follow what the other person is saying by taking your cues from him. Do not jump from subject to subject or interrupt him. If you cannot think of anything to say, go back to something he said earlier in the conversation and ask him a question about that.

Interpersonal Process Recall

Kagan (1971) developed a process by which professionals may better understand their own inner experiencing in a helping relationship. A major objective of the model is to develop one's ability to introspect about an interview shortly after it is over. Another objective is to develop the ability to sense and respond, if appropriate, to unverbalized perceptions and feelings present *during* an interview. Kagan's studies reveal that professional helpers have feelings and make observations during interviews that they are aware of at some level, but apparently their awareness of more subtle aspects of an interview is not as acute as it might be.

The fact that helpers (and also helpees) experience much more during an interview than is ever verbalized can be demonstrated by asking, right after a conference, what was experienced during the meeting. Being keenly aware of one's feelings and thoughts is related to the notion of immediacy. As Egan (1975) observes, "Once [the teacher] sees the richness of this unused material, he can learn to step back from the interview during the interview itself, see what the [parent] is doing, see what he himself is feeling and doing [or not doing], and use what he notices immediately, if it is appropriate" (p. 177).

Lister (1966) developed a concept of internal awareness and how it can help in interpersonal situations. (In reading the quotation below the reader might substitute the word "teacher" for "counselor" and "parent" for "client.")

> Counselors have focused on clients' experiencing as a guide to their behavior during an interview. Most counselors feel that they can function more effectively when they know what is "going on" within another person. It seems that experiencing can also pro-

vide the counselor with a kind of "intrapersonal communication" which aids him in detecting and modifying within the immediate present subtle, moment-by-moment nuances of feelings within himself which disrupt his communication with his client. [p. 55]

Lister contends that outward signs of discomfort or threat are often preceded and accompanied by identifiable internal states. For example, when a teacher feels threatened (internal), her throat may tighten (external), causing a pinched, anxious tone in her voice; or she may become aware that certain voluntary muscles have been tense for some time, which was preceded by a feeling of anger.

Although being able to *respond* with immediacy during an interview is the primary goal of Kagan's Interpersonal Process Recall (IPR) model, a teacher's *awareness* of her feelings toward a parent may be enough. To illustrate, a teacher may realize that a particular parent generates feelings of guilt and anger with comments like "I wish you'd spend more time with my son" or "George always used to talk about Mrs. Grayson, his third-grade teacher, and how she used to make him feel like he had a second mother."

Instead of openly dealing with the parent's remarks or interpersonal style, which the teacher won't be able to alter anyway, her awareness of the effect the parent has on her (anger or guilt) gives her some significant data upon which to build a set of hypotheses about the parent. She may hypothesize that what she is experiencing probably isn't unique to her and that others are treated in the same fashion and have similar responses. These insights may provide cues about the parent's child, for example, why other children tend to avoid him. The interpersonal style of the parent may reveal why the child responds with feelings of shame, guilt, and fear in relating to you or other children. Conversely, a parent's warmth and caring and your subsequent feelings of comfort in his presence help you understand why his child, who may be severely handicapped, seems so much better adjusted psychologically than the other child.

The following process, which uses Kagan's IPR model in role playing, allows some general insights into the often unexpressed feelings and perceptions of both teacher and parent.

1. Divide the group or class into pairs.
2. Each pair engages in a five-minute interview (you may wish to construct an interview, to use situations alluded to in other sections, or draw upon the critical incidents in Chapter 7).

3. At the end of the interview, each pair meets with another pair.

4. The parent from pair *A* meets separately with the one from pair *B*. They help each other explore their feelings and perceptions about the interview, namely, what each parent thought and felt about himself, about the teacher, and about the interaction generally but did not verbalize.

5. At the same time, the two teachers meet and do the same thing.

6. After about ten minutes all four members meet together. The two members of pair *B* help the two members from pair *A* share their thoughts and feelings that were not verbalized.

7. The process outlined in number 6 above is repeated with pair *A* helping pair *B*.

8. Discuss the process and what you learned from the exercise in the larger group.

Paraphrasing

Paraphrasing is the technique that constitutes the core of good interviewing because it captures the essence of understanding: *empathy*. Good listening and attending are its necessary prerequisites.

Ivey and Gluckstern (1974) believe that paraphrases serve three purposes: (1) they convey to the parent that the teacher is trying to understand what is being said; (2) they crystallize a parent's comments by making them more concise, thus giving better direction to the interview; and (3) they provide a check on the accuracy of the teacher's perceptions.

Ivey and Gluckstern (p. 26) distinguish paraphrasing from simple restatement:

> *Helpee:* I don't know about him. One moment he's nice as can be, and the next minute he is a real bastard.
> *Helper 1:* He's a real bastard. [restatement]
> *Helper 2:* He's pretty inconsistent then.

or

> His inconsistent behavior makes it difficult to trust him. [Both of *Helper 2's* responses are paraphrases in contrast to the restatement from *Helper 1*.]

Paraphrases, then, go beyond restatements and tend to capture the core of what someone is saying.

Brammer (1973) breaks down paraphrases (he uses the term "reflections") into feeling and content. *Content* paraphrasing repeats, in fewer and fresher words, the essential *ideas* of another person. It is used to clarify ideas that the parent may be expressing with some difficulty. In reflecting, the teacher tries to find the essence of what is being said rather than just restating the words.

Two examples of *content* paraphrases follow:

Parent: Sometimes Ron seems close to us and affectionate and at other times he is distant and preoccupied.

Teacher: He tends to move in and out of your relationship with him. His behavior can be kind of puzzling.

A simple restatement, which is not to be considered a poor response, might be

Teacher: Sometimes Ron is close to you and at other times more distant.

The paraphrase goes beyond the restatement by focusing on the *relationship* between Ron and his parents and not just Ron's behavior. It also reflects what must be a confusing situation for Ron's parents ("His behavior can be kind of puzzling").

Parent: Every time I come here to talk with you I feel like a burden . . . as if you have other things you have to do.

Teacher: You seem to be saying to me that I give off signals that tell you that I would rather be doing something else than talking with you. Can you tell me a little more about this so that I can better understand?

This paraphrase focuses on possible cues the parent is picking up from the teacher's behavior. The comment may give the teacher some insight into her own unrecognized behavior, or it may suggest that she is dealing with a parent exceptionally sensitive to the slightest indication of inattentiveness. Only additional conversations will reveal whether the teacher should take a closer look at her nonverbal cues or proceed gingerly with a parent prone to misinterpretation. This paraphrase also asks the parent to elaborate on his response to allow the teacher full understanding.

A *feeling* paraphrase "involves expressing in fresh words the essential feelings, stated or strongly implied, of the helpee. The purpose of reflecting feelings are to focus on feeling rather than content, to bring vaguely expressed feelings into clearer awareness and to assist the helpee to "own" his feelings" (Brammer 1973, p. 90).

Brammer cautions that to be helpful to others with their feelings one must understand one's own. For reasons too complex to discuss at length here, some people are cut off from their emotional life, having learned early, for example, that feelings lead to a loss of control. The result probably is suppression, a conscious defense mechanism that keeps unpleasant events, thoughts, etc. somewhat below one's awareness, yet not completely inaccessible (unconscious). Teachers and counselors who chronically suppress their feelings tend to discourage affective expression by those they are in a position to help. If feelings are considered dangerous, they are dangerous whether expressed by oneself or by others.

Egan (1975) concurs with Brammer that to help others clarify their feelings one must understand one's own. He suggests that prospective helpers can better understand how their feelings manifest themselves by reflecting on the concomitants of certain emotions. To illustrate, when I feel *accepted*, I

feel warm inside
feel safe
feel free to be myself

and when I feel *scared*, I

feel like running away
feel vulnerable
feel like crying

In a small group each person should be allowed to discuss the relationship between a feeling (e.g., fear) and how it is manifested (e.g., feeling vulnerable).

1. anger
2. anxiety
3. boredom
4. competitiveness
5. confusion
6. defensiveness
7. frustration
8. guilt
9. hurt

    10. loneliness
    11. love or warmth
    12. rejection
    13. confidence

A review of the two incidents presented above suggests that the following *feelings* may be inferred from the parents' comments:

Parent: Sometimes Ron seems close to us and affectionate, and at other times he seems distant and preoccupied.

[*Possible feelings:* confusion, upset, disappointment, frustration, ambivalent, manipulation.]

Parent: Every time I come here to talk with you I feel like a burden, as if you have other things you have to do.

[*Possible feelings:* rejection, hurt, anger, inferiority.]

A *feeling* paraphrase to these comments might be

I think you're telling me that you feel as if you are not important [rejected, hurt] and therefore feel like you're bothering me [a burden]. It's almost as if I don't care to talk with you.

Unless their relationship with a parent is fairly close, teachers should allude to feelings indirectly (e.g., "you are not important") rather than exposing them directly by using words like "hurt" or "rejection." Some words or phrases may cut too deeply when a parent is not accustomed to relating to a teacher in a more intimate fashion. The critical aspect is that the teacher can sense the feeling hidden behind the words.

Feeling paraphrases must be used judiciously as they challenge a teacher's sense of timing and judgment more than any other response. When a parent is in trouble, teachers are there to be supportive, not to uncover deep feelings best dealt with by a trained psychotherapist.

Timing

Timing in an interview is a combination of experience and good judgment. Responses to parents are based on one's generalized knowledge of people as well as knowledge of the specific situation. For example, if a parent is anxious and excessively concerned about teacher would certainly not initiate a discussion of his academic progress.

Losen and Diament (1978) equate timing in a parent conference with timing as it is used in chess, where one wishes to make initial moves that afford the greatest latitude or number of alternatives for later courses of action.

> . . . The timing of questions and of when *not* to question should always be based upon consideration of what response (or question) is most likely, at what point, to elicit the broadest range of exploration data for further, later study. [p. 60]

Some believe that timing in interpersonal situations can make the difference between the acceptance or rejection of an opinion or idea. When parents are in a projecting (blaming others) stage or mood, simple listening and responding (paraphrasing) may be the best course of action. When the same parents begin to adjust to their handicapped child and appear to be ready to take on responsibility for extended classroom activities, the teacher should include ideas and suggestions to which the parents are now responsive. Conversely, parents who are coping well and who wish to learn a specific teaching strategy to better work with their child require more of an action relationship with the teacher and less of a supportive one.

Teachers concerned about proper timing may become excessively self-conscious, especially beginners. Even though it may be inhibiting in some respects, it does serve to caution the teacher that an utterance may be far more effective at one point in a relationship than at another. The self-consciousness decreases as teachers learn to trust their own intuitive sense of timing. Those who seem to have problems in timing, however, need good supervision.

How To and When To Be Supportive

One way to get a perspective on supportive responses is to consider their opposites: probing, interpreting, advising, cajoling, lecturing, or judging. In contrast, supportive comments inform parents that teachers understand their predicament and that they will not be abandoned during trying periods. Supportive statements often implicitly encourage someone who is troubled to continue in the face of adversity. Reassurance, a component of support, connotes that the situation with which one is struggling has an attainable goal.

In using supportive responses the teacher should have determined that the parent is undergoing a concern of some magnitude or a crisis that requires some type of support. Following are some supportive responses:

> *Parent:* I don't know what I'm going to do. Alice has become so moody and difficult to deal with that I find it more and more difficult to be nice to her.
>
> *Teacher:* I hear you saying that Alice's moodiness seems to be making it harder to interact with her in a positive way. I can sense your frustration in coming to grips with the situation. It must be difficult for you.
>
> *Parent:* We learned last week from our pediatrician that what we were afraid of these past few years is true. Dr. Ferguson told us that Tommy will never be able to walk.
>
> *Teacher:* That must have been quite a blow to have your worst fears confirmed. I feel badly that the news wasn't more positive, but over time I feel certain that some of the things that Tommy *can do* will stand out.

These responses contain definite elements of reassurance. However, the teacher should beware of cutting short a period of mourning that the parent needs to go through. If the parent appears to accept the reassurance provided, she should continue in that way; if not, she should revert to something like the initial supportive reflection ("That must have been quite a blow to have your worst fears confirmed.")

> *Parent:* As you know Timmy will be going to a new school next year. We are worried that he will not continue to get the kind of education and attention he has gotten here.
>
> *Teacher:* I can sense your concern and can appreciate your feelings of uneasiness in facing a new and unknown situation. I know of several other parents who have faced similar situations who told me that their youngster eased into the new school very nicely and that they were pleased that the move didn't hamper their child's learning.

In general, try to remain supportive without being suffocating: e.g., "Don't worry, Mrs. Wilson, I know everything will be OK so you need not worry about a thing." In your quest to be helpful be wary of making statements that only someone in another profession (e.g., medicine) can make. For example, in the second situation above, a teacher may comment: "I wouldn't take Dr. Ferguson's diagnosis seriously. I've seen boys with Tommy's condition before and sooner or later they begin to walk." Such remarks are said more to ease the teacher's anxiety (by lessening the parent's grief) than to be of genuine help. That statement is not supportive but misleading.

Do not confuse sympathy with support. Support conveys understanding, whereas sympathy connotes pity. Few of us tolerate the condescending communication of sympathy from another.

Below are a few examples of supportive and sympathetic responses. Give some thought to how you would feel or react as a recipient of these comments.

1. *I sense that you are concerned about Tommy's progress in school.* [*supportive*]

   It must be terrible to always be anxious of how Tommy is doing in school. [*sympathetic*]

2. *That must have been quite a blow to have your worst fears confirmed.* [*supportive*]

   I really feel sorry for people when they get such tragic news. [*sympathetic*]

3. *Hearing that from your husband must have hurt.* [*supportive*]

   Oh, you poor thing. It's a pity that a good person like you has to tolerate such language from her husband. [*sympathetic*]

How and When To Be Assertive and Firm

There are instances in one's personal life when it is necessary to be firm. A roommate's tendency to shirk the responsibility for cleaning up, buying the groceries, and managing the finances requires that one eventually confront a situation that is generating anger. A discussion with one's roommate is in order, during which one must listen to his *perception* of the situation. Perhaps in his view the existing situation is comfortable and not subject to change. In such an instance, one may wish to discuss the limits within which one will continue to share an apartment; that is, one is *asserting* one's right as an equal partner in the shared apartment.

The words firm, assertive, and confrontive are often used to convey essentially the same meaning: displeasure with an existing situation (recognition of a feeling), the desire to openly discuss it (being confrontive or assertive), and the intention of setting up limits should the discussion fail to achieve a mutually acceptable compromise (being firm).

On occasion teachers find it necessary to confront a situation of long standing. Consider, for example, the parent who volunteers as an aide in the classroom. Most teachers would welcome some help in the classroom, but within limits. This hypothetical parent, because of her compulsive or monopolizing manner, has a tendency to take over. She initiates activity without the teacher's consent or approval, and in her zeal to be helpful, has lost her perspective on her role as a volunteer. When the aide becomes more of a burden than an asset, the teacher needs to confront the situation by pointing out the role of both teacher and aide in the classroom. The aide should be allowed to express her views and her reaction to the teacher's confrontation. If she accepts the teacher's observations, then the teacher can outline the ways in which the two parties may complement each other in the classroom. Parents who are totally insensitive to their role may require a firmer response:

I very much appreciate your desire to be helpful to me in the classroom, but I feel that I work best when I can inform you how you might be able to help best when you are here. If you feel comfortable with this I would very much welcome your help, but if you feel too constrained by what I am suggesting, then I would ask that you reconsider working with me.

Fortunately, such firmness is generally unnecessary, but when it is required, it is better to be assertive than to internalize one's anger and growing sense of frustration.

We have all been in situations where an assertive response on our part would have been gratifying, but we often withdraw because of some felt risk. Therefore, confrontation is considerably easier to talk about than to implement.

Consider the following incidents which commonly arise in daily living and require some type of assertive response.

1. A friend or colleague that you are very fond of has a habit of ———— [think of a real and annoying habit, if you can]. The habit is so annoying that you feel you have to discuss [with your friend] the effect it has on you.

2. You feel that your supervisor consistently treats you in a condescending manner. You believe that this behavior is unwarranted and you plan to discuss it at your next conference.

3. You have been treated shabbily and in a demeaning manner by a sales clerk. You feel justifiably angry and you are about ready to assert yourself in this situation.

Consider the parent-teacher situations below, real ones, or your own hypothetical ones, using assertive and firm responses (in each instance assume that the situation requires this response):

1. At every conference the parent makes an issue of the fact that you are using inappropriate materials for your students. Because you are conscientious, you sought feedback from your peers and researched the materials extensively. You even experimented with other materials and are now convinced that those you selected are the most appropriate.

2. A parent insists that you are the only one who can help him with some serious personal problems. You've tried subtly to tell the parent you are not trained to help him with these problems, to no avail.

3. The parent continually moans about the lack of progress her child has made. You feel strongly that the child needs to work on his deficiencies outside of class to reinforce gains made in class. The parent, however, refuses to spend any time working on academics with her child and feels that such activity should remain in the classroom.

4. Whenever father and mother meet with you for a conference they begin to fight with each other, revealing some definite interpersonal problems that you feel can be dealt with effectively by a professional counselor. You've witnessed this situation often and have been reluctant to suggest marital counseling; now you have come to the conclusion that you will deal with this issue at the next conference.

It is crucial to recognize some differences between assertive responses (expressing oneself appropriately) and aggressive responses (unbridled release). Alberti and Emmons (1970) believe that assertive behavior may be characterized as follows:

1. increases feelings of self-worth as well as self-worth of others
2. expresses what one feels and thinks and encourages others to do so; usually conveys friendly, affectionate, nonanxious feelings
3. usually achieves goal and encourages other to achieve their goals

4. makes one feel less anxious and more competent; others feel comfortable and at ease in expressing themselves
5. generates feelings on part of others that one is not punitive and is more likely to rationally evaluate events
6. in response to unreasonable requests politiely refuses and explains reasons.

In contrast, aggressive responses have the characteristics described below, according to Alberti and Emmons:

1. increases self-worth but denies worth of others; others feel disparaged and even humiliated
2. expresses what one feels and thinks but denies opportunity for such expression by others
3. achieves goals by downgrading others; thus others usually do not achieve goals
4. depreciates others so that they feel hurt, defensive, and incompetent
5. in response to an unreasonable request tends to refuse angrily, which makes others either defensive or angry.

The Use of Questions

It is a foregone conclusion that questions constitute a large portion of the interview—or is it? Benjamin (1974) believes that interviewers ask too many questions, often meaningless, and ones an interviewee cannot possibly answer. Questions are often posed that actually confuse or interrupt the interviewee or that the interviewer doesn't want answered, resulting in responses he doesn't hear. By asking questions and getting answers, asking more questions and getting more answers, a teacher may be setting up a pattern from which neither parent nor teacher can become extricated.

The ultimate test for asking a question may be stated thusly: "Will the question I am about to ask further or inhibit the flow of the interview?" In using questions, Benjamin (1974, p. 67) suggests that:

1. We should be aware of the fact that we are asking questions.
2. We should challenge the questions we are about to ask and weigh carefully the desirability of asking them.

3. We should examine carefully the various sorts of questions available to us and the types of questions we personally tend to use.
4. We should consider alternatives to the asking of questions.
5. We should become sensitive to the questions the interviewee is asking, whether he is asking them outright or not.

First let us examine the types of questions available to us.

OPEN VERSUS CLOSED QUESTIONS

According to Benjamin *open* questions tend to be broad; allow the interviewee full scope; widen his perceptual field; solicit views, opinions, thoughts, and feelings; and widen and deepen the contact. For example,

> *Jerry appears to be quite active these days. He seems to be at an age where there is much to stimulate him. What do you think?*
> *You don't seem to be your usual self today. Anything happen?*
> *Some kids really like school and others are turned off by it. How do you think Jerry feels about school?*

In contrast, *closed* questions are narrow, limit respondent to a specific answer, curtail one's perceptual field, demand cold facts only, and circumscribe the contact. For example:

> *How old is Jerry?*
> *When is he going to camp?*
> *Does Jerry seem to like school?*

Another type of *closed* question includes the answer, or at least strongly implies that the respondent agree:

> *Isn't it obvious that Karen doesn't care about the kids she teaches?*
> *Everyone knows that Mr. and Mrs. Snyder are real pains, isn't that so?*
> *It's perfectly clear that this school is the worst one to teach in, isn't that so?*

This type of questioning does not allow parents to indicate alternate views.

DIRECT VERSUS INDIRECT QUESTIONS

Direct questions are obvious queries, whereas indirect questions inquire without seeming to do so and are more open. The latter do not end in a question mark, yet it is evident that a question is being asked.

Direct: Isn't it rough working with such unmotivated kids?
Indirect: It must be rough working with kids who have trouble motivating themselves.
Direct: How do you like your new teaching job?
Indirect: I wonder how the new teaching job seems to you.
Direct: What do you think of the new token economy system we're using?
Indirect: You must have some thoughts about our new token economy system.
Direct: How does it feel to be in your new school today?
Indirect: I'd sure like to know how you feel about your new school.

Even more than open questions, indirect questions allow for a variety of responses.

DOUBLE QUESTIONS

Double questions limit the parent to one choice out of two. Some examples follow:

Do you want to set up an appointment for two or three weeks?
Would you like to have coffee or tea?
Do you want Jimmy to be a teacher or social worker?
Do you want to sit near Darrel or Kevin?

Simple double questions like these curtail a parent's perceptual field and response and should be avoided *when other alternatives exist.* Of course, where only two possibilities are available one should not imply that more exist.

Examples of more elaborate *double questions,* which tend to confuse, are as follows:

Have we covered everything we wanted to today and what do you think about scheduling an appointment for our next conference?
Is Jimmy more controllable now at home and how is his toilet training coming along?

Did you get a chance to see an orthopedic surgeon about Karen's hip and what did the eye doctor say about her vision?

A simple solution to this problem is to ask each question singly.

"WHY" QUESTIONS

Benjamin views "why" questions as the most useless and potentially destructive type because they often connote disapproval or displeasure. Thus, whenever someone hears the word "why," he may feel the need to defend himself, to withdraw and avoid the situation, or to go on the offensive. However, this type of reaction is generally less likely when rapport between two people is favorable, that is, when trust and respect are present.

It is interesting to note that for children, "why" has two drastically different meanings. As suggested above, it often has a pejorative connotation. On the other hand, children often ask "why" questions as a key to unlock the world about them; thus "why" is used to gain information.

In adult-to-adult relationships "why" is too often perceived as "Don't do that" or "You ought to be ashamed." As a result, a parent may withdraw into herself, attack or rationalize, with the consequence of distancing herself from the teacher. The parent will not feel free to explore and experience but will feel threatened and resort to defending herself as best she can.

Below are some examples of "why" questions that often are perceived in a negative way. Discuss in your group what your feelings would be as a recipient of these questions:

Why don't you have your Halloween bulletin boards in black and orange?

Why are you late to our conference today?

Why doesn't Bruce wear warmer clothing during the winter months?

Why doesn't Rita read better than before after we discussed her home reading program last time?

These kinds of questions can be framed so that they will have less bite by being asked in a more indirect way:

I noticed that Bruce seems to be cold during class and I was wondering if there might be something he could wear so that he would feel more comfortable.

I noticed that Rita hasn't improved her reading very much since our last conference. I wonder what we could do that would motivate her to read more often.

You must have run into that terrible downtown traffic on your way here.

During the next few weeks, try to become aware of the *types of questions* you tend to ask and under what circumstances you ask them. You might also wish to develop a more acute awareness of your response (internal and verbal) to questions that are posed to you, as well as the types of questions people around you tend to ask and the types of responses they receive.

Interpretation: Pros and Cons

In counseling the technique of interpreting behavior or feelings has met with a mixed response. Interpretation is the hallmark of Freudian-oriented counseling—which is not to say that it is the sum and substance of Freud's theory, but interpretive responses constitute the basic therapeutic technique. In contrast, client-centered counseling (developed by Carl Rogers) eschews interpretation, believing that building relationships and positive personality growth is achieved by an empathic, warm, and genuine counselor. Thus, interpretations, or perhaps more accurately, insights, are made by the client.

Interpretations made by the counselor convey his perceptions, not the client's, and therefore their value as a facilitative technique in building rapport is limited. Some argue that reflections, summarizations, and paraphrases are indeed interpretations, but more subtle ones. Be that as it may, the purpose of this section is to show how interpretation may be of practical help in some situations and useless or even destructive in others.

Interpretation serves the function of providing information without mistake or distortion. For example, when a parent confers about his child's test scores, the teacher will want to interpret them accurately. Interpretation often lessens the parent's sense of uncomfortable ambiguity.

Sure, Mr. Good, I'd be happy to go over Jimmy's reading test results with you. On the vocabulary section he scored on the _____ percentile, meaning that _____ percent scored above

*him and ———— percent scored below Jimmy. On the compre-
hension section of the test he scored ————, again telling us
that ———— percent did better than he did compared to
thousands of others who took the test and scored lower. In
general, his test scores at this point tend to indicate that he
would have difficulty in a straight academic program in high
school. At this point I'd be interested in your observations,
thoughts, and questions.*

Sometimes when parents are at a complete loss about their
child's behavior they may come to the teacher for help. Should the
teacher feel that her perspective can be of assistance, she may proceed to interpret what she believes is responsible for the child's
behavior, but in a way that allows parents to respond to her observations:

*It's quite possible that Amy is acting up these days because of
the birth of her baby brother. It is not unusual for a child to
behave differently when she realizes that she won't get as much
attention as she used to and feel left out to a certain extent.
What do you think, Mr. Phillips, does this make sense to you?*

Interpretations of behavior can be of immense value to a parent,
but they also have a dangerous aspect. People often resent having
their feelings and behavior interpreted. For example, how would
you feel if a teacher you didn't know well commented:

*Boy you sure do let quiet, shy Joan have it full blast. I think the
reason you're so harsh on her is because she reminds you of your
mother's introverted behavior that you hated. In a way it's like
striking back at her through Joan.*

*Now I understand why Jeff is so emotionally disturbed. It's hard
for a child to feel secure in a home like yours where everyone is
yelling and blaming each other for things.*

*Your anxiety about George's lack of progress is unfounded. What
is happening is that you're putting your own need to achieve on
your son and by doing that you're placing undue pressure on
him and making him a nervous wreck.*

Although they are sometimes accurate, such interpretations almost always generate feelings of anger and defensive responses.
"Anxiety" is an emotionally laden term and should be avoided unless parents use it to refer to themselves. To declare that parents'
feelings are "unfounded" is to make them feel silly or stupid in
having them. Fears and anxieties are not necessarily based on obvious

events; some people can be as fearful of a friendly crowd as others are of a deadly snake. By starting a sentence, "What is happening is . . ." the teacher is implying that her word is above question. Interpreting a parent's own need to achieve (although it may be correct) can certainly make him feel uncomfortable for a variety of reasons—not the least of which is the fact that he is not meeting with the teacher for personal psychotherapy. A remark that the parent is putting a great deal of pressure on his son can only lead to feelings of guilt, feelings that the parent may already experience. Finally, suggesting that the son is a "nervous wreck" either reinforces or arouses in the parent's mind the possibility that the boy is unstable.

All in all, these responses are most destructive. By *reflecting*, not interpreting, material the parent has already provided, a teacher can facilitate awareness without generating guilt, resentment, anger, and lowered self-esteem. For example:

> *I hear you saying that you have a tendency to be hard on yourself and you're wondering whether you might also be hard on George.*

The teacher is paraphrasing what the parent has, in his own words, alluded to; the *core meaning* is reflected back.

Home Conferences

Teachers do not have time, nor is it necessary, to make frequent home visits. However, there are times when such conferences should be seriously considered, and one ought to keep the following aspects, as discussed by Duncan (1978), in mind:

1. Do not schedule such a meeting until you have proposed it to the parents.

2. Never drop in on a parent for a brief visit. Parents should know about and be involved in the scheduling of a home conference or a brief visit.

3. Be on time. Parents may not be prepared for an early arrival, and they would resent anxiously awaiting the arrival of a teacher who is significantly late.

4. To the extent possible, keep to the time schedule you initially established with the parents.

5. Don't overdress or wear the jeans with which you clean up the house. The clothes you normally wear in class should suffice.

6. Refusing to eat or drink what parents offer may hurt their feelings. If you do not wish to indulge, a comment should be made about having eaten shortly before the visit. It is customary to be offered some repast when visiting in someone's home, and it is generally considered disrespectful to refuse.

7. Try not to cancel a home visit. Parents spend a considerable amount of physical and mental energy preparing for it. A cancellation can hurt morale, especially for the heretofore uncooperative parents who are making an initial attempt to establish a relationship with the teacher.

8. Be prepared for distractions. Children running and shouting, phone calls, and visitors dropping by may interrupt the conference. You are now in the parents' territory and have little control over the environment. For most parents there will be other, distraction-free conferences at school where the teacher can discuss more serious matters.

The home visit is best used to help the teacher establish or continue rapport with the parent and to become more knowledgeable about the family.

Referrals

Thus far in this volume the recommendation that the teacher refer the parent to other professionals for help was made a number of times. For some professionals (e.g., physician, social worker) referrals are made rather easily and often because they frequently are expected. However, parents may be less likely to expect a referral from a teacher, which makes the process somewhat touchy. Referrals for psychological reasons are particularly sensitive as both parties must deal with what such a referral implies to them.

Barsch (1969) considers three options available to teachers who have concluded that psychological intervention is needed. The first is to communicate the problem to the principal, school psychologist, or social worker in the hope that they will either modify the parents' behavior through their own efforts or discuss with the parent appropriate community referral. The second option is to adopt the role of a psychotherapist or counselor and assume the responsibility for positive change. The third and most pessimistic alternative is to regard the situation as unchangeable and, therefore, to do nothing. A fourth possibility not addressed by Barsch but recommended by me is for the teacher to make the referral.

In Barsch's view the referral process is fraught with so many pitfalls that the reasonable solution is to regard the parent as an ally or associate and enlist him in the teaching enterprise regardless of his psychological problems. Barsch's solution has merit when the problem resides in the interaction of parent and teacher, and when the interpersonal situation seems intractable (although other solutions for such impasses are suggested elsewhere in this book). It is my opinion that if the parent is having obvious difficulties, teachers can do more harm than good by not making an appropriate referral.

Barsch does not consider the second and third alternatives as viable ones. The teacher is not a qualified psychological counselor, even though transitory problems can be effectively dealt with by professional helpers possessing solid, basic counseling skills. In this regard, it would be helpful if teachers learned to be less fearful of parents' feelings and their problems. The third option, to regard the situation as unchangeable, is in almost all cases an unthinkable stance for a professional teacher to adopt. In fact, because of their status in the community and their contacts with parents and their children, teachers often are in an excellent position to make referrals.

Teachers should be sure the community has the necessary resources to accomplish the goals of the referral. Discretion is required in introducing the subject to a parent, and it should be done in a warm, caring manner. The justification for the referral should be clear to the teacher and must be communicated unambiguously to the parent. Finally, it is most helpful if the parent personally recognizes the need for a referral and that the time and means are available for carrying out the recommendation.

Counseling for significant personal problems is a long-term process if positive and lasting effects are to be obtained. Thus, the teacher should not be impatient to see problems diminish or vanish but should remain supportive of the parents' efforts to seek help, no matter how long it takes or how difficult the process.

SELF–HELP ORGANIZATIONS

Although peer self-help groups are currently enjoying enormous popularity, Konopka (1972) points out that small therapeutically inclined groups parallel the history of social services as they evolved within a changing society. The older social services, which distinguished sharply between the giver and receiver, were generally referred to as philanthropy. As people moved from farm to city and from foreign countries to the United States, mutual self-help groups sprang up to meet the ever increasing need for aid, identity, and support. For example, there were the brotherhoods that developed their own centers, such as the Jewish Community Centers and settlement houses for various nationalities. These groups were initially conceived and run by outsiders, but they gradually took on their own responsibilities as they developed.

Self-help groups were, and to some extent still are, characterized by a desire for citizen action to improve their own lot or to help improve that of others. The recreation movement as well as the formation of unions supplied additional impetus to the idea.

> One of the more potent arguments for homogeneous grouping is suggested by the success of groups of peers that initially assemble because of common problems. The understanding generated by having experienced common concerns is a strong force in the success and increasing popularity of peer self help groups. Such groups certainly reinforce the notion that peers with similar problems can be of significant help to each other and . . . are feasible resources for each other. [Seligman 1977, p. 7]

In writing about self-help organizations for parents of exceptional children, Wirtz (1977) notes that:

> . . . one of the most important aspects of program development in the United States in recent years has been the development of parent associations. By and large these are truly organizations of parents helping parents. The schools serving handicapped children should capitalize on the existence of these organizations, and if they are not there, should establish some of their own. [pp. 63–64]

In an effort to provide much needed help to parents of exceptional children in the Lexington, Kentucky, area, Project Cope was born, and the Parent Club was formed as an outgrowth of group counseling under its auspices. The goals, operations, and functions of the Parent Club, as described by Taylor (1976), parallel to a large extent other parental self-help groups. The club had three primary objectives: (1) to provide social activities, (2) to provide educational opportunities through speakers in various professional fields, and (3) to develop projects to increase parents' identity as a group and provide some avenue for self-awareness and leadership for their children. The Parent Club was instrumental in establishing a state bureau of special education and a law permitting public schools to purchase services from private agencies. It was also active in various fund-raising projects.

In a more general sense, self-help organizations evolve as a consequence of the perceived needs of parents for mutual support, inspiration, education, and social action. Self-help groups may also be of practical assistance, by providing baby-sitting arrangements and transportation for members. Because such organizations can be an enormous help to parents of exceptional children, it would be most advantageous for teachers to know of the ones in their community—particularly for a new parent in the community or one who may be bewildered by or not aware of the array of educational possibilities, care-taking facilities, and medical- and health-related services available.

Telford and Sawrey (1977, p. 153) summarize the attributes of peer self-help organizations:

1. Gaining facts and information concerning their [shared] conditions and problems
2. Exchanging information concerning ameliorative and coping devices
3. Providing mutual motivation and support
4. Receiving feedback from others to assist in evaluating one's status and progress
5. Gaining a group identification that reduces one's feelings of isolation and alienation
6. Obtaining satisfaction from members' mutual altruistic concern

The Appendix lists a number of peer self-help groups that are recognized nationally. Teachers may wish to become familiar (even to the extent of attending meetings) with groups in their particular community.

PARENT VOLUNTEERS

In addition to self-help, parents can be a significant resource to teachers. Kroth and Scholl (1978) contend that teacher training programs rarely consider the competencies required to organize, supervise, and manage ancillary personnel in the classroom. Of particular interest is the mobilization of volunteer parents who may be helpful to teachers in a number of ways:

1. For certain activities the pupil-teacher ratio can be reduced, benefiting both teachers and pupils.

2. Because of special knowledge or expertise that parents may have, an additional learning dimension can be brought into the classroom. For example, parents may have specialized capabilities in such areas as art, music, dance, or mechanics that the teacher may use to augment the educational program.

3. Parents can help with noninstructional activities (for example taking attendance, supervising playground activities, duplicating materials), and in so doing make it possible for the teacher to use her time more effectively.

4. Assisting with instructional activities should not be ruled out. Under minimal teacher supervision, parents may help in correcting papers, giving spelling words, and reading.

5. Some parents gladly help out with field trips and student club activities.

6. Involvement allows the parent to achieve a closer and perhaps a more positive perspective on the child's learning environment. In addition, active involvement is good public relations from the school's point of view. Probably the most effective source of public relations is parents speaking positively to other parents about the schools. Such cooperative endeavors help to eliminate communication barriers between parents and school personnel.

7. Parents often derive a sense of being useful and productive in assisting teachers. Some of the sting of feeling impotent and guilty is alleviated by such active participation.

Kroth and Scholl (1978) believe that it is useful to survey teachers around needs that parent volunteers could help meet. For example, noninstructional needs might include help with coats and hats, duplicating materials, taking attendance, helping with snack breaks, and collecting lunch money; instructional needs may be helping with music, art, or special-interest areas, grading papers, and showing flash cards; extracurricular needs can include organizing and supervising fieldtrips, special class presentations, and helping with club activities.

A survey of existing needs makes it easier to solicit parent volunteers around activities where needs have been identified. Parents will then be offering to help with specified activities instead of volunteering to assist with vaguely defined objectives.

To reduce the possiblities of failure, the initiation of parent volunteer programs should be preceded by an orientation. Open dialogue between teachers and parent volunteers should be encouraged during the orientation which could include such areas as discipline, instructional involvement, attendance, school policy, and confidentiality. Followup meetings are encouraged to reinforce the open dialogue initiated during the orientation and to allow for discussion of problems as they arise.

In summary, parent volunteers can be an enormous resource to teachers if used judiciously. Of value also are the personal benefits derived by parents who feel they are productively involved in the school. And finally, it is the children who will be the ultimate benefactors of the positive relationships established between parents and teachers. As Harris (1978), who discusses an innovative parent involvement program, notes, parental involvement and cooperation tend to have a very positive effect on students' attitudes toward school.

BIBLIOTHERAPY

Bibliotherapy is a fancy word for a rather simple technique—the use of reading material to help someone better understand a condition or situation or to provide support, encouragement, and a sense of universality (a feeling that others have similar problems). Parents of exceptional children, especially those who like to read and/or those who desire information about their child's condition, can benefit from the judicious referral to reading material. Some parents, as well as children, also achieve insights and encouragement by reading biographies and classical literature involving a handicap. The teacher should remember that although for some people such books are inspiring, for others they may symbolize unattainable achievements.

Written sources may inform the parent of legislation related to their child's exceptionality, where needed services may be sought as well as the exact nature of these services, or how to effectively deal with a particular situation (e.g., toilet training, dressing and undressing).

Although bibliotherapy is generally viewed in a positive fashion, McWilliams (1976) is more cautious in her endorsement. She asserts that reading materials for parents of exceptional children are a mixed blessing. They are often so brief as to be misleading, include too much too soon, or are written from the point of view of a specific philosophy that may conflict with what is planned for a particular child.

Bibliotherapy does not simplify a professional's responsibilities. McWilliams cautions that the professional should be knowledgeable about published material so that appropriate and excellent selections are recommended. Recommended readings should include those that are most objective, least misleading and biased, and compatible with the goals one has set forth in working with a parent of an exceptional child as well as the goals formulated for the child. After recommending a book or article, the teacher should give parents the opportunity to discuss what they have read.

Slavson (1958) shares McWilliams' caution regarding the value of bibliotherapy for parents, especially for significantly troubled parents. However, he believes that the availability of appropriate reading materials may help them feel less alone and may contribute to their general knowledge about their problems.

In a recent publication Fassler (1978) builds a convincing case for using carefully selected books and stories to provide parents with useful bibliographic resources to help their children cope with significant life changes. Such, Fassler believes, serve as springboards to constructive parent-child discussions about significant events.

In the Appendix a list of available readings is grouped into specific categories. In order to make appropriate referrals to the readings, teachers should be knowledgeable about their content and quality. It is therefore recommended that the teacher keep apprised of new articles, books, and journals that may be of value for parents. Finally, it is not the task of the teacher to monitor what a parent reads, but to make referrals to appropriate sources when it seems advisable or when a parent requests it. It is also helpful if the teacher makes herself available to discuss an article or book. Some reading materials require interpretation or elaboration by a professional, and others stimulate thoughts and ideas that parents may wish to share with their child's teacher.

CHAPTER 6

Working with Problem Parents

Sometimes teachers perceive parents accurately, as they really are; other times, they are seen in a distorted way because of cultural stereotypes and personal anxiety. It is probably true that the dynamics of most parent-teacher encounters are a combination of reality and distortion. It is important to be aware of the causal factors that influence perceptions because it is only through such understanding that teachers will be in a better position to appraise parents' behavior.

As noted in Chapter 2, the general conclusion appears to be that teachers view parents more negatively than parents see teachers, for many reasons. Parents who behave in certain ways or possess certain attributes are considered to be "problem parents" and challenge the teacher's interpersonal skills. However, a parent who might be a problem for one teacher may not be for another. Personality needs and the interpersonal style of teacher A meeting with parent A may be *much* more compatible than if parent A met with teacher B, whose characteristics would clash with those of the

155

parent. Therefore, for some, the designation "problem parent" is inaccurate. What is reflected in a *problem situation* are differences attributable to the interaction.

The following discussion was written with some trepidation. Parents of exceptional children have been categorized and characterized in a most unfavorable light in the literature, a situation that creates negative attitudes toward them and feeds existing stereotypes. In addition, there is danger of generalizing when singling out troublesome characteristics of any particular group of people. It is important to keep in mind that the problem parents examined in this chapter constitute a small percentage of the total that present themselves to teachers.

Hostile Parents

The apparent source of the parent's angry feelings may be the teacher, the school, or the curriculum. Anger might, of course, be directed toward institutions or people unrelated to the school the child attends (e.g., a physician or social worker). Apparent sources of anger may camouflage underlying or unconscious ones as such defense mechanisms as denial or projection may be operating. It is sometimes difficult to determine whether a parent's angry remarks can be taken at face value or whether they are manifestations of unconscious feelings related to factors unknown to the parent. Knowledge of family dynamics and coping mechanisms (Chapter 3) contribute to more accurate appraisals of the causes of anger.

Perhaps the most anxiety-provoking angry parent is the one who openly criticizes the teacher. The teacher may be accused of failing to cope with, teach, or in some other way meet the needs of the child. Criticism may be expressed in a rational, articulate fashion or with considerable emotion and animation. Although the teacher may perceive the anger as an attack on her person, in most cases, anger is projected; and what appears to be angry feelings toward the teacher are really feelings that have been deflected. There are, of course, instances where anger is rightly placed at the teacher's feet.

Angry feelings directed at the school or teacher may indicate anxiety over the apparent lack of progress the child has made—through no fault of the teacher. It is sometimes easier to project blame onto another source than to face the reality of the handicap.

Some parents may be angry before they even meet their child's teacher because of past negative experiences with other professionals. Parents may legitimately be angered at the school for their inflexible policies or because they feel that their needs as exceptional parents are always neglected. Direct expressions of anger may also be indicative of the teacher's seeming lack of interest in them or their child. Some parents may be frustrated, feeling that the teacher places little value on their observations.

A particularly sensitive area and a frequent source of parental hostility is when parents are told that their child will be transferred to another classroom or school. Such moves—where their child will be exposed to a new teacher, new peers, and generally a different environment—leads to considerable anxiety because the new situation involves a host of unknowns.

The teacher must be cognizant of veiled or indirect expressions of anger toward herself, the school, or the program in which the child is involved. The unexpressed portion of a parent's comments about his child's general lack of progress may relate to perceived dissatisfaction with the teacher. However, such underlying feelings are difficult to discover, and it is generally best not to assume blame or interpret the parent's comments as an indication of his dissatisfaction with the teacher or school until he expresses it directly. In other words, the teacher may incorrectly reflect, "I think your unhappiness with Jim's progress really indicates your dissatisfaction with me." A response that would allow the parent to go in whichever direction he desired is, "I sense your dissatisfaction with Jim's progress. Do you have any thoughts about why this is the case?"

In such instances parental anger and impatience can be relieved when the teacher indicates areas in which the child is making gains. Sometimes, in their impatience to see dramatic achievements, parents do not recognize the smaller gains their child has made.

The key to working with an angry parent is to avoid responding in a hostile or defensive way. Such responses contribute to a spiraling negative encounter, where both parties accuse each other of negligence and neither person listens to the other.

When a parent is uncharacteristically angry, a useful response would be a paraphrase and an open invitation to convey one's perceptions.

Mrs. Koerner, I can certainly sense your feelings of frustration and anger. You seem to be concerned with your daughter's behavior, which seems to have gotten worse since she has been in school. I wonder if you have any thoughts about why her be-havior has changed?

After listening to the parent the teacher may wish to contribute her observations in an objective, noncontentious way. There will be times when the observations of parent and teacher coincide, as well as instances when they do not resemble each other at all. It is helpful to view differing perceptions in terms of supplementary and not contradictory observations. Observations are cumulative, adding to a more comprehensive picture of the child.

One of the more productive reactions to angry expressions directed at sources outside of the school is listening and paraphrasing. For example, parents might be furious about a community incident that painfully highlights their child's exceptionality. The angry feelings in such instances reflect both anger and hurt. In addition to attentive listening and paraphrasing, the teacher may wish to contribute comments of a supportive nature.

Parents who are characteristically critical and hostile are sometimes disarmed by a teacher who doesn't respond in kind but who reacts in an understanding way. At other times, chronically hostile parents respond to a teacher who takes a firm and assertive stance (Chapter 5). There is no easy way to learn assertive responses except through practice and self-monitoring. The tremendous growth of assertiveness-training workshops indicates the difficulty overly passive or excessively hostile people have in expressing their feelings in this manner. (The reader should have several opportunities to practice such responses through role-playing exercises in Chapter 7.)

Angry parents threaten the teacher more than any other problem parent. More often than not the anger reflects annoyance, frustration, or impatience at someone or something other than the teacher. By keeping this in mind, teachers will be less likely to feel inadequate. By the same token, they must consider the validity of parents' observations, and when they have inadvertently erred, admission of the error reflects maturity.

Uncooperative Parents

In addition to children who find various means to convey their lack of interest and cooperation in the classroom, parents may likewise, by their uncooperative behavior, be the source of considerable frustration for teachers who genuinely wish to form an alliance with them. It is useful to understand the reasons why parents may choose to be uncooperative in an endeavor designed to be of help to their handicapped child.

In a minority of cases, parents may simply not have the time and energy to care. They may be preoccupied with family problems or other problems of living. In other instances, they do care, but because of overwhelming burdens they are in fact doing all they can to keep their lives together.

Anxiety can account for absences at parental conferences; hearing about or working with a child's deficiencies are painful reminders of his handicap. Also, parents may agree to carry out a home program but find it difficult to implement. Avoidance (or withdrawal) may be the parent's way to keep anxiety at a manageable level.

The teacher may be faced with emotionally disturbed or mentally retarded parents, whose involvement may be minimal. Invitations should be offered on occasion and suggestions must be made in a concrete fashion, depending on the parent's resources. (This topic will be discussed in more detail later in this chapter.)

Avoidance behavior may indicate that the parents are still hiding from the truth of their child's situation. During this period, the teacher ought to approach the parent cautiously, by realistically pointing out areas where the child requires special help and others where the child demonstrates strengths. When the teacher senses denial, a greater focus on what the child does well rather than what she does poorly is recommended. Timing is especially critical here. The teacher wants to attract parents, not frighten them, to remain realistic yet optimistic. It is not the teacher's duty to thrust painful reality upon a parent in the interest of developing parent-teacher cooperation.

Some parents may feel that conferences are a formality, a school ritual of little substance. Others may be concerned that because of their modest education they will not be looked upon favorably by the teacher and/or understand what he says. Still others, because of faulty mail deliveries or because of frequent moves, are simply not notified of parent conferences.

Teachers must be wary of developing negative attitudes toward parents who miss conferences. To try to understand why, the teacher should gently and occasionally inquire, being careful not to imply wrongdoing.

Lack of cooperation may be a barometer of the relationship

between parent and teacher, as most of us tend to avoid unpleasant interpersonal situations. Should the teacher be unable to ascertain the source of an impasse, an inquiry about the relationship is in order.

Parents, at times correctly and at other times incorrectly, feel or perceive that teachers consider them to be a burden, and as a consequence, avoid all contact with school personnel. They do not feel welcome and therefore are reluctant to collaborate with the teacher. The teacher should examine her own attitudes toward parents to determine whether there may be some truth to this perception. When the parent clearly misconstrues the teacher's attitudes and she is aware of it, she should undertake special efforts to make the parents feel welcome. They can be encouraged to attend conferences, to help out in circumscribed ways in the classroom or with special activities and field trips, or to observe their child in school.

Some parents are so preoccupied with demanding jobs and/or community activities that involvement in school would exceed their available time and energy. However, excessive energy in other activities may be an excuse not to become involved with the child. This is a coping mechanism that needs to be understood, not challenged. Other parents who give of themselves on the job and in the community provide a caring environment for their child at home, but because of their marginal involvement with the teacher, appear to be disinterested and uncooperative. The teacher should try to get to know these parents on the rare occasions they meet, but she should not pressure them for more frequent conferences.

Teachers may wish to consider writing a note to the parent. Notes should convey interest in meeting with the parent and a concern for the child, not a veiled threat or a scolding. Infrequent phone calls are another available resource. Parents who are unable or do not wish to attend conferences in person may be willing to talk to the teacher over the phone. For some parents, phone conferences may be a stepping stone for future in-person meetings.

As an overriding rule, the teacher should keep in mind that parents will more willingly attend meetings when they know they will be conferring with a teacher who is knowledgeable, who listens, and who cares. There is no easy solution for the resistance of some parents, however, and the teacher must be alert to her sense of apathy and resignation which may follow repeated attempts to gain their cooperation. One can only benefit the child by trying again.

Perfectionist Parents

In contrast to parents who eschew involvement with the school, perfectionists may be overly involved, or at least overly involved with their child. Perfectionism can sometimes be traced to childhood, when performances that were less than perfect were subject to criticism or ridicule. Even if the parent recognizes at some level the deleterious effect his behavior has, the compulsion to demand perfection from others as well as from himself remains.

The perfectionist parent expresses dismay to the child and the teacher when tasks are accomplished in a less than acceptable (usually perfect) fashion. The consequences of this type of behavior for a handicapped child are particularly severe as the child is driven to achieve beyond his capabilities. Also, a handicapped child can be enormously frustrating to the perfectionist. Excessive tendencies of this kind can result in emotional problems for the child, which complicate existing impediments.

Almost certainly the child will begin to hate schoolwork because of the barrage of criticism he receives whenever his performance falls below his parents' standard. The child's self-esteem suffers, further blocking whatever potential he may possess.

It would be a mistake for the teacher to work toward a relaxation of the parents' unrealistically high standards. They should be made aware, however, in clear and understandable terms, the nature of the child's learning problems, her limitations, and her potentials. An examination of the situations where the child functions optimally and those where she doesn't should make the parents realize that their child's progress is related to both psychological and cognitive factors. For example, without putting the parent on the defensive, the teacher might mention that when the child senses pressure in the classroom, her performance drops off considerably; conversely, when pressure is minimized her performance generally improves. The teacher might try to explain that children respond differently to pressure; some thrive on it and others, finding it unbearable, react in an adverse way. Finally, the teacher might mention that praise and support when the child does well is a potent source of motivation. The parents might even be invited to observe their child in the classroom, but only if the teacher has some assurance that their presence will not have an adverse effect on the child, or vice versa.

If the teacher senses that only one of the parents is a perfectionist, she should try to encourage both parents to attend conferences. This, of course, is a good practice to follow in any event, but in such instances the more rational parent can have a positive effect on the perfectionist spouse.

It is important for the teacher to avoid indicating that the parent is at fault for the child's performance. The parent may already be dimly aware of this and will gain further self-insight as the child performs better under less demanding circumstances.

Professional Parents

Professional parents may be as threatening to a teacher as the teacher is to some parents. Much of the problem lies with the teacher's sense of awe; but there are professional parents who consciously or unconsciously use their knowledge in a condescending way, or because of their position, demand special attention or favors for their child.

Professional parents may be more likely to get their way because school personnel want to please them for social and/or political reasons or because they are more sophisticated at manipulating the system than those with less education. One can hardly blame parents for wanting the best for their exceptional child, and yet excessive and unrealistic demands should not be tolerated.

Professional parents who seem to annoy teachers most are those who feel that their knowledge about school, teaching, or exceptional children gives them license to be unduly critical of the teacher or the curriculum. These parents may be motivated by their excessive concern for their child, their unconscious wish to impress the teacher with their knowledge, or simply their need to exert influence. Parents who are frustrated teachers, somewhat knowledgeable but without credentials, may also fall into this category.

When receiving unsolicited advice from professional parents, as well as other parents, the teacher should weigh the advice to determine its merit and not automatically cast it aside. When the parent has a need to pass on her knowledge but does so in a sensible way, the teacher may wish to consider her involvement in the classroom. Another possibility would be to tell the parent what suggestions she has made that have actually been implemented in the classroom.

Parents who are knowledgeable, as well as those who think they are, and incessantly interfere with the teaching program, the curriculum, or methods of discipline require a different approach than interested parents who form helpful alliances with the teacher. Some interfering parents are appeased when given some small responsibilities to carry out; others become worse.

Scolding or arguing with parents yields little, but the teacher may need to set firm limits on what the parent does in the classroom. The teacher also has a right to assert her feelings that the conference is to be used for making plans to help the child and not as a forum for constant criticism of the educational program. Although the parents' observations are welcome, the central focus of the conference is the child.

The advantage in this approach (of setting limits) is that the parent respects the professional expertise and integrity of the teacher. Also the parent may covertly welcome the limits because they allow him to relax his feeling that he must demonstrate, whenever possible, his genuine concern and involvement for his child or his feeling that the best way to demonstrate his knowledge is to exhibit it to the teacher whenever possible.

The potential risk of this response is to make the parent feel like a fool, a busybody who had no right to convey his observations. The parent may complain to the principal or withdraw from the school altogether. In either case, the teacher should try to continue the dialogue so that feelings and perceptions of both parties become clear. Confrontations and setting limits should be considered only when other possibilities have failed.

For the most part professional parents do not act substantially different from other concerned parents. The disparity in status perceived by the teacher tends to be more of a problem than the actual behavior of the parents. In such instances, the teacher should remember that she is a trained specialist in teaching children, whereas the parent may be a specialist in another field. Information about their child, as well as support and encouragement, are as important for these parents as they are for others.

Dependent Parents

The dependent parent characteristically asks questions about virtually every aspect of the child's (and sometimes even the parent's) life. The dependent parent finds it difficult to assume the responsibility of making decisions, and therefore, enlists the help of the teacher in both minor and major matters. Because of a basic insecurity, the parent will solicit the teacher's opinions instead of risking her own. One might find single-parent families in this category, although many operate as well or better than those that are intact.

Dependent parents generally cooperate with the teacher, although only when the teacher, not the parent, assumes responsibility for decisions and courses of action. A teacher who is working with a dependent parent sometimes wonders whether she is dealing with a child or an adult; overly dependent people do, in fact, resemble young children clinging to parents for direction and guidance.

Perhaps responsibility was never given to the parent as a child, or even after marriage, the spouse who was atttracted to a dependent person may have further reinforced the immature behavior. Thus, the dependent parent rarely has had an opportunity for independent thinking and subsequent responsibility.

Perhaps the parent feels that important decisions she made in the past have turned out disastrously, and the resultant sense of responsibility or guilt was more than she could bear. Finally, perhaps the parents temporarily feel that they cannot cope with their handicapped child and rather than risk another mistake, will try to involve the teacher in future decisions. This type of dependency is rarely a persistent problem because feeling guilty, indecisive, and psychologically burdened is a normal human emotion when it occurs sporadically.

Excessively dependent parents are frightened parents. The teacher's task is not to heighten their anxiety by turning away from them but gradually to wean them away from their dependency.

Decisions made and actions taken by parents should be reinforced. When a parent asks for the teacher's opinion or when she is asked to help make a decision, statements like the following might prove helpful:

> *I can appreciate that its difficult to know what to do but I don't think my opinion is any better than yours. What do you think should be done?*

> *That's a tough predicament. I'm not certain that I'd know what to do if I was faced with that situation. I'm wondering what your thoughts are?*

For the parent who *insists* that the teacher offer an opinion or make a decision:

> *It might seem like a difficult decision to make. I'd like to be of help as much as I can, but I really believe that people feel better about themselves when they make tough decisions, even if they don't always turn out right. I know I feel better when I do.*

Teachers might be particularly susceptible to dependent parents. People in the helping professions thrive on the dependence or conferred authority others place on them, which allows them to do their job and meet their need to be helpful. Therefore, they can easily be seduced into a relationship with someone who has strong dependency needs.

Finally, because of their propensity to teach others and give advice, teachers may inadvertently turn independent parents into dependent ones. *Telling* parents what to do instead of developing a cooperative relationship quickly informs them of their place. In working with parents, the teacher's traditional role has definite pitfalls.

Overly Helpful Parents

Helpful parents can be a real asset to the teacher, not only with their own children but also in the classroom. However, the *overly* helpful parent, energetic and well meaning, can become a burden (see also the discussion in Chapter 5).

Excessively helpful parents are motivated by their need to be useful—a need that is often not satisfied in other relationships—and not allowing them to help would be unjust. The major problem is not so much the parent's desire to be helpful, but the teacher's inability to communicate, in a sensitive way, that only a limited amount of assistance is needed. Parents generally catch on quickly when confronted by the teacher, and they may feel hurt and rejected by his comments. Below are two ways of telling a parent that her assistance is appreciated yet more help is being offered than can be constructively used:

> *Mrs. Green, sometimes I don't know what I would do without you. You've been a tremendous help on numerous occasions. However, there are times when I feel things are very much in*

*control, and there is little to be done. I wonder if we can reduce
the amount of time you spend with us? What do you think?
I know you want to be helpful and the kids really enjoy you, but
there are times when I feel that I don't need as much help as
I have been given by you and other parents. I very much appreciate your assistance, but a more reduced time schedule would
work out better. What do you think?*

Overprotective Parents

Overprotective parents are typically anxious about their child's
welfare. They worry about his academic progress, yet their central
concerns center around protection against physical or psychological
harm. This behavior is often a reflection of being warned as children to be careful about accidents, disease, befriending certain
peers, and the like, thus culminating in a fearful attitude about most
things. They are careful in what they eat and tend to be conservative in what they do. They worry and fret and when something
they have been concerned about (which is just about everything)
occurs, their fearfulness seems justified and is further reinforced.

Because of guilt feelings, parents of exceptional children may
be particularly susceptible to overprotection. Typically they shield
the child from tasks he is capable of performing successfully, from
social interactions considered to be harmful, and from situations in
which he might be hurt physically.

Existentialists believe that the primary cause of man's anxiety
is represented by the thin line between life and death. Therefore,
a type of low-keyed but pervasive anxiety about many situations
is normal, and for most of us, anxiety is not unbearable. An existen-
tialist might say that overprotective parents have a heightened
sense of their precarious existence and protect against further
tragedy by excessive care.

From another point of view, overprotection is seen as a com-
pensatory behavior to make up for socially undesirable feelings,
such as rejection. That is, overprotection is the exaggerated response to unacceptable negative feelings toward the child. Other
parents feel that the existing handicap must not be compounded
by other difficulties. The child, they feel, is already significantly
impaired, so that strenuous efforts must be made to minimize the
possibility of other problems.

More often than not overprotectiveness inhibits growth, as the child is protected from a variety of situations which normally expand horizons and add to one's knowledge. Overprotected children often develop fears not found among children who have been granted reasonable freedom within a loving family, thereby adding to and exacerbating the existing handicap.

Overprotective parents are not likely to change their behavior easily, if at all. Nevertheless, the teacher owes it to the child and the family to suggest the use of more realistic, growth-promoting practices. Whenever possible, independent actions initiated by the child should be reinforced so that he will continue the behavior. At conferences, the parents ought to be told of the child's gains, especially acquired skills or behaviors that will facilitate independent thinking and living. The teacher might show *her* delight at these achievements. Activities that help develop the child's self-esteem and ability to cope should also be pointed out. Some parents are so convinced that their child is generally incapable that they are delightfully surprised to hear from the teacher or to see in the classroom achievements they thought were impossible.

When parents seem unwilling to modify their smothering behavior, which clearly is detrimental to the child, the teacher may wish to relate her observations in a clear and firm fashion. For example:

> *I think I understand your desire to help Lois and to protect her, but I wonder if it might do her more harm than good in the long run. Parents have a natural tendency to want to protect their children. This is good, but sometimes too much protection can keep a youngster from developing skills that she will need later on in life and will help her to feel good about herself.*

Overprotective parents who are particularly resistant to change are those whose needs are being met by such behavior. Unconsciously, the parents may wish to keep the child at an infantile level, enabling them to give and receive love and to feel useful. After all, an independent, virtually self-sufficient child is hardly gratifying to parents who require people to be dependent upon them. It is difficult for the teacher to exercise much leverage in this case. One hopes that the parents will begin to experience more pleasure in the child's achievements than they did in his dependency. Also, as the parents' circumstances change, their sense of loneliness or lack of love from others may be gratified in new, fulfilling relationships or in other ways.

Neglectful Parents

Nothing is more heart-breaking to the teacher than a child, clearly in need of love and proper care, who is barely attended to by his parents. They may be so preoccupied with other family members or problems that they cannot extend themselves further. They may reject the child because of his unbearable handicap or for such reasons as the birth of an unwanted child. (It is important to note that rejection can be reflected in at least two contradictory ways: overprotection due to intense guilt or outright neglect.)

In some instances, parents may equate neglect with independence, or neglect may be the consequence of their life style—in which attending to their children is secondary to other pleasures or problems (e.g., alcoholism). Neglected children, because of the potentially severe psychological ramifications, are now considered to fall under the general rubric of "battered children." In any event, child neglect is a serious problem and one of which the teacher must be aware. The circumstances surrounding neglect will dictate the difficulties that might be expected. For example, the parent who mistakenly equates neglect with independence is quite different from the one who rejects the child or is otherwise preoccupied.

In severe cases it is advisable to inform the school social worker, who would then try to work with the parents to achieve behavioral changes and greater involvement. The social worker may ask the teacher about her observations of the child from time to time.

Other than informing the social worker and perhaps the principal, the teacher's recourse when neglect is significant and of long standing, is to help compensate to the extent possible for what the child is not receiving at home. The teacher can demonstrate concern for the neglected child both verbally and on occasion, when appropriate, physically (a hug or pat on the back). She may also set up situations in the classroom in which the child is included in group activities and occasionally assumes a position of leadership.

Neglectful parents resemble uncooperative parents except in one significant way: the latter generally provide the love, attention, and support the child needs at home. Neglectful parents, however, compound their lack of cooperation with school personnel by not providing the essential emotional ingredients for the healthy development of their child.

Because parents who neglect their children are not motivated to cooperate with the teacher, access to these parents is difficult. Sometimes the social worker can facilitate a parent-teacher meeting, but no matter how frustrating and unrewarding, attempts to engage the parent should be continued by the teacher. The possibility of a home visit should not be ruled out if the parent appears willing.

Numerous efforts to involve the parent may eventually bear fruit. At such time the teacher is confronted with the admittedly difficult task of what to say or do when the parent is present. Incidentally, some neglectful parents routinely attend parent conferences, believing that in doing so they have met their parental obligation.

In conferring with the parents, the teacher should avoid blaming them for the child's problems. Only when she believes the situation to have grave consequences for the child, and the parents seem not to be aware of it or consciously continue to neglect the child, should she confront the issue in open, honest terms. Before more drastic measures are taken, the teacher might point out to the parents the contrast in the child's response when he is attended to and when he is not. The child may thrive on positive attention and caring from the teacher and others and show discouragement and unruly behavior when he is ignored.

Incidents involving the withholding of food, adequate shelter, clothes, and love require a more direct approach. The teacher should make every attempt to make the parents cognizant of the impact neglect has on the child, even at the risk of offending them and generating guilt. In fact, extreme neglect may in part be the result of the parent's inability to experience what might be called "normal guilt," a situation demanding more help than the teacher can provide. Damaging and intractable neglect may be dealt with by saying something like the following:

> *I realize that you face numerous problems at home, but Susie is just crying out for any signs of love she can get. Before the situation gets worse, where your child will need more help than you and I can give her, I would urge you to try to let her know that you care.*

> *I really feel uncomfortable commenting on Jerry's dress and behavior, but I believe that if I don't, no one will, and the situation will continue. I've been aware that Jerry comes to school disheveled most of the time. He doesn't seem to be getting enough to eat, and whenever another child has some candy Jerry is always there attempting to get some. I've been wondering if*

Jerry is ill or whether he is not getting enough food at home. He looks tired and frequently falls asleep in the classroom. Have you observed the same things and if so what do you think?

Some of us have been witness to remarkably destructive relationships within families. Fortunately, child neglect, especially the neglect of exceptional children, is rare. Nevertheless, as involved outsiders, teachers must make every effort to positively influence situations in which children are the victims of psychological or physical neglect. Sometimes other school personnel need to be involved; at other times observations must be conveyed to parents in an open and direct way. Fortunately, neglectful parents are rare; unfortunately, when this situation does arise, there often is little a teacher can do.

Parents as Clients

Because of the press of personal problems, parents may seek the help of the teacher. Such problems often center around acute or chronic concerns related to the handicapped child, but they may range from transient feelings of frustration and anger over minor incidents to situations that severely threaten family integration (e.g., divorce).

In engaging a colleague or friend to listen to our problem and, conversely, by offering our help to a friend who needs a concerned ally, we all at different times have assumed the roles of both counselor and counselee. The great difference between being an empathic listener and a trained professional counselor, however, requires the teacher to make this important distinction by wisely using his professional judgment.

Temporary problems, which at the time appear to the parent to be significant but really constitute expected and easily resolved crises, can often be dealt with by the teacher. A parent's frustration over toilet training her child rarely calls for psychological help. (However, the word "rarely" is important because a child's inability or unwillingness to become toilet trained may be caused by psychogenic* factors.) Often, concerns that appear bothersome but are

---

* Psychogenic refers to underlying psychological causes of problems that are manifested psychologically (e.g., being fearful to step out of one's house) or physically (e.g., developing ulcers).

temporary and not debilitating merely require the occasional presence of a concerned listener.

However, one needs to be cautious of situations in which a parent, having significant problems, either overtly or covertly coaxes the teacher into the role of a professional counselor or psychotherapist. Teachers who are seen as warm and skilled interviewers and who make themselves accessible to parents are potentially attractive counselors. On a positive note, the fact that friends and parents come to a teacher for help because she is a good listener is an excellent endorsement for anyone in a people-oriented profession. However, teachers who are good listeners and convey a sense of caring also must be able to distinguish between minor problems and those of more major proportions. For the most part, one's judgment improves with experience, but some cues to look for in significantly troubled parents would be helpful. Before discussing this topic, though, we will examine some of the reasons parents look to teachers for counseling.

Some parents may seek help from their child's teacher because she is physically accessible, whereas others are not aware of where else to go. Parents may know of the existence of professional assistance but are confused by the array of titles (psychologist, psychiatrist, social worker, counselor) and wonder whether a certain type of professional may be more to their advantage than another. In discussing different professional disciplines with parents, teachers can provide a brief description of their academic background and whatever other accurate information they happen to know about their professional training. Referrals should be based on the reputation the person has in the professional community, including what is known about his ethical conduct, the personality "fit" with the parents, and the cost. Finally, parents may be reluctant to seek the help of a psychologist or psychiatrist because of the stigma attached to doing so. Some people are greatly troubled by the implications of needing help for psychological problems, although interestingly, in some segments of society and in some geographical areas, having one's own therapist is a status symbol.

Parents with the following complaints often require professional psychological assistance:

1. deep and unrelenting depression, which may be accompanied by insomnia or nightmares; suicidal thoughts might be expressed

2. strong feelings of rejection toward the handicapped child (a factor which may contribute to number 1 above)
3. indications that family unity is being threatened (comments about significant and continuous arguments; discussion of impending separation and divorce)
4. comments about the considerable difficulty a normal sibling has adjusting to the handicapped child
5. remarks suggesting severe neglect of the child or physical abuse
6. indications that the handicapped child is developing psychological problems

Parents must be dissuaded from seeking a teacher's help in resolving any long-standing or significant problems. The teacher must communicate his concern (not sympathy) over the parents' plight, yet decline to assume a counseling role. He must make the parents aware that ther problem(s) appear to need psychological attention and that he is not professionally prepared to be of assistance. If this fact is communicated sensitively and in a caring manner, parents may then be able to ask where professional help is available. (It is not uncommon for a recommendation to be acted upon months after the referral is suggested.)

The teacher should have at her disposal the names of community mental health clinics and private psychotherapists. Community clinics are considerably cheaper, but some people prefer a private practitioner. Professional counselors and psychotherapists who have a good reputation for dealing with exceptional families are a particularly good resource to have available.

Parents who subtly imply or forcefully insist that the teacher provide the kind of help needed to resolve major problems might be informed that it would be improper for her to assume such a role:

> In a way I get the feeling that you are asking me to help you with a problem for which I am not trained. I am really flattered that you trust me enough to confide in me, but because I can't really be of help to you I'd like to suggest a few possibilities where you can get assistance from trained professionals. In any event, I'd like us to continue to schedule our parent conferences to discuss Joan's progress in school. I'd also be interested in knowing how the problem we discussed is coming.

This comment communicates several important themes: the teacher is aware of the problem and the parents' desire to be helped by her; she knows her professional limitations but is concerned about the parents; she is willing to help the parents locate an appropriately trained professional; she wants to continue to meet with the parents but shifts the major focus of future meetings to the child; she retains an interest in the problem as an interested friend, not as a therapist.

Fighting Parents

A number of authors have commented about the importance of having both parents at conferences, and this point cannot be overemphasized. In this way both parents and teacher are involved in planning for the child, and any differing perceptions or opinions are subject to examination during the meetings. Such meetings, however, challenge the interpersonal skills of the teacher more than any other.

The teacher should not look negatively upon parents who argue with each other during conferences. If nothing else, it allows the teacher to gain a fuller understanding of family dynamics, which may help to explain behavior not previously understood. Such interaction highlights conflicts that exist in the family and are related to the psychological adjustment of their handicapped child, as well as of normal offspring.

Sometimes the teacher will find himself in the uncomfortable position of listening to a heated argument between parents and not knowing how or whether to intervene. Since this is an infrequent occurrence and is not expected, discomfort with fighting parents is to be expected. There are, however, a few guidelines that the teacher might find helpful.

Teachers are not marriage counselors, and parents whose interactions suggest significant family problems should be referred to a qualified professional. The teacher should avoid involvement in heated arguments that are symbolic of deep-seated problems. Even highly qualified professionals find interventions during an animated interchange between parents a challenge of significant proportions.

However, some parental disagreements are mild and reflect an easily resolved difference of opinion. In some cases, the arguments may be the consequence of having partial information or information that is perceived differently. Sometimes, the teacher can see that both perspectives are valid, and a sensitive comment can change a competitive situation to one of cooperation and understanding. For example, a teacher may respond as follows to a mother who feels more emphasis should be placed on her child's appearance and social behavior and a father who values the importance of academic achievement:

> *In sitting here and listening to you, I can't help but agree with both of you. In looking to the future, Karen's behavior, appearance, and schoolwork will be important. I wonder if instead of concentrating on one or two of these concerns we can, without pushing Karen too much, work on all three. What would you think of a program that balances the three areas?*

When arguments are based on incomplete or inaccurate information, the teacher might comment:

> *I can understand that with the information you have been given, your confusion about whether Bobby will be able to go to college is growing. I'm not sure if this will help, but let's review and discuss the available information.*
>
> *According to his tested IQ score, Bobby should be able to compete successfully in college. What clouds the picture somewhat are the indications of specific learning disabilities which interfere with his learning now and, if not corrected, will get in the way in college. Therefore, our efforts should be to correct to the extent possible the deficiencies we already know about so that his learning will not be as frustrating for him in the future as it is now. If his motivation to go to college is high and we are able to decrease the impact of existing learning problems, Bobby should do well in college. I don't know if this helps to make things clearer. Do you have any questions?*

Whether parents are fighting over family concerns of some importance or whether they are arguing about an easily resolvable issue, the cardinal rule for the teacher to follow is to *avoid taking sides*. If the teacher is to get involved at all, she should seek a compromise solution. She will have a most difficult problem to contend with if parents pick up the fact that she favors one or the other of them. The tendency needs to be guarded against most assiduously when the teacher privately does side with one of the parents.

Finally, teachers are sometimes shocked and frightened by some parents who characteristically relate to each other in an animated fashion. What the teacher perceives may run counter to her own experiences with her parents, which contributes to her sense of astonishment. It is essential for the teacher to discriminate among the expression of major family problems, minor disagreements, and different styles of interpersonal interactions. Some family members deal with each other in a quiet, rational manner, and others are more vocal and emotional. One style of interaction is not better or healthier than the other; just different.

Mentally Retarded and Emotionally Disturbed Parents

Parents who themselves are handicapped may show characteristics similar to any of the problem parents discussed so far. Yet because of their own limitations and the special dilemmas they present to the teacher, mentally handicapped parents warrant separate discussion.

In working with these parents the teacher should avoid difficult and abstract terminology; also, she may have to communicate information more than once because of the parents' limited ability in abstract reasoning or their preoccupation. Although the same dimensions of good interpersonal relationships apply to handicapped parents, more patience may be needed and language should be commensurate with their comprehension. This is not to say that teachers should talk down to parents but that they should use understandable concepts—a practice that really needs to be taken seriously with all parents.

Mentally handicapped parents may require more help than the teacher can provide. Emotionally disturbed parents may already be receiving help from a psychologist or psychiatrist, and mentally retarded parents may likewise be receiving help from other sources.

When excessively unrealistic expectations, neglect, overprotection, and so on are evident, the teacher may wish to enlist the aid of the school social worker or the school psychologist. When other school personnel are involved, open communication between them and the teacher is essential so that all available information is shared. This cooperation tends to decrease erroneous perceptions based on partial information and allows for coordinated efforts toward the goal of assisting both child and parents. Unfortunately, professional jealousies and personality conflicts sometimes interfere with maximum team efforts—an unfortunate by-product of professional teams that the teacher must guard against. The main focus of team interaction must be the child and the family and not issues of a more egocentric nature.

Lack of cooperation and hostile reactions from mentally handicapped parents may be symptomatic of other problems they face and are not to be construed as a direct and personal attack on the school or the teacher. Misunderstanding or misconstrued comments may result in reactions difficult for the teacher to comprehend. For example, an emotionally disturbed parent who characteristically projects blame onto others may, to the teacher's amazement, project his child's disturbed behavior onto a perfectly normal grandparent who interacts positively with the child. As time goes on, the teacher may learn that other problems are attributed to the grandparent, who appears to be a convenient scapegoat. It is not the teacher's task to correct the parent's perceptions, but to be aware of them so that the parent is appraised more accurately.

Mentally handicapped parents may exhibit inconsistent feelings and behaviors. Once the teacher realizes that this inconsistency will occur with particular parents, she will be in a better position to understand and work with them. One might surmise that such behavior affects the child negatively, and yet there is little the teacher can do about it except for insuring that her own behavior with the child and the parents remains consistent, thereby providing a positive model for the parent and a source of stability for the child. Whenever possible, the teacher might drop hints to the parents about the advantage of consistent behavior.

Mood changes can accompany other problems or be the major psychological aberration of the parent. Radical mood swings also contribute negatively to a child's sense of security, but once again the teacher is in the unfortunate position of having little effect on the parent. A good rule to follow is to stay away from potentially depressing discussions when the parent is depressed and engage him in cooperative endeavors when he views life more positively and has increased energy.

To summarize in working with mentally handicapped parents, the teacher ought to utilize the facilitative skills used with other parents, be patient, expect behaviorial and mood shifts, and communicate in an understandable but not condescending manner. At times, an inordinate amount of tolerance for frustration is needed. If the parents' behavior is thought to have a significantly adverse effect on the child (e.g., neglect), other personnel better equipped to deal with these issues should be consulted.

Involved Uninvolved Parents

Teachers will, from time to time, be confronted with parents who say all the right things and convey a strong sense of cooperation during conferences yet fail to carry out agreed upon courses of action. Such behavior can be confusing and frustrating for the teacher, but an examination of the possible motives behind it should prove helpful.

As with the other problem parents, the reasons for any particular behavior differs from parent to parent and, for certain actions, may be multi-determined; that is, more than one causal factor contributes to a specific behavior.

The parent's wish to please the teacher or other school personnel with his positive intentions and general willingness to be cooperative may account for his behavior. The parent may feel that he has to convey interest so that the child will continue to be accepted in the program or so that the teacher will view the parents, and therefore the child, in a positive way.

Some parents may genuinely want to be helpful and cooperative and have every intention of pursuing activities decided upon with the teacher, but somehow they find them impossible to initiate. For some parents, the demands of other members of the family and jobs may be so great that good intentions are difficult to implement. For others, engaging in mutually agreed upon activities with their child serves to highlight their child's deficiencies, thereby increasing their anxiety and subsequent withdrawal.

Although they may agree with the teacher that certain activities should be done at home, some parents may actually feel that these programs fall within the scope of the classroom. Such parents resent engaging in activities they feel the teacher is trained to conduct. Other parents think they cannot adequately perform the tasks agreed upon and, therefore, will not risk failure or harm to the child.

Discovering what lies behind the parents' failure requires sensitivity and tact. The teacher must be sure that her own frustration and anger do not become an impediment to effective communication. She must not blame the parents for the child's slow progress or imply that they are liars, lack responsibility, or are untrustworthy. It does little good to point out the discrepancy between what the parents said they would do and what they actually do. However, in some situations the teacher must find some way of communicating her concern to the parent.

> *I know it must be difficult at times with the other responsibilities you have, but if one of you could spend about one-half hour three times a week with Joan in a reading activity, I believe it would help her retain whatever gains she has made in school.*

> *I'm sure it must be hard to constantly be reminded of the things Jimmy does not do well and it must be frustrating to have him do things over and over again with little to show for it, but I believe that if we work together and be consistent with him at home and at school he will begin to make small gains. It's discouraging not to see more progress, yet I feel that some progress has been made and that more is possible but I very much need your help. What do you think—can we work together on this?*

In both responses the teacher recognizes the parents' underlying feelings (of frustration and discouragement), which tells them that she is trying to understand their problems. In the first response the teacher describes the advantages of having academic activities reinforced at home. Also, she depicts the demands on the parents' time as modest and shared so that working with the child is not seen as overwhelming. In the second response, parental feelings are again recognized and communicated. Also, the parents are asked to become allies with the teacher in the interest of their child. The teacher takes an optimistic view of past gains and future achievements without promising significant and unrealistic progress. Finally, the parents are asked how they feel about the teacher's comments.

In contrast, responses that would probably result in increased resistance follow:

> *Mrs. Greenwald, I don't know how many times I've asked you to reinforce John whenever he goes to the bathroom. Unless you do what I keep telling you to do John may never learn to be toilet trained. What's the matter, don't you care enough about your son to do this little thing that I ask?*

> *I don't know what's going on at home but I just don't understand what is keeping you from being more consistent with Leslie at home. It's really a very simple thing that I'm asking you to do. The next time we meet I hope to hear that you are working consistently with Leslie.*

> *I'm getting tried of hearing about all the great activities you*

lpers regardless of their professional affiliation. In this regard, achers must be careful about who is privy to confidential information and who is not. Breaches of confidentiality can be detrimental to both the children and the parent as well as to the teacher. onfidential leaks tend to occur most often under two circumstances: (1) when the teacher is angry at a child or parent and ants revenge, or (2) when the teacher is unaware under what ircumstances confidential information can or cannot be shared.

All professionals encounter parents or clients that provide significant challenges. Some parents take up inordinate amounts of ime and energy or are constantly complaining about some facet of their child's education, and as a consequence, they generate feelings of frustration, anger, or anxiety in the teacher. A natural and often a helpful tendency under such conditions is to vent one's feelings to a colleague or friend. Little harm is done in discussing, in a general way, a frustrating situation, but the discussion must avoid content that would in any way identify the parent. Such discussions are safer with a professional colleague or supervisor, where confidentiality is less of an issue and the teacher can openly vent her feelings and also be in a position to receive feedback if necessary. Breaches of confidential information to friends and acquaintances is a serious matter, one that raises questions of appropriate professional conduct (Schulman 1978).

Information shared between parent and teacher must remain private unless other *involved* professionals in the school (e.g., school social worker) are consulted. Test and/or anecdotal information retained in files is likewise considered confidential to uninvolved professionals as well as to people outside of the school. Consultants and other professionals may have access to confidential information only if the parent signs a release-of-information form. In such instances, parents should be fully informed as to who will have access to the information and for what purposes.

Recent legislation, long overdue, makes it mandatory that parents have available to them information about their child. This ruling, which enables parents to examine information previously hidden from them and to respond to any inaccuracies found in the files, makes it incumbent for those making entries to consider carefully and accurately report any information about the child and parent.

As mentioned in an earlier chapter, the use of recording devices

> *promise to do with your son but never carry out.*
> *that you take some action on what you say you ar*

These responses—examples of cajoling, rudeness
can easily lead to guilt, defensiveness, and hostilit
tunately will take their toll on the child. The teache
terested in the reasons for the parents' behavior or
and he converts his own angry feelings into a scold

Parents who wish to please the teacher with ver
tions, may, within the context of a good relationship,
him with actual deeds. Others who do want to help
siderably burdened should be asked to cooperate onl
and manageable basis. There are times when an ove
parent should not be asked for more, or for anything,
ful situation is eased.

Parents who believe that learning activities shoul
only in a classroom may change their minds if a teach
time to explain how gains made at school can be increas
These parents may need to know that additional help
particularly important for exceptional children and that
ents now work with their children in collaboration with t
This last point can be construed as an attempt to appl
on parents, but it gives them a perspective on contempor
school relationships.

Parents who feel they cannot successfully work with
dren might be willing to try if the demands are not too
if they have success, thereby increasing their self-confi
may be helpful for the parents to understand that the
harm the child through home activities

Ethical Concerns

Contrary to what many believe, ethics refer more to iss
professional judgment than to legalistic implications, altho
breach of ethics can lead to legal problems. Personal jud
(good sense) and judgment based on ethical codes of conduc
veloped by professional organizations (e.g., the National Educ
Association) should guide teachers' behaviors with those they s
The ethical issue of confidentiality is important to professi

should only be used when the parent knows of the recording, the reason for it, who will be listening to it, and how it will be used. The only legitimate reason for recording parent-teacher conferences is for learning purposes, and it is not to be used for the collection of "evidence" under any circumstances.

Performing in a professional manner activities generally ascribed to one's role is an ethical matter. Subsumed in this category is a commitment to working as effectively as possible with children and parents. Using principles of good interpersonal relationships is important, as is making oneself accessible to parents. In general, the teacher owes it to herself and the children and parents to take her job seriously, with dedication and enthusiasm, even though at times her level of motivation is low. She should consider other professions if her interest and motivation wane since the teaching profession, with its enormous demands, requires the services of people with high principles, desire, interest, and knowledge.

When teachers are not sure of the propriety of their actions, they often find it helpful to consult the code of ethical standards developed by the professional organization to which they belong. Such codes have been prepared for the specific purpose of providing guidance to the professional.

Teacher Burnout

The diverse and sometimes contradictory demands placed upon teachers can, over extended periods of time, lead to what has in other professions become a recognized phenomenon that is currently being given serious attention, namely, professional burnout. Burnout has become a particularly critical issue in counseling, where there has been a significant movement of counselors out of full-time positions and to other occupations. According to Warnath and Shelton (1976), the problem is serious.

> Our contacts with numerous counselors and our own experience in agency counseling leads us to the conclusion that full-time professional counselors simply "burn out." [p. 172]

In regard to our schools, Lisbe (1978) makes the following observations:

I have seen idealism easily transformed into disenchantment in many interns or other students I have supervised. Apprentices in social work, psychology, administration, counseling, and teaching all want to make their unique impact on the slow-moving monolith of the public schools. . . . Too soon, when the pressures become greater, the question "How many mountains *should* be moved?" becomes "How many *can* be?" Eventually, if all energy is drained, the question may become, "How can *I* survive?" [p. 239]

Warnath and Shelton believe that a number of factors contribute to counselor burnout. Because of similarities between counselors and teachers (e.g., they both work with children and adults in a learning–helping capacity), these reasons may also apply to teachers. Therefore, although the following discussion is influenced by Warnath and Shelton's article, the situations used will be those commonly experienced by teachers.

The seeds of disillusionment are sown during the teacher's experiences in college. Students read about and are informed by their professors of the high ideals they should bring to their chosen profession—ideals that tend to become tarnished in the day-to-day encounters with students, supervisors, and parents. Educators of teachers must be more aware of the significant gap between college ideals and reality, which is a major source of disappointment to novice teachers. Also, some professors who talk about the importance of productive interpersonal relationships are themselves distant, closed, and manipulative in their contacts with their students— hardly a proper social model for students who look to their professors for guidance, which is often accomplished through emulation.

Disillusionment grows in the realities of the job. Teachers are often confronted with high demands and low rewards. For example, new teachers are ill-prepared to face the high cost in terms of psychological and physical fatigue. Each day brings its quota of problems, from students who lack the motivation for learning to parents who are critical, demanding, and uncooperative. Obvious progress is infrequently evident, and mistakes are pounced upon with unnerving regularity.

In many classrooms high student-teacher ratios and discipline problems allow little opportunity for more personal relationships between student and teacher. It is of some consequence to note that the selection of a people-oriented profession is motivated by a need for close interpersonal relationships, a need often frustrated in the classroom.

Positive feedback from students and parents, a major source of fulfillment, is intermittent and not particularly reinforcing. This situation, coupled with the lack of reinforcement from supervisors, is most discouraging. Teachers' professional esteem may be additionally challenged as they are asked to assume new roles and implement new school policies and mandated laws.

Sooner or later teachers are exhausted to the point where they no longer look forward with anticipation to their work. It is little wonder that burned-out teachers are seeking professional opportunities in other areas. Those teachers who feel they are not in a position to change careers spend much time complaining about their negative experiences to colleagues or tolerate their jobs by ingesting tranquilizers or visiting psychotherapists. In any event, teaching is viewed with more dread than positive anticipation, a situation culminating in significant problems of morale.

The following recommendations, extrapolated from and added to the possible solutions by Warnath and Shelton, may counteract teacher burnout:

1. School administrators should be required to teach, putting them in a better position to empathize with the teacher, as well as to lighten her work load.

2. Before graduation, students should be required to spend one *full-time* term in the classroom, with their responsibilities increasing with time and proficiency. Such an experience would give the prospective teacher a more realistic view of her chosen profession.

3. Each student should be required to enroll in a course that focuses on issues related to teachers in the classroom. In this way teachers can be better prepared to deal more effectively in their role.

4. Teachers should be given greater voice in the formulation of policy. At minimum, they should be given opportunities (e.g., in faculty meetings) to voice their opinions about their jobs and be guaranteed that their comments will not be held against them. Having a voice in one's destiny is an important builder of morale.

5. Schools should make provisions for teachers to spend time away from the classroom during the school year. For example, teachers should be relieved periodically for a period of time to pursue more relaxing activities or hobbies. These minisabbaticals can often serve as an opportunity for renewal. At the very least,

they give the teacher the impression that the system, which is often viewed as an adversary, is concerned about their welfare.

6. Teachers should have a chance to present for consideration areas in which they feel deficient so that in-service training programs are built around their perceived needs. This input should greatly increase interest and motivation to attend such programs.

CHAPTER 7

Parent-Teacher Conferences: Critical Incidents for Role Playing and/or Discussion

It is helpful to know how problem situations develop, to understand their dynamics, and to learn about alternative solutions, but cognitive knowledge and understanding are only partial answers to their successful resolution. Discussion with others and especially role playing difficult encounters help one to anticipate how to deal with a particular situation. Such active involvement and practice in working through, in a nonthreatening context, commonly encountered experiences contribute to a reduction of anxiety and a sense of confidence that one can perform successfully. Although less helpful than simulation and active role playing, thinking through a critical incident to possible solutions can also be useful. At the very least, thoughtful consideration of a problem can help the teacher anticipate how she would respond as well as alert her to potential troublesome situations.

Critical incidents related to parent-teacher conferences have inherent advantages in role playing and can be used in several different ways. The points below allude to both advantages and methods of implementation:

1. The discussion or role playing of a particular critical incident often goes beyond the specific incident to an exploration of other issues. For example, recognizing that her typical response to hostile parents is to withdraw, the teacher might then examine, in a more general sense, why she reacts in this fashion when confronted by angry people.

2. Moving from the *discussion* of a critical incident or problem to role playing is accomplished easily and helps bridge the gap between how one might respond to a particular situation and how one *actually does* react to the incident in a simulated context. As Schwebel (1953) notes, role playing provides a safe atmosphere in which participants can try out different strategies without harming an actual parent-teacher relationship.

3. Although one may elect to move from discussion to role playing, an alternative strategy would be to do the opposite. Even if discussion precedes role playing, it is extremely useful to allow time for discussion *after* as well, when insights gained from feedback and suggestions related to alternative approaches often occur.

4. It is enlightening for the teacher to examine closely how he responds to a number of critical incidents. Such examination helps develop a rough profile of his *typical* way of relating to parents. For example, a teacher may find that he typically begins a conference by conveying test results and behavioral information about a child before both parties are settled in.

5. Critical incidents are flexible and may be used on a one-to-one basis, in a group context or by oneself, as noted earlier. The technique is extremely productive in groups, where the incidents generate considerable discussion and valuable feedback.

6. The critical incidents that follow are far from exhaustive so the reader may wish to write out two or three incidents that are particularly relevant and use them in role playing or for discussion.

7. One problem with critical incidents is that they never seem to supply enough information and are thus a minor source of frustration. A simple way to correct this situation is to add concrete information that will help create, as accurately as possible, the problem one wishes to address. Also, eliminating and adding to the information provided allows one to consider whether relatively minor changes result in significantly different configurations which necessitate different interventions. For example, by changing the child's handicap from blindness to mental retardation or by changing the parents socioeconomic level, one may find that the situation has been altered considerably.

8. Although the introduction of evaluative procedures tends to heighten anxiety and for some interferes with normal interaction, one may wish to evaluate the role player on dimensions discussed in Chapters 4 and 5. A series of simple rating scales, anchored at each end, can be developed. Here are a few samples:

Timing Scale

(Circle number)	Poor				Excellent
	1	2	3	4	5

Verbal Following Behavior Scale

(Circle number)	Needs much work	Needs some work	An adequate job	Above average	Super job
	1	2	3	4	5

Overall Performance Scale

Poor	Below average	Average	Above average	Excellent
1	2	3	4	5

9. The scales relating to different behavioral dimensions should have the same descriptors, thereby adding needed consistency. Some instructors may wish to make students' final grades in a course partially dependent on their performance. Others use rating scales exclusively for the edification of the students. Ratings are collected *by the student* who performs simple statistical procedures (mean, mode, range) so that the teacher may review the collective perceptions of the observers.

Peer ratings can be very useful. However, if an instructor elects to use them for grading, she should remember that the role player was rated by peers, who had limited experience themselves.

It is helpful to have peer ratings on more than one incident. Ratings from two or three different role-played situations allow the student to see whether gains have been made over time; they probably have, both from role playing oneself and from observing others.

Introducing the Technique

Although the implementation of this procedure may be handled in various ways, the instructions below represent two methods in which it may be structured.

INSTRUCTION 1

The following critical incidents have been developed primarily for *discussion*. There are no right or wrong answers; however, some responses may be considered more facilitative than others. The incidents represent situations commonly encountered by teachers who confer with parents.

After reading and reflecting upon the incident, write down one or two strategies or responses that you believe best represents what you would do in that particular situation. Be prepared to discuss your opinion.*

INSTRUCTION 2

The following critical incidents have been developed for *role playing*. There are no right or wrong answers; however, some responses may be considered more facilitative than others. The incidents represent situations commonly encountered by teachers who confer with parents.

The instructor may call upon two people in the group or ask for volunteers. They should leave the room for a few minutes to reflect upon the situation and decide who would take the roles of parent and teacher. Upon entering the room the two people can begin the simulated conference.

Role-Playing Considerations and Strategies

Role playing tends to provoke anxiety, primarily because one is being evaluated in public, and any mistakes are generally obvious to the role player and observers alike. Most people fear making mistakes and therefore often spend considerable energy to keep errors hidden from others.

Although anxiety cannot be eliminated, it can be reduced. The judicious application of the interpersonal skills one has learned should be used when commenting on someone else's role playing.

---

* Written responses to incidents may also be turned in to the instructor if so desired.

Thus participants have opportunities continuously to practice facilitative behavior. Role-playing groups should give open, honest feedback delivered in a humane and facilitative manner. Light-heartedness and humor, without becoming giddy, is to be encouraged—humor tends to help ease situations. Following is an example of a facilitative and a nonfacilitative response to a role-played situation:

> *Nonfacilitative:* Karen, you talked so much in the interview that the "parent" hardly had a chance to get a sentence in. In general, you were rude and insensitive and I think you have a lot to learn!
>
> *Facilitative:* My feeling is that you were talking about some issues that are important to the parent. However, in putting myself in the parent's place, I was beginning to feel a little annoyed because I wanted to respond to what you said. I wonder if next time you might bring up some of the issues you did during the first conference but allow the parent to be a bit more expressive.

Because his expertise is not at issue, the person taking the parent's role will find that it provokes less anxiety than that of the teacher. It is important that all the people in the group be given opportunities to play the teacher's role since this is the position they will have or already do have. However, participants playing parents may achieve important insights into parental perspectives during parent-teacher conferences—insights that should be discussed openly.

Although it may not seem like a long time, four to six minutes is generally sufficient for role playing, as many data are available to the role players and observers after that length of time. Five minutes of role playing can lead to a half hour's discussion. Occasionally the role playing is interrupted after a few minutes for comments, but in general, they should be avoided unless a conference has reached a natural conclusion, the role players wish to stop, or an alternate strategy is being introduced (e.g., role reversal).

As indicated above, the most useful aspect of role playing is often the discussion that takes place afterward. Time should always be made available for debriefing, since it is during this period that important feedback is provided and relevant issues surface.

A useful role-playing strategy is the *alter-ego* technique. Each role player has someone sitting behind him commenting on unexpressed material (e.g., underlying feelings) that the alter ego believes the role players are not aware of or are not addressing for some reason. The alter egos can comment whenever they wish, but the role players cannot address comments directly to them. The role players, of course, hear and may wish to incorporate what their alter egos have said, but *without addressing the alter egos.* This technique is useful in uncovering feelings or content that seem to be present but is not expressed by either role player. In other words, the alter ego speaks what he imagines to be the role player's inner thoughts. To avoid excessive distraction, the alter egos may wish to intervene only occasionally. They are placed as follows:

Teacher Alter Ego   Teacher   Parent   Parent Alter Ego

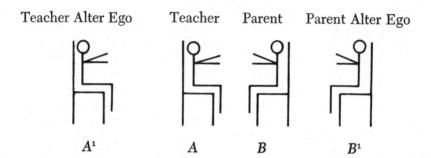

A¹   A   B   B¹

The alter-ego technique is an excellent role-playing strategy, but because four people are involved, a sensitive coordinator needs to observe and direct the action. For example, alter egos might be introduced after three minutes if it is obvious to the coordinator (and perhaps to others) that superficialities are keeping important conversation hidden.

Another useful technique, *role reversal,* is to interrupt the action at some point and have the two people switch roles in midstream, as it were. They then continue from the point of interruption. Role reversal forces the role players to see the situation from the other's point of view. It is also used when one or the other player becomes stuck and cannot continue.

The final strategy, the *mirror technique,* can be used to help develop self-awareness. For example, the "teacher" may sit aside and watch another person interact with the "parent" in the same way he had done previously. This technique is particularly useful when a role player is blocked or wishes to see how someone else might deal with a particular situation.

The reader should now be ready to begin role playing. What follows is a series of critical incidents with accompanying questions for thought and discussion.

INCIDENT 1

Mr. and Mrs. Smithfield have recently been informed that their handicapped son will have a new teacher next year, a change they had not anticipated. Their son's current teacher (you) plans to retire, and a new teacher will be hired in your place. The Smithfield's perception of you is highly positive. They feel their son has made significant progress under your tutelage, and they have always felt comfortable in your presence.

The reality that their son and they themselves will be relating to a new and unknown quantity, so to speak, has the Smithfields in a state of considerable apprehension. They are coming to you to discuss their concerns.

DISCUSSION QUESTIONS

1. Why are the Smithfields apprehensive about the change?
2. Why might the Smithfields be reluctant to let go of you?
3. How do you think their son might feel about the change?
4. How will you begin the conference?
5. What are your goal(s)?

INCIDENT 2

Freddie has exhibited behavior that is clearly suggestive of a disturbed child. For example, he would defecate in his pants, blow his nose without a tissue, refuse to work, scream, and throw objects around the room. In several meetings with the parents you've learned that they appear to love him deeply.

Freddie's parents never mentioned any problems they may have had with him at home. Whenever you mention the problems you've observed in the classroom, the parents appear genuinely surprised. Thus far, your impression is that Freddie's parents believe his misbehavior is insignificant and does not manifest problems that need special attention.

You feel that it is necessary for the parents to view their child's problems more realistically, and you also feel that more can be done for the child with their support and assistance.

You have an appointment to meet with Freddie's parents in an hour.

DISCUSSION QUESTIONS

1. Why do you think the parents are not acknowledging behavior that clearly falls outside normal limits?
2. Is it possible that Freddie may behave differently at home than at school? If so, why?
3. What precautions should you keep in mind when conferring with Freddie's parents?
4. What do you plan to say?

INCIDENT 3

After a faculty meeting two months ago it was determined that Raymond should be placed in a learning disabilities classroom. The child's verbal skills are very good, but teachers' comments on his referral sheet note that he shows the following: impulsiveness, visual-perceptual inefficiency, poor awareness of his body and general clumsiness.

These clinical observations need to be supplemented by test data but the parents refuse to consent. They appear not to understand the difference between mental retardation and learning disability. Since his verbal skills are good, they find it hard to believe that he has any problems at all and are resisting attempts to have him placed in a more appropriate class.

Since you are Raymond's teacher and the parents know you well, you've been asked to meet with them to discuss the situation.

DISCUSSION QUESTIONS

1. What may be behind the parents' resistance to the testing?
2. What might be some of the reasons for their confusion about mental retardation and learning disabilities?
3. How would you explain the differences between the two to Raymond's parents?
4. What would you do or say if, after you've explained the importance of the testing and the new placement, the parents still do not want their son tested or placed elsewhere?
5. What are your primary goals of the conference?

INCIDENT 4

About a month ago you suggested to Jill's parents that they use a specific behavior-modification technique to reduce her excessive attention-getting and disruptive behavior both at school and at home. The parents appeared pleased with your suggestion and promised to carry out this plan.

Since then, Jill's behavior has not gotten better. In fact, her usual classroom antics were supplemented by behaviors not seen before, and she has generally become more disruptive.

Although you are not certain, you suspect that Jill's parents misconstrued the strategy you had discussed with them, and have, in fact, implemented an approach contradictory to the one used in school.

Because the problem is getting worse and you suspect that Jill's parents and you are inadvertently working at cross-purposes, you've asked them to come in for a conference.

Discussion Questions

1. What are your objectives in the forthcoming conference?
2. What may have caused the different perceptions of the strategy you outlined during the earlier meeting?
3. Even if you and Jill's parents are relating differently to the child, what would account for the significant change in her behavior?

INCIDENT 5

Jean is a ten-year-old celebral palsied girl with normal intelligence. Academically, she performs as well as other nonhandicapped students in your class. Even so, you believe that she is an exceptionally creative child who may be even brighter than her tests indicate. She tends to be somewhat introverted and does not relate well to her classmates.

Your meetings with Jean's parents have revealed that they care very much about their daughter but tend to view her as having limited abilities. They have even suggested that she may be misplaced and should perhaps go to school in a special classroom with mentally retarded children "who are more like her."

As her teacher you can see that Jean's parents perceive their child unrealistically, and that with encouragement from her parents she might be able to develop latent abilities. Their perception that Jean belongs in a mentally retarded class would appear to be most inappropriate and potentially damaging.

Jean's parents have called you for a conference. You suspect that they wish to pursue with you the possibility of a different placement for their child.

DISCUSSION QUESTIONS

1. What are your immediate and long-range goals with Jean's parents? (Remember *they* called for the conference.)
2. Why do you think they see their daughter so unrealistically?
3. Why might they prefer to have her placed in a different setting?
4. What might you do in school to help Jean with her shyness?
5. What effects, if any, might her parents' perceptions of her have on Jean?

INCIDENT 6

Rachael will be fifteen years old before the end of the next school year. She is close to completing her fourth year at your school. Previously she had two unsuccessful years at public school, where she experienced considerable difficulty in learning accompanied by problems in behavior.

Rachael's behavior, which is felt to impede her learning, is characterized by uncontrolled giggling, childish mannerisms, ritualistic neatness, perseveration, and fantasizing. She is generally gentle and a bit shy but unable to relate well to her peers; she was often picked on by other children.

The teachers who had worked with her, the social worker, and the district psychologist felt that she had made gains but that four years was about a maximum stay at your school and that another school, already specified to the parents, would now help her more.

Rachel's parents are as conscientious and caring about her as they are about their two normal, younger children. The family atmosphere appears to be a comparatively happy one where enriching family experiences are valued.

At the last conference, in which the new special class was mentioned to the parents, they said that although Rachael has some behavioral and academic problems, she would catch up with her age group and be perfectly able to compete with other students in college.

The conference you are about to have with Rachael's parents is intended to review the content of the last meeting. Your hope is that the parents will view their child more realistically and accept the recommendation made earlier. Intuitively, however, you feel that they will gently but firmly reject your recommendation.

DISCUSSION QUESTIONS

1. Given your expectations of how Rachael's parents may respond, how will you start the conference?
2. What factors may contribute to the parents' unrealistic view of their child?
3. Rachael's parents seem to be rational, not emotional, in their reaction to the recommendation. How do you account for that?
4. What is your recourse if, after the conference, the parents still refuse to follow the recommendation?

INCIDENT 7

Dr. Morgan, an educational psychologist, and her husband, a local television personality, meet with you periodically to discuss their exceptional child. In their conference with you the Morgans typically grill you about testing procedures, how you made your observations, the validity of the tests used to measure the child's academic progress, etc. The meeting, in your view, is not an exchange of information and observation about their child but a cross-examination of the methods used in assessing children. Advice about how you might otherwise obtain your test data and conduct your class is given regularly.

The parents appear to view their behavior as helpful. They act more like your consultants than parents of a child in your class. They ask questions and dispense advice calmly and not in an authoritarian or emotional fashion.

The net result is to make you feel that you've lost control of the conferences. The advice, although seemingly given without malice, makes you feel ill-prepared to assume the duties of a teacher. You feel frustrated and angry, have a lowered sense of self-esteem, and become quite anxious when you are scheduled to meet with the Morgans. In addition, because the conversation, although ostensibly about their child, tends to focus more on your methods, a thorough examination of the Morgans' child is never undertaken—which you feel is a disservice to the child.

Your scheduled meeting with the parents is coming up shortly. You are upset to the point of finally confronting your general sense of exasperation with them.

Discussion Questions

1. What purpose(s) might the Morgans' behavior serve?
2. What hypotheses would you make about how they feel about their child?
3. How might you characterize the relationship between the parents and the child?
4. What underlying feelings might these parents have about their circumstances?
5. What would you like to do in the upcoming conference, and does it differ from what you feel you ought to do?
6. How would you characterize the relationship you have with the parents?
7. What are your goals for the conference?

INCIDENT 8

Mrs. Sweetness is an exceptionally nice and pleasant person. She always attends conferences, praises you for the superb job you do, and welcomes any suggestions you have about how she might be of help to her child at home.

You strongly suspect that her promises to work with her child on specific tasks are rarely, if ever, carried out. In addition, her excessive sweetness is obnoxious to you and appears to be phony. However, her niceness contributes to the difficulty you have in confronting her with the discrepancy between what she claims she does and what she actually carries out.

You feel that if you and Mrs. Sweetness continue to relate to each other as you have in the past, your negative feelings toward her will grow more intense and valuable time that could help her child will be lost.

In your next conference, you intend to deal with the issues that trouble you about this relationship.

Discussion Questions

1. What aspects of the relationship do you intend to deal with?
2. What is your understanding of Mrs. Sweetness' behavior?

3. Are you going to or should you express your frustration and anger at Mrs. Sweetness?
4. What are your thoughts about feeling frustrated and angry at this parent?
5. Speculate on how she relates to her children and husband.

INCIDENT 9

Mrs. Gibbons is recently divorced and the mother of two children, one normal and the other severely handicapped. While married, Mrs. Gibbons and her husband would attend parent conferences. They seemingly dealt with their circumstances well as a family unit, but you often sensed that Mrs. Gibbons lacked self-confidence.

Since the divorce, Mrs. Gibbons seems to have fallen apart. During conferences she ruminates with you about her handicapped child, the effect the divorce is having on her other child, and her pervasive sense of inadequacy in dealing with the circumstances confronting her. In addition, she is despondent and lonely and has mentioned two persistent nightmares that haunt her.

Your rapport with Mrs. Gibbons has been very good. However, you are becoming increasingly uncomfortable because of the apparent severity of her problems and your feeling that you are ill equipped to deal with them. You have decided to discuss this matter with Mrs. Gibbons at your next conference.

DISCUSSION QUESTIONS

1. Taken together, what are the factors contributing to Mrs. Gibbons' depression?
2. Why do you think she is entrusting you with her problems?
3. What precautions should you take when you confer with her?
4. Can you expect any behavioral changes from her child? If so, what might they be and why?
5. What are your goals for the conference?

INCIDENT 10

Mr. and Mrs. Shaw anxiously await their conferences with you. They typically ask you for advice and request games, activities, and books which they might use to help their child. Although they are always pleasant, they subtly urge you to push their son, David, in his academic subjects.

You have met with the Shaws enough times to know that they are pressuring their son to do better to the point where it is becoming destructive. You sense the existence of a pervasive compulsion to get as much into their son's head as is humanly possible. The Shaws seem to believe that incessant pressure facilitates rather than impedes progress.

David, who is twelve years old, does not do well academically. You feel that he could do much better if his fears about failure were lessened. He persists at assignment until he either succeeds, which is infrequent, or begins weeping uncontrollably, seemingly ashamed that he could not complete the task or assignment. He is so preoccupied with trying to succeed and so fearful of not succeeding that he has no energy nor motivation to develop necessary social relationships with classmates.

You plan to discuss the situation as you see it at your conference with the Shaws.

DISCUSSION QUESTIONS

1. What may account for the Shaws' anxieties?
2. What strategies might you use in the classroom to help David?
3. How do you picture David's home life?
4. How do you think the Shaws feel about David?
5. How do you plan to approach the conference?

INCIDENT 11

Mrs. Johnson, the mother of a handicapped daughter, appears to enjoy spending time in the classroom as a volunteer aide and you are appreciative of her help. She has been a volunteer for about five months. Although she is not really needed that often, Mrs. Johnson spends the equivalent of two entire days at school. She appears motivated to work with children and has good rapport with them.

In the past Mrs. Johnson was an aide in the true sense of the word; that is, she worked under your supervision and was guided by the activities that were scheduled for the period. Lately, however, she has assumed a coequal position in the classroom by initiating her own activities and subtly suggesting ways in which you might structure classroom activities. Mrs. Johnson has developed a different way of disciplining the children, using an approach you disagree with and which seems to confuse the children, who were accustomed to a consistent form of discipline.

You have been feeling increasingly uneasy about Mrs. Johnson's changing role in the classroom and you plan to discuss it with her at the conference.

DISCUSSION QUESTIONS

1. What are your *feelings* toward Mrs. Johnson?
2. Should you discuss your feelings with her? If so, how would you do it?
3. What may have caused Mrs. Johnson's change of behavior in the classroom?
4. How do you think Mrs. Johnson feels about you?
5. What might prompt a parent to take such an avid interest in the classroom?
6. How do you plan to approach Mrs. Johnson?
7. What are your goals for the conference?

INCIDENT 12

Since the beginning of the school year you have been very much aware of nine-year-old Jeff Peters. Invariably, he comes to class dirty, odorous, and disheveled. On a number of occasions, Jeff has come to class with bruises and welts on his face and neck. You've noticed that he gobbles up his hot lunches as if he hadn't eaten in some time and then scrounges around for extra food that others leave on their trays.

Although he responds to you fairly well, he has a tendency to strike out physically at his classmates, especially when he construes a comment to be suggestive of his intellectual or physical inadequacy. Academically he is functioning far below his capabilities. From your observations and from the comments of others who know him, you are certain that Jeff is a neglected child, if not a physically battered one. You have met once with his mother and father. They appeared to be uncomfortable during the conference and anxiously awaited its termination. The Peters referred to the hard life they lead in bringing up Jeff, his three brothers, and one sister. The parents claim that they see little of Jeff at home, and that he is usually wandering around the neighborhood with his friends, of whom they claim to disapprove.

You are concerned about Jeff from both an educational and psychological point of view, but foremost is your suspicion that he is being totally neglected by his parents and may even be subject to beatings. You plan to discuss these concerns at your next conference.

DISCUSSION QUESTIONS

1. What factors may contribute to Jeff's neglect?
2. What precautions should you exercise in discussing this issue with the parents?
3. What would be your overriding objective for the next conference?
4. Would you consider getting other school staff involved? If so, whom would you consult?
5. What would you do if the parents deny being neglectful or physically abusive?
6. What would you do if they admit to neglecting Jeff?

INCIDENT 13

After Jamie had been in your classroom for about six months, his behavior confirmed your initial impression that he was capable of considerably more independent activity than what he would do voluntarily. Jamie is an educable mentally retarded nine-year-old, who manifests a psychological dependence on you. His dependence takes the form of asking unnecessary questions related to his work, requesting help in finding and putting on his clothing, and generally asking questions in a repetitive fashion to the point of distraction.

In your three conferences with Jamie's parents you have become aware of the overprotective, smothering manner of relating to their son. You feel that Jamie is capable of more independent thinking and activity and firmly believe that his growth is being impeded by his parents' behavior.

As a consequence you have decided to call a conference to discuss what you believe is a significant barrier to the child's development.

DISCUSSION QUESTIONS

1. What cues indicate that Jamie is capable of greater independence?
2. What did you perceive in the parent conferences to lead you to believe that Jamie's parents are overprotective?
3. What factors do you feel contributed to the parents' considerable concern for their son?
4. If Jamie has more independence, how do you think he will respond? How do you think his parents will respond?
5. How do you think your observations will be received by Jamie's parents?
6. How would you communicate your observations to Jamie's parents?
7. Should the parents concur with your observations, how will you proceed?
8. Should they resist, how will you handle their reaction?

INCIDENT 14

Jonathan is the son of a physician in the local community and a prominent professor at the university. He is a nine-year-old educable mentally retarded child who, in addition, manifests a number of specific learning deficiencies. In school he is performing well, given his intellectual abilities, but appears overly intense when doing his schoolwork, which he characterizes as dumb and stupid. Jonathan, incidentally, has a younger brother who by all accounts is exceptionally bright.

During parent conferences, Jonathan's parents are visibly uncomfortable and appear marginally interested. They always attend scheduled conferences, ask questions about their son's academic progress, and then make a rapid exit.

Your goal with Jonathan's parents at this point is to inform them of your observations of their son and get to know them better.

DISCUSSION QUESTIONS

1. Given the information above, what do you think about Jonathan's level of self-esteem?
2. What factors do you feel contribute to his self-concept?

3. What may be the sources of Jonathan's anxiety about his work?
4. Speculate about the reasons for the parents' uneasiness during conferences.
5. Would you deal with the parents' uneasiness during the conference? If so, how?
6. Do any of your behaviors or attitudes contribute to or are the cause of the parents' discomfort?
7. Consider your feelings prior to a conference in which you will be conveying certain information to a physician and a professor.

INCIDENT 15

You have met with Mr. and Mrs. Reynolds twice since the beginning of the school year. They have been amiable and appear cooperative. On both occasions you have been aware that the Reynolds' are much more talkative when the focus of the discussion is not directly on their son's schoolwork and behavior. They fall silent and become embarrassed when these topics are broached, even though they are aware that their son's overall performance will be addressed in the conference.

Their son, John, is a fifteen-year-old mentally retarded child with cerebral palsy who falls within the lower limits of the EMR range on standardized IQ tests. His learning problems are significant, but he continues to make progress in certain areas. He is a likeable person who tends to be rather sedentary and quiet, but not sullen. John relates well to his peers, although his interaction with other children occurs infrequently.

You are aware that Mr. and Mrs. Reynolds find it difficult to discuss their son and his circumstances and yet they continue to come to scheduled conferences. You are concerned about their reactions, but you are not sure what you should do about it at the upcoming conference.

DISCUSSION QUESTIONS

1. What factor(s) may account for the parents' reaction?
2. What *feelings* do you think they have when they discuss their son's situation?
3. How would you deal with the parents' reaction?

4. Would you work with the parents differently at first than you would later?
5. What do you think about *not* addressing the problem?
6. What are your goals for the upcoming conference?

INCIDENT 16

Since Rita began as your *paid* aide, you have not been pleased with her work. You must remind her frequently to follow your instructions. When she decides to help, she does so reluctantly, often with glances that convey her displeasure with your request. When Rita is not being told directly and specifically what to do, she may be found working with a child productively, and she generally appears to enjoy interacting with the children. The problem is that you need her to engage in specified activities at certain times. On occasion, however, you will catch her daydreaming or otherwise preoccupied.

To date you have not discussed with her your views and reactions. You plan to do so at a conference to be held shortly.

DISCUSSION QUESTIONS

1. What is the crux of the problem for you?
2. How does the fact that Rita is paid alter the situation?
3. What might account for Rita's behavior?
4. How do you plan to broach the problem with her?
5. If she is receptive, what type of cooperative relationship would you propose to Rita?

INCIDENT 17

Gordie's mother, Mrs. South, has been to two previously scheduled conferences with you. She has been pleasant to work with and motivated to collaborate with you in any way she can. At your last meeting with Mrs. South, she mentioned that her husband was anxious to meet with you to discuss their son's progress. Unfortunately, he is unable to come to a regularly scheduled conference at school because of unusually awkward working hours. Mrs. South suggested, and you agreed, to have the next conference at their house at a mutually convenient time.

1. What conditions might you expect during your home conference with the Souths?
2. What precautions should you bear in mind during the conference?
3. How does the location of the conference alter your expectations, change the issues you plan to discuss, or change the way you would conduct yourself? Or does the location make no difference?

INCIDENT 18

You are in a conference with Mr. and Mrs. Bradford. They are generally pleased with their son's school and his progress and adjustment. The Bradfords are, however, somewhat upset over what they consider to be a shift in his affection from them to you. They are puzzled and seem hurt over their son's frequent references to you. According to the Bradfords, all they hear about is "my teacher" does this or "my teacher" does that. Even when they are entertaining friends, their son frequently talks about how wonderful you are.

You have just heard the parents' concern and are about to respond (remember you are *in* the conference).

1. How do you intend to explain their son's behavior, or do you?
2. How do you think the Bradfords feel about you?
3. What will your goal(s) be during the conference?

INCIDENT 19

(For this incident develop a hypothetical Individualized Educational Program for a fourteen-year-old girl who falls into the educable mentally retarded category, is mildly cerebral palsied, and periodically manifests behavior suggestive of emotional disturbance. Part of the role playing should include your interpretation of the IEP to the parents as well as future recommendations.)

Mr. and Mrs. Golden have just heard your report of their child's progress to date as well as your recommendations for objectives to be achieved during the remainder of the school year. Although they have not expressed their reaction to your recommendations yet, you sensed that they were becoming increasingly uneasy during this part of the conference.

After completing your recommendations and upon asking the Goldens for their reaction, they emotionally begin to question you about the propriety of the goals you have set forth. In general, they are concerned that your expectations are far beyond what they feel their child can achieve. They are concerned that the goals are too ambitious and should be scaled down considerably.

You had given careful thought to these objectives and believe that they reflect what the child can realistically accomplish. After listening to the parents' concerns you are ready to respond.

DISCUSSION QUESTIONS

1. What nonverbal cues might the Goldens have shown to demonstrate their unease with your recommendations before they verbally told you?
2. How do you explain the parents' modest view of what their daughter can achieve?
3. Might your goals in fact be unrealistic?
4. What will you try to accomplish with the Goldens during the conference?

Resources to Help Teachers Help Parents

Sometimes parents of exceptional children will need help to resolve acute personal crises as well as long-term problems. At other times parents will need concrete information, inspiration, support, and insight. The following resources have been developed so that teachers may have available to them referral sources and reading materials to better serve the parents with whom they work.

It should be noted that the sources and references listed in this chapter are far from complete. The reader should supplement these lists with other useful references and with resources that exist in the teacher's community. All reading material recommended to parents, whether referred to in this chapter or not, ought to be read by the teacher. Also, before recommending readings and making referrals to agencies, the teacher should be knowledgeable about the parents so that their recommendations are appropriate.

Social Service Agencies

American Association of Marriage and Family Counselors, 225 Yale Avenue, Claremont, Cal. 91711 (714 621-4749).

Referrals to qualified marriage and family counselors may be obtained by writing or telephoning the AAMFC. A directory of AAMFC-qualified counselors is available to professional people for referral at a cost of five dollars.

State branches of the American Psychological Association compile directories of professionals who have met state requirements for licensure in clinical and counseling psychology. Qualified psychologists are generally described in terms of their specialty.

Family Service Association of America publishes a *Directory of Member Agencies,* which lists family assistance agencies in many cities in the United States.

Jewish Family Service, 33 West 60th Street, New York, N.Y. 10023.

Jewish Family Service (JFS), which has been in existence for over one hundred years, is a counseling agency for individuals and families. JFS also provides family-life education and legal services. They are located in many communities.

The National Directory of Private Social Service Agencies, 211-03 Jamaica Avenue, Queens Village, N.Y. 11428.

This is an up to date loose-leaf directory of private social agencies in the United States, classified by services offered and listed by states and cities.

The National Association of Social Workers, 1425 H Street NW, Washington, D.C. 20005. NASW publishes a directory that lists and describes both national and international social service and information agencies.

Tansey, Anne M. *Where to Get Help for Your Family.* St. Meinrad, Ind., Abbey Press, 1977.

A good general directory of agencies for people having family-related problems. One hundred and fifty-seven agencies are described in considerable detail.

Most communities publish catalogues of comprehensive and current information about service agencies within the community. For example, in Pittsburgh, up-to-date and accurate information is provided in a compendium called, *Where to Turn,* where all existing agencies, along with vital information about them, are included. In New York City, such information is contained in their continually updated volume, *Directory of Social and Health Agencies of New York City,* published by Columbia University Press.

Teachers should be aware of similar sources in their communities. Libraries generally have such books in their collection, as do professionals who work in service agencies.

Self-Help Groups

Teachers may wish to know about the self-help groups in their respective communities. At least in the more populated areas, such groups tend to exist for parents of children with different handicaps. For example, in Pittsburgh, an active parent group engaged in self-help and advocacy activities is the Pennsylvania Association of Retarded Citizens, a state branch of the National Association of Retarded Citizens. Other parent self-help groups include the Association for Children with Learning Disabilities, Mothers of Young Mongoloids, and National Association for Autistic Children.

Gartner, A., and F. Riesman. *Self-Help in the Human Services.* San Francisco: Jossey-Bass, 1977; Katz, A. H., and E. I. Bender. *The Strength in Us.* New York: Watts, 1976.

These books provide further insights into the purposes and dynamics of self-help groups. In addition, the book written by Gartner and Riesman lists existing self-help groups in the United States.

Hurvitz, N. "Peer Self-Help Psychotherapy Groups and Implications for Psychotherapy." *Psychotherapy: Theory, Research, and Practice* 7 (1970): 41–49.

Hurvitz provides an excellent overview of the dynamics of self-help groups. His observations are based on many years of experience.

Parents Anonymous, 2810 Artesia Boulevard, Redondo Beach, Cal. 90278. (Toll free outside Cal.: 800 421-0353; in Cal.: 800 352-0386.)

P.A. is a self-help crisis-intervention program to help parents prevent damaging relationships between themselves and their children. P.A. groups exist all over the United States and have toll-free help-lines for parents who need information, help, or wish to locate a P.A. group in their community. They also publish a chapter directory.

Parents Without Partners, Inc., 7910 Woodmont Avenue, Suite 1000, Washington, D.C. 20014.

P.W.P. is devoted to the interests and welfare of single parents and their children. Over 850 chapters exist in the United States and Canada.

Information and Assistance for Parents of Children with Specific Disabilities

The national organizations listed below should prove helpful for parents who require assistance or information related to their child's exceptionality.

Organization providing assistance to the parents of all exceptional children: Council for Exceptional Children, 1920 Association Drive, Reston, Va. 22091.

Arthritis: The Arthritis Foundation, 475 Riverside Drive, New York, N. Y. 10027.

Autism: National Society for Autistic Children, 169 Tampa Avenue, Albany, New York 12208.

Blindness: American Association of Workers for the Blind, Inc., 1511 K Street, NW, Washington, D.C. 20005; American Foundation for the Blind, 15 West 16th Street, New York, N. Y. 10011; The Library of Congress, Division for the Blind and Physically Handicapped, 1291 Taylor, NW, Washington, D.C. 20042.

Cancer: American Cancer Society, Inc., 777 Third Avenue, New York, N. Y. 10017.

Cerebral palsy: United Cerebral Palsy Association, Inc., 66 East 34th Street, New York, N. Y. 10016.

Communication disorders: American Speech and Hearing Association, 9030 Old Georgetown Road, Washington, D.C. 20014; Information Center for Hearing, Speech, and Disorders of Human Communication, 10 Harriet Lane Home, The Johns Hopkins Medical Institutions, Baltimore, Md. 21205.

Deafness: Alexander Graham Bell Association for the Deaf, 3417 Volta Place, NW, Washington, D.C. 20007; National Association of the Deaf, 814 Thayer Avenue, Silver Springs, Md. 20910.

Diabetes: American Diabetes Association, 600 Fifth Avenue, New York, N. Y. 10020.

Epilepsy: Epilepsy Foundation of America, 1828 L Street, NW, Washington, D.C. 20036.

Heart disease: American Heart Association, 7320 Greenville Avenue, Dallas, Tex. 75231.

Learning disabilities: Association for Children with Learning Disabilities, 5225 Grace Street, Pittsburgh, Pa. 15236.

Mental illness: National Institute of Mental Health, 5600 Fishers Lane, Rockville, Md. 20852.

Mental retardation: American Association on Mental Deficiency, 5201 Connecticut Avenue, NW, Washington, D.C. 20006; National Association for Retarded Citizens, 2709 Avenue East, Arlington, Tex. 76001; Retarded Infants Services, Inc., 386 Park Avenue South, New York, N.Y. 10016.

Multiple sclerosis: National Multiple Sclerosis Society, 257 Park Avenue South, New York, N.Y. 10010.

Muscular dystrophy: Muscular Dystrophy Association of America, Inc., 810 Seventh Avenue, New York, N.Y. 10019.

Myesthenia gravis: Myesthenia Gravis Foundation, Inc., 238 Park Avenue, New York, N.Y. 10017.

Orthopedic: Institute for the Crippled and Disabled, Rehabilitation and Research Center, 340 East 24th Street, New York, N.Y. 10010; The National Easter Seal Society for Crippled Children and Adults, 2023 West Ogden Avenue, Chicago, Ill. 60612.

Paraplegia: National Paraplegia Association, 333 North Michigan Avenue, Chicago, Ill. 60601.

Respiratory disorders: Tuberculosis and Respiratory Disease Association, 1670 Beverley Boulevard, Los Angeles, Cal. 90026; American Lung Association, 1740 Broadway, New York, N.Y. 10019.

General Information About Books and Reading

The Great Books Foundation, 307 North Michigan Avenue, Chicago, Ill. 60601.

The foundation selects and publishes noteworthy books for adults and juniors. The Junior Great Books Program develops the ability of students to think reflectively and independently. The foundation is actively engaged in training discussion leaders.

Reading is Fundamental (RIF), L'Enfant 2500, Smithsonian Institute, Washington, D.C. 20560.

The aim of RIF is to create the desire to read among all children at an early age by showing them that reading is fun. The role of RIF is to help establish and guide local projects throughout the country. Currently there are more than 400 local RIF projects operating in forty-seven states.

Literature Related to Legal Rights of Parents of Handicapped Children

Digest of State and Federal Laws, 1974 ed. The Council for Exceptional Children, 1920 Association Drive, Reston, Va. 22091.

The *Digest* is concerned with the status of state and federal laws through December 1974. This volume may be of particular assistance to teachers who wish to be more familiar with education-related legislation in their own as well as in other states.

Exceptional Children (Nov. 1976).

This issue has as its main focus a discussion of existing federal programs for exceptional children with particular emphasis on the implementation of PL 94–142.

Know Your Rights, Fall 1977 (6 pages). Closer Look: The National Information Center for the Handicapped, P.O. Box 1492, Washington, D.C. 20013.

Brief but comprehensive review of parent rights.

Losen, S. M., and B. Diament. *Parent Conferences in the Schools.* Boston: Allyn and Bacon, 1978.

Pages 257–72 focus on the major aspects of PL 93–380 (Education Amendments Law of 1974) and PL 94–142 (Education for All Handicapped Children Act of 1975). The authors also address the implications of these important pieces of legislation as they relate to parents' rights vis-à-vis the school.

Martin, E. W., Jr. "Rights and Coalitions." *Exceptional Parent* 3 (Mar.-Apr. 1973): 9–10.

Author advocates a national coalition for civil rights legislation for the handicapped.

Literature for Children About Handicapped People and Conditions

Alcott, L. M. *Little Men.* Any unabridged edition. Intermediate through young adult.

An emotionally disturbed boy attends Jo's school in this fictionalized account of the author's experiences.

Baskin, B. H., and K. H. Harris. *Notes from a Different Drummer: A Guide to Juvenile Fiction Portraying the Handicapped.* New York: R. R. Bowker, 1977.

The authors have compiled a comprehensive guide and annotated bibliography reflecting concerns of handicapped persons. Juvenile fiction written between 1940 and 1975 is included for readers in the young child (5–8 years old) to mature adolescent (16–18 years old) age range.

Beim, J. *Across the Bridge.* New York: Harcourt, 1951. Primary, including preschool, through intermediate.

This is a story about a child with a visual handicap.

Bishop, C. *Lonesome End.* Philadelphia: Lippincott, 1963. Elementary through young adult.

The loss of two fingers puts Jim's high school football career in jeopardy.

Bro, M. H. *Su-Meis' Golden Year.* Garden City, N.Y.: Doubleday, 1950. Elementary through intermediate.

A young girl and her crippled father save the village harvest in this story of Chinese life during World War II.

Burmingham, J. *Cannonball Sump*. Indianapolis, Ind.: Bobbs-Merrill, 1967. Primary, including preschool.

Byars, B. *The Summer of Swans*. New York: Viking, 1970. Elementary through young adult.

Sara survives her fourteenth summer with the help of her brain-damaged brother and his near-tragic adventures.

Dahl, B. *Finding My Way*. New York: E. P. Dutton, 1962. Intermediate through young adult.

This autobiographical work describes the thoughts and actions of a middle-aged teacher and author after a serious operation in which she lost her vision.

DeJong, M. *Wheel on the School*. New York: Harper and Row, 1954. Elementary through intermediate.

An amputee in a wheelchair is the instrument of heroism.

Downes, A. M. *Speak to Me, Brother*. Philadelphia: Lippincott, 1954. Young adult.

Forced to take care of their family, a sister and crippled brother each find their own fulfillment after struggle, injustice, and hardship.

Dunnahoo, T. *Ann Sullivan: A portrait*. Chicago: Reilly and Lee, 1970. Elementary through intermediate.

The story of Helen Keller's teacher is retold for the young.

Farber, N. W. *Cathy's Secret Kingdom*. Philadelphia: Lippincott, 1963. Elementary through intermediate.

Cathy's emotionally disturbed, socially retarded stepsister joins in a mystery and adventure.

Friis, B. *Kristy's Courage*. New York: Harcourt, 1965. Intermediate.

A badly disfigured girl faces and overcomes the teasing of others.

Graff, S., and P. Anne. *Helen Keller: Toward the Light*. Champaign, Ill.: Garrard, 1965. Elementary.

This is a story for the young about Helen Keller.

Herman, W. *Hearts Courageous, Twelve Who Achieved*. New York: Dutton, 1949. Young adult.

Milton, Beethoven, Franklin Roosevelt, Charles Steinmetz, and Glen Cunningham are among the "twelve who achieved" in spite of their handicaps.

Hodges, C. W. *The Namesake*. New York: Coward-McCann, 1964. Elementary through intermediate.

Despite his handicap, Alfred-the-one-legged becomes involved in the destiny of a Britain war-torn by the wild Vikings.

Konigsburg, E. L. *Inviting Jason*. New York: Atheneum, 1971. Elementary through intermediate.

Dyslexic Jason, clumsy and odd, is finally accepted by his schoolmates. Dyslexia is explained simply.

Lawrence, M. *The Shining Moment*. New York: Harcourt, 1960. Intermediate through young adult.

A young girl copes with a scarred face and a scarred personality.

Little, J. *Mine for Keeps*. Boston: Little, Brown, 1962. Elementary through intermediate.

Sal's efforts on behalf of others help her overcome her own fears and the physical limitations of cerebral palsy.

———. *Take Wine*. Boston: Little, Brown, 1968. Elementary through intermediate.

Laurel is "prodded" into getting help for her retarded younger brother and into making a normal life for herself.

Mirsky, R. P. *Beethoven*. Chicago: Follett, 1957. Elementary through intermediate.

This biography for young people tells of the musical genius whose "ears were sealed to the outside world."

Mullins, J., and S. Wolfe. *Special People Behind the Eight-Ball*. Johnstown, Pa.: Mafex, 1975.

Pace, M. M. *Juliette Low*. New York: Scribner's, 1947. Intermediate.

The founder of the Girl Scouts was handicapped by deafness.

Van Stockum, H. *Mogo's Flute*. New York: Viking Press, 1966. Intermediate.

Because of his ill health, an African boy must learn to use another talent besides strength in order to be accepted by the tribe.

Literature for Parents

FOR INSIGHT, INFORMATION, AND PRACTICAL SUGGESTIONS

Buck, P. S. *The Child Who Never Grew*. New York: John Day, 1950.

A beautifully written account of Pearl Buck's experience with her adopted mentally retarded child.

Carroll, T. J. *Blindness: What It Is, What It Does, and How to Live with It*. Boston: Little, Brown, 1961.

A readable account of the problems associated with blindness.

Crawford, J. A. *Children with Subtle Perceptual-Motor Difficulties*. Pittsburgh: Stanwix, 1966.

Describes problems of learning and suggests activities for parents and teachers.

Fassler, J. *Helping Children Cope*. New York: Free Press, 1978.

Discusses the pros and cons of books and stories meant to be used to assist youngsters in mastering stressful situations of all kinds. A thorough, reasoned, and enjoyable review of the best, worst, and so-so literature available, by a knowledgeable practitioner. Illustrated.

Green, H. *I Never Promised You a Rose Garden*. New York: New American Library, 1971.

A biography of a young girl who suffers a nervous breakdown. The book describes her feelings before the breakdown and her recovery in a mental hospital.

Hewett, S., and J. Newson. *The Family and the Handicapped.* Chicago: Aldine, 1970.

This book deals with the variety of problems cerebral palsy produces in family life. Also includes services available for families of cerebral palsied children.

Jones, B., and J. Hart. *Where's Hannah?* New York: Hart, 1968.

The book traces the psychological as well as the instructional aspects of helping a brain-injured child at home and at school.

McMichael, J. K. *Handicap: A Study of Physically Handicapped Children and Their Families.* Pittsburgh: University of Pittsburgh Press, 1971.

Educational and emotional problems encountered by physically handicapped children and their parents.

Mullins, J., and S. Wolfe. *Special People Behind the Eight-Ball.* Johnstown, Pa.: Mafex, 1975.

An excellent annotated bibliography of books (and some articles) related to handicapped children and adults. The literature is classified by handicapping conditions.

Myklebust, H. R. *Your Deaf Child.* Springfield, Ill.: Thomas, 1950.

Although somewhat dated, most of the information in the book is still relevant. Basic information on causes and types of deafness is provided as well as concrete ways to help the young deaf child.

Spock, B. *Caring for Your Disabled Child.* New York: Macmillan, 1965.

A handbook with practical suggestions for planning education, recreation, and training. A list of community resources is included.

Strauss, S. *Is It Well with the Child?* Garden City, N.Y.: Doubleday, 1975.

A mother's story of her mentally retarded autistic child includes many practical suggestions on ways of locating diagnostic services, day schools, and residential schools, as well as dealing with daily problems.

West, P. *Words for a Deaf Daughter.* New York: Signet, 1973.

A father's view of the early years of his deaf daughter's life, the problems encountered, and his feelings are given through chapters addressed to the child.

BIOGRAPHIES, AUTOBIOGRAPHIES, AND FICTION ABOUT PEOPLE WITH HANDICAPPING CONDITIONS

Axline, V. M. *Dibs: In Search of Self.* Boston: Houghton-Mifflin, 1965.

A boy, deprived of emotional contact with his parents, searches for his identity with the help of his psychotherapist.

Berg, M. A. *Wednesday's Child: A Tale of Love and Courage.* Philadelphia: Muhlenberg, 1960.

In this novel, a sister of a cerebral palsied girl writes of childhood experiences with her and their family.

Bloom, F. *Our Deaf Children.* London: Herneman, 1963.

The author, a sociologist, writer, and chairman of the National Deaf Children's Society, gives an account of her own experiences— her difficulties, frustrations, and triumphs.

Bourgeon, R. *In Darkness.* New York: William Morrow, 1969.

A story about the main character's conflicts with blindness. (Fiction.)

Brown, C. *My Left Foot.* New York: Simon & Schuster, 1955.

Cristy Brown, able to control only his left foot because of cerebral palsy, writes his autobiography.

Buck, P. *The Gifts They Bring.* New York: John Day, 1965.

There is an emphasis on love and understanding of the mentally retarded and suggestions for their care.

Dickens, C. *A Christmas Carol.* Any unabridged edition.

Dickens tells his classic story of a miser, three ghosts, and the crippled boy, Tiny Tim. (Fiction.)

Garry, V. "Mainstreaming: Children's Books About Children with Disabilities." *Exceptional Parent* 2 (April 1978): 8–12.

Garry reviews numerous recently published books about children who have made the most of their disability. The reviews, although brief, capture the central theme of the book and indicate appropriate reader age range. The areas covered are deafness, blindness, mental retardation, physical disability, learning disability, and physical size.

Gershe, L. *Butterflies Are Free.* New York: Random House, 1970.

This novel was inspired by Harold Krents, a blind student at Harvard University.

Greenberg, J. *In This Sign.* New York: Holt, 1970.

A young deaf couple leave a home for the handicapped and try to live in the world of the hearing. (Fiction.)

Hugo, V. *The Hunchback of Notre Dame.* Any unabridged edition.

Quasimodo, the hunchback, is deaf from years of ringing Notre Dame's thunderous bells. (Fiction.)

Johnson, M. "Our Daughter Is Blind." *McCall's* May 1953, p. 4.

This article shows how one family helped its blind child to live in a bright world.

Jones, B., and J. Hart. *Where's Hannah?* New York: Hart, 1968.

Coauthored by the mother and the teacher of a brain-injured child, the book covers the psychological as well as the instructional aspects of helping the child at home and at school.

Kipling, R. *The Light that Failed.* Any authorized edition.

The hero of Kipling's novel, an artist, works courageously against the time of his complete blindness.

Park, C. C. *The Siege.* Gerrards Cross, England: Colin Smyth, 1968.

A mother writes of the problems living with an autistic child and the methods used to help her.

Plath, S. *The Bell Jar.* New York: Harper, 1971.

This novel was written by a poet just before her own suicide. It has great insight into emotional disturbance.

Spencer, E. *The Light in the Piazza.* New York: McGraw-Hill, 1960.

The author writes a fictional, romantic account, as seen through the eyes of her mother, of a brain-damaged girl, who has become a handsome young woman.

Steinbeck, J. *Of Mice and Men.* Any unabridged edition.

The tragic and compassionate story of a retarded man and his friend. (Fiction.)

Thomas, G. *My Mind a Kingdom.* New York: E. P. Dutton, 1938.

In this diary, a family copes with muscular disease with courage and faith.

Tucker, C. D. *Betty Lee.* New York: Macmillian, 1954.

The mother of a brain-damaged child tells of her own experiences.

Wheeler, O. *Ludwig von Beethoven and the Chiming Tower Bells.* New York: Dutton, 1942.

The author tells of the younger life of the deaf composer.

Literature for Children About Handicapped Athletes

Boynick, D. K. *Champions by Setback: Athletes Who Overcame Physical Handicaps.* New York: Crowell, 1954. Young adult.

Stories about formerly handicapped athletes.

Campanella, R. *It's Good to Be Alive.* Boston: Little, Brown, 1959. Intermediate through young adult.

Roy Campanella, the well-known baseball star, was paralyzed after an automobile accident.

Graham, A. *It Takes Heart.* New York: Harper and Row, 1959. Intermediate through young adult.

Stories of athletes who overcame handicaps to become champions.

Graham, F. *Lou Gehrig: A Quiet Hero*. New York: Putnam, 1942. Intermediate.

This story of Lou Gehrig tells of his brave adjustment to multiple sclerosis and his later work on the New York Parole Board.

Hirshberg, A. *The Man Who Fought Back: Red Schoendienst*. New York: Messner, 1961. Intermediate through young adult.

A noted baseball player conquers tuberculosis.

Piersall, J., and A. Hirshberg. *Fear Strikes Out—The Jimmy Piersall Story*. Boston: Little, Brown, 1955. Young adult.

A major-league baseball player conquers his nervous condition.

Scott, J. *Bob Mathias, Champion of Champions*. Minneapolis, Minn.: Denison, 1963. Young adult.

This is the story of a small-town boy who overcame anemia to become a great all-around athlete.

References

ACKERMAN, N. W. *The Psychodynamics of Family Life: Diagnosis and Treatment of Family Relationships.* New York: Basic Books, 1958.

ALBERTI, R. E., and M. L. EMMONS. *Your Perfect Right.* San Luis Obispo, Cal.: Impact, 1970.

AMIDON, E., and E. HUNTER. *Improving Teaching.* New York: Holt, Rinehart, and Winston, 1967.

ANDERSON, K. A., and A. M. GARNER. "Mothers of Retarded Children: Satisfaction with Visits to Professional People." *Mental Retardation* 1 (1973): 36–39.

ASPY, D. N. "The Effect of Teacher-Offered Conditions of Empathy, Congruence, and Positive Regard Upon Student Achievement." *Florida Journal of Educational Research* 11 (1969): 39–48.

———. *Toward a Technology for Humanizing Education.* Champaign, Ill.: Research Press, 1972.

———. "Toward a Technology Which Helps Teachers Humanize Their Classrooms." *Educational Leadership* (March 1971).

ASPY, D. N., and F. N. ROEBUCK. "An Investigation of the Relationship

Between Levels of Cognitive Functioning and the Teacher's Classroom Behavior." *Journal of Educational Research* (May 1967).

ASPY, D. N., and W. HADLOCK, "The Effects of High and Low Functioning Teachers Upon Students' Performance." In *Beyond Counseling and Psychotherapy*, edited by B. Berenson and B. R. Carkhuff, p. 297. New York: Holt, Rinehart and Winston, 1967.

BAILARD, V., and R. STANG. *Parent-Teacher Conferences.* New York: McGraw-Hill, 1964.

BARNEBEY, N., and E. RUPPERT. "Parents of Chronically Ill or Physically Handicapped Children." In *Helping Parents Help Their Children*, edited by L. E. Arnold, pp. 174–82. New York: Brumer/Mazel, 1978.

BARSCH, R. H. *The Parent of the Handicapped Child: The Study of Child-Rearing Practices.* Springfield, Ill.: Thomas, 1968.

———. *The Teacher–Parent Partnership.* Arlington, Va.: The Council for Exceptional Children, 1969.

BAUM, M. H. "Some Dynamic Factors Affecting Family Adjustment to the Handicapped Child." *Exceptional Children* 28 (1962): 387–92.

BAXTER, D. "An Open Letter to Those Who Counsel Parents of the Handicapped." *J. of Rehab. of the Deaf* 10 (1977): 1–8.

BELL, N. W., and E. F. VOGEL, eds. *A Modern Introduction to the Family.* Glencoe, Ill.: Free Press, 1960.

BENJAMIN, A. *The Helping Interview.* 2nd ed. Boston: Houghton-Mifflin, 1974.

BERGIN, A. E. "The Effects of Psychotherapy: Negative Results Revisited." *Journal of Counseling Psychology* 10 (1963): 244–55.

BERNSTEIN, L., R. S. BERNSTEIN, and R. H. DANA. *Interviewing: A Guide for Health Professionals.* 2nd ed. New York: Appleton-Century-Crofts, 1974.

BERNSTEIN, N. R. "Mental Retardation." In *The Harvard Guide to Modern Psychiatry*, edited by A. M. Nicholi, Jr. Cambridge, Mass.: Harvard University Press, 1978.

BERSCHEID, E., and E. H. WALSTER. *Interpersonal Attraction.* Reading, Mass.: Addison Wesley, 1969.

BIBRING, G. L., T. F. DWYER, D. S. HUNTINGDON, and A. F. VATENSTEIN. "A Study of the Psychological Processes in Pregnancy and the Earliest Mother-Child Relationships." *Psychoan. Stud. Child* 16 (1961): 9–72.

BISSELL, N. E., "Communicating with the Parents of Exceptional Children." In *Professional Approaches with Parents of Handicapped Children*, edited by E. J. Webster. Springfield, Ill.: Thomas, 1976.

BLAKE, H. E. *Creating a Learning-Centered Classroom: A Practical Guide for Teachers.* New York: Hart, 1977.

Bowlby, J. "Separation Anxiety." *Int. J. Psycho-Anal.* 41 (1960): 89–113.

Brammer, L. M. *The Helping Relationship: Process and Skills.* Englewood Cliffs, N.J.: Prentice-Hall, 1973.

Branan, J. M. "Negative Human Interaction." *Journal of Counseling Psychology* 19 (1972): 81–82.

Brown, G. I. *Human Teaching for Human Learning.* New York: Viking Press, 1971.

Buscaglia, L. *The Disabled and Their Parents: A Counseling Challenge.* Thorofare, N.J.: C. B. Slack, 1975.

Caldwell, B., and S. A. Guze. "A Study of the Adjustment of Parents and Siblings of Institutionalized Retarded Children." *Amer. J. Ment. Def.* 64 (1960): 845–61.

Calvert, D. R. "Dimensions of Family Involvement in Early Childhood Education." *Exceptional Children* 37 (1971): 655–59.

Carberry, H. "Parent-Teacher Conferences." *Today's Education* 65 (1975): 67.

Carkhuff, R. F. *Helping and Human Relations.* New York: Holt, Rinehart and Winston, 1969.

Carkhuff, R. R. "Differential Functioning of Lay and Professional Helpers." *Journal of Counseling Psychology* 15 (1968): 117–26.

Chevigny, H. *My Eyes Have a Cold Nose.* New Haven, Conn.: Yale University Press, 1946.

Clements, S. L. "What Is Man?" In *The Complete Essays of Mark Twain,* edited by C. Neider. Garden City, N.Y.: Doubleday, 1963.

Cohen, K. M., and F. G. Kimmerling. "Attitudes Based on English Dialect Differences: An Analysis of Current Research." (ED 056 579.) Cambridge, Mass.: Language Research Foundation, 1971.

Combs, A. W., R. A. Blume, A. J. Newman, and H. L. Wass. *The Professional Education of Teachers: A Humanistic Approach to Teacher Preparation.* Boston: Allyn and Bacon, 1974.

Combs, A. W., and D. W. Soper. "The Helping Relationship as Described by Good and Poor Teachers." *Journal of Teacher Education* 14 (1963): 64–68.

Connor, B. C. "An Evaluation of Alcohol Education Methods." Unpublished doctoral dissertation, University of Pittsburgh, 1974.

Cooley, C. H. *Human Nature and Social Order.* New York: Schocken, 1964.

Council for Exceptional Children (CEC), *Working with Parents of Exceptional Children* (undated).

Cowan, E. L., R. P. Underberg, and R. T. Verrillo. "The Development and Testing of an Attitude to Blindness Scale." *Journal of Social Psychology* 48 (1958): 297–304.

DUNCAN, D. "The Impact of a Handicapped Child Upon the Family." Paper presented at the Pennsylvania Training Model Training Sessions, Harrisburg, Pa., May 1977.

———. "The Conduct of Home Conferences." Unpublished manuscript, University of Pittsburgh, March 1978.

DUNCAN, L. W., and P. W. FITZGERALD. "Increasing the Parent-Child Communication through Counselor-Parent Conferences." *Personnel and Guidance Journal* 47 (1969): 514–17.

EGAN, G. *Exercises in Helping Skills.* Monterey, Cal.: Brooks/Cole, 1975.

———. *Interpersonal Living: A Skills/Contract Approach to Human Relations Training in Groups.* Monterey, Cal.: Brooks/Cole, 1976.

EKMAN, P. "Body Position, Facial Expression and Verbal Behavior During Interviews." *Journal of Abnormal and Social Psychology* 68 (1964): 295–301.

EYSENCK, H. J. "The Effects of Psychotherapy: A Reply." *Journal of Abnormal Social Psychology* 50 (1955): 147–48.

FANTINI, M., and G. WEINSTEIN. *Toward Humanistc Education.* New York: Praeger, 1970.

FARBER, B. "Effects of a Severely Mentally Retarded Child on Family Integration." *Mongr. Soc. Res. Child Devel.* 24 (1959).

———. "Effects of a Severely Retarded Child on the Family." In *Readings on the Exceptional Child,* edited by E. P. Trapp and P. Himelstein, pp. 227–46. New York: Appleton Century Crofts, 1962.

FASSLER, J. *Helping Children Cope.* New York: The Free Press, 1978.

FELDMAN, M. A., R. BYALICK, and M. P. ROSEDALE. "Parents and Professionals: A Partnership in Special Education." *Exceptional Children* 41 (1975): 551–54.

FLANDERS, N. *Analyzing Teacher Behavior.* Reading, Mass.: Addison-Wesley, 1970.

FLECK, S. "An Approach to Family Pathology." *Comprehensive Psychiatry* 7 (1966): 307–20.

FOTHERINGHAM, J. B., M. SKELTON, and B. A. HODDINOTT. *The Retarded Child and His Family: The Effects of Home and Institution.* Monograph Series No. 11. The Ontario Institute for Studies in Education, 1971.

FOX, M. A. "The Handicapped Family." *The Lancet* 2 (Aug. 1975): 400–401.

FOX, R., M. B. LUSZKI, and R. SCHMUCK. *Diagnosing Classroom Learning Environments.* Chicago, Ill.: SRA, 1966.

FREUD, A. *The Ego and the Mechanisms of Defense.* London: Hogarth Press, 1948.

GARRETT, A. *Interviewing: Its Principles and Methods.* New York: Family Service Association of America, 1972.

GILDEA, M., J. C. GLIDEWELL, and M. B. KANTOR. "Maternal Attitudes and General Adjustment in School Children." In *Parental Attitudes and Children's Behavior,* edited by J. C. Glidewell. Springfield, Ill.: Thomas, 1961.

GLASS, S. D. *The Practical Handbook of Group Counseling: Group Work with Children, Adolescents, and Parents.* Baltimore, Md.: BCS Pub. Co., 1969.

GORHAM, K. A. "A Lost Generation of Parents." *Exceptional Children* 41 (1975): 521–25.

GORHAM, K. A., C. DESJARDINS, R. PAGE, E. PETTIS, and B. SCHEIBER. "Effect on Parents." In *Issues in the Classification of Children,* edited by N. Hobbs. San Francisco: Jossey-Bass, 1975.

GREENBERG, H. M. *Teaching with Feeling.* Toronto, Ont.: Macmillan and Co., 1969.

GROSSMAN, F. K. "Brothers and Sisters of Retarded Children." *Psychology Today* 5 (Apr. 1972): 82–84, 102–104.

GUR, T. "Problems of Counseling Parents of Retarded Children." Unpublished manuscript, University of Pittsburgh, 1976.

HAMMOND, D. C., D. H. HEPWORTH, and U. G. SMITH. *Improving Therapeutic Communication.* San Francisco: Jossey-Bass, 1977.

HARRIS, J. A. "Parents and Teachers Inc." *Teacher* (Sept. 1978), 85–87.

HENSIE, L. E., and R. J. CAMPBELL. *Psychiatric Dictionary.* 4th ed. London: Oxford University Press, 1970.

HETZNECKER, W., L. E. ARNOLD, and A. PHILLIPS. "Teachers, Principals, and Parents: Guidance by Educators." In *Helping Parents Help Their Children,* edited by E. L. Arnold, pp. 363–78. New York: Brunner/Mazel, 1978.

HOBBS, N., ed., *Issues in the Classification of Children.* San Francisco: Jossey-Bass, 1975.

HOLLINGSWORTH, C. E., and R. G. PASNAW. *The Family in Mourning: A Guide for Health Professionals.* New York: Grune and Stratton, 1977.

HOPPOCK, R. *Occupational Information.* 3rd ed. New York: McGraw-Hill, 1967.

IVEY, A. E. *Microcounseling: Innovations in Interviewing Training.* Springfield, Ill.: Thomas, 1971.

IVEY, A. E., and N. B. GLUCKSTERN. *Basic Attending Skills: Participant Manual.* Amherst, Mass. 1974.

JAKUBOWSKI-SPECTOR, P., R. DUSTIN, and R. GEORGE. "Toward Developing a Behavioral Counselor Education Model." *Counselor Education and Supervision* 10 (1971): 242–50.

JOHNSON, D. E., and M. J. VESTERMARK. *Barriers and Hazards in Counseling.* Boston: Houghton-Mifflin, 1970.

KAGAN, N. *Influencing Human Interaction.* East Lansing: Michigan State University CCTU, 1971.

KAMER, L. "Parents' Feelings About Retarded Children." *Amer. J. Ment. Defic.* 57 (1953): 375–83.

KELLY, E. J. "Parental Roles in Special Education Programming—a Brief for Involvement." *Journal of Special Education* 4 (1973): 357–64.

KERSHAW, J. D. *Handicapped Children.* London: Heinemann, 1973.

KHAN, S. B., and J. WEISS. "Teaching of Affective Responses." In *Second Handbook of Research on Teaching,* edited by R. M. W. Travers, pp. 759–804. Chicago: Rand McNally, 1972.

KINGSLEY, L. V. "Parents Can Help with School Difficulties." *Exceptional Parent* 1 (1971): 13–15.

KLAUS, M. H., and J. H. KENNELL. *Maternal-Infant Bonding.* St. Louis, Mo.: Mosby, 1976.

KLEIN, S. D. "Brother to Sister: Sister to Brother." *The Exceptional Parent* 2 (1972): 10–15.

KNAPP, M. L. *Nonverbal Communication in Human Interaction.* New York: Holt, Rinehart and Winston, 1972.

KOHL, H. *The Open Classroom.* New York: Random House, 1969.

KONOPKA, G. *Social Group Work: A Helping Process.* 2nd ed. Englewood Cliffs, N.J.: Prentice-Hall, 1972.

KROTH, R. L. *Communicating with Parents of Exceptional Children: Improving Parent-Teacher Relationships.* Denver, Col.: Love, 1975.

KROTH, R. L. and G. T. SCHOLL. *Getting Schools Involved with Parents.* Reston, Va.: The Council for Exceptional Children, 1978.

KÜBLER-ROSS, E. *On Death and Dying.* New York: Macmillan, 1969.

LANGDEN, G., and I. W. STOUT. *Teacher-Parent Interviews.* Englewood Cliffs, N.J.: Prentice-Hall, 1954.

LEIGH, J. "What We Know About Counseling the Disabled and Their Parents: A Review of the Literature." In *The Disabled and Their Parents: A Counseling Challenge,* edited by L. Buscaglia, pp. 39–63. Thorofare, N.J.: Slack, 1975.

LEVINE, S. "Sex-Role Identification and Parental Perceptions of Social Competence." *American Journal of Mental Deficiency* 70 (1966): 907–12.

LIKERT, R. *New Patterns of Management.* New York: McGraw-Hill, 1961.

LISBE, E. R. "Professionals in the Public Schools." In *Working for Chil-*

dren: Ethical Issues Beyond Professional Guidelines, edited by J. S. Mearig, pp. 239–61. San Francisco: Jossey-Bass, 1978.

LISTER, J. L. "Counselor Experiencing: Its Implications for Supervision." *Counselor Education and Supervision* 5 (1966): 55–60.

LORTIE, D. C. *Schoolteacher: A Sociological Study.* Chicago: University of Chicago Press, 1975.

LOSEN, S., and B. DIAMENT. *Parent Conferences in the Schools.* Boston: Allyn and Bacon, 1978.

LOVE, H. D. *The Mentally Retarded Child and His Family.* Springfield, Ill.: Thomas, 1973.

LUSZKI, M. B., and R. SCHMUCK. "Pupil Perceptions of Parental Attitudes Toward School." *Mental Hygiene* 49 (1965): 296–307.

LYON, H. C. *Learning to Feel—Feeling to Learn.* Columbus, Ohio: Merrill, 1971.

McCAULEY, B. L. "Evaluation and Authority in Alternative Schools and Public Schools." (ED 064 787.) Palo Alto, Cal.: Stanford Center for Research and Development in Teaching, Stanford University, 1972.

McGOWAN, J. F. "Developing a Natural Response Style." *Education* 4 (1956): 246–49.

MACKEITH, R. "Parent Counseling." *Devel. Med. and Child Neurology* 15 (1973): 525–27.

McWILLIAMS, B. J. "Various Aspects of Parent Counseling." In *Professional Approaches with Parents of Handicapped Children,* edited by E. J. Webster. Springfield, Ill.: Thomas, 1976.

MADOFF, J. M. "The Attitudes of Mothers of Juvenile Delinquents Toward Child Rearing." *Journal Consult. Psychol.* 23 (1959): 518–20.

MEADOW, K. P., and L. MEADOW. "Changing Role Perceptions for Parents of Handicapped Children." *Exceptional Children* 38 (1971): 21–27.

MEDINNUS, G. R., and R. C. JOHNSON. *Child and Adolescent Psychology: Behavior and Development.* New York: Wiley, 1969.

MILLER, E. A. "Cerebral Palsied Children and Their Parents." *Exceptional Children* 24 (1958): 298–302.

MURRAY, M. A. *Needs of Parents of Mentally Retarded Children.* National Association for Retarded Citizens (undated).

NAEGLE, K. D. "Clergymen, Teachers and Psychiatrists." *Canadian Journal of Economics and Political Science* 22 (1956): 46–62.

NAPIER, R. W., and M. K. GERSHENFELD. *Groups: Theory and Experience.* Boston: Houghton-Mifflin, 1973.

OLSHANSKY, S. "Chronic Sorrow: A Response to Having a Mentally Defective Child." *Social Casework* 43 (1962): 190–93.

PALOMARES, G. D. "The Effects of Stereotyping on the Self-Concept of

Mexican-Americans." (ED 056 806.) Albuquerque, N.M.: South-western Cooperative Educational Laboratory, 1970.

PECK, J. R., and W. B. STEPHENS. "A Study of the Relationship Between the Attitudes and Behaviors of Parents and That of Their Mentally Defective Child." *American J. Ment. Deficiency* 64 (1960): 839–43.

"Principals Move to the Top in School Studies." *The Pitt News*, February 13, 1978.

RADKE, M. J. "The Relation of Parental Authority to Children's Behavior and Attitudes." Series No. 22, *University of Minnesota Institute of Child Welware Monograph*, 1946.

RAINWATER, L., R. P. COLEMAN, and G. H. HANDEL. *Workingman's Wife: Her Personality, World, and Life Style*. New York: Oceana, 1959.

REIK, T. *Listening with the Third Ear*. New York: Farrar, Straus, and Giroux, 1972.

REPLOGLE, B. L. "What Help Do Teachers Want?" *Educational Leadership* 7 (1950): 445–49.

REYNOLDS, M. C., and J. W. BIRCH. *Teaching Exceptional Children in All America's Schools*. Reston, Va.: Council for Exceptional Children, 1977.

RINGNESS, T. A. *Mental Health in the Schools*. New York: Random House, 1968.

ROE, A. "Early Determinants of Vocational Choice." *Journal of Counseling Psychology* 4 (1957): 212–17.

ROGERS, C. R. *Counseling and Psychotherapy*. Boston: Houghton-Mifflin, 1942.

ROOS, P. "Parents of Mentally Retarded People." *Int. J. Ment. Health* 6 (1977): 96–119.

ROSS, A. O. "Family Problems." In *The Exceptional Child: A Functional Approach*, edited by R. M. Smith and J. T. Neisworth. New York: McGraw-Hill, 1975.

ROSS, A. O. *The Exceptional Child in the Family: Helping Parents of Exceptional Children*. New York: Grune and Stratton, 1964.

ROWE, M. "Psychoanalytic Insights for Parent Guidance." In *Helping Parents Help Their Children*, edited by L. E. Arnold, pp. 37–45. New York: Brunner/Mazel, 1978.

RUBIN, Z. *Liking and Loving*. New York: Holt, Rinehart and Winston, 1973.

SACHS, B. *The Student, the Interviewer and the Curriculum: Dynamics of Counseling in the School*. Boston: Houghton-Mifflin, 1966.

SAMLER, JOSEPH. "Change in Values: A Goal in Counseling." In *Counseling: Readings in Theory and Practice*, edited by John F. McGowan and Lyle D. Schmidt. New York: Holt, Rinehart and Winston, 1962.

SARASON, S. B. *Psychological Problems in Mental Deficiency.* New York: Harper and Row, 1959.

SCHAEFER, E. S. "A Circumplex Model for Maternal Behavior." *J. of Abn. Soc. Psychol.* 59 (1959): 226–35.

SCHILD, S. "The Family of the Retarded Child." In *The Mentally Retarded Child and his Family,* edited by R. Koch and J. C. Dobson, pp. 454–65. New York: Brunner/Mazel, 1976.

SCHLEIFER, M. J. "Let Us All Stop Blaming the Parents." *The Exceptional Parent* (Aug./Sept. 1971), 3–5.

SCHLESINGER, B. *The One-Parent Family.* Toronto: University of Toronto Press, 1969.

SCHMID, R. E., J. MONEYPENNY, and R. JOHNSTON. *Contemporary Issues in Special Education.* New York: McGraw-Hill, 1977.

SCHULMAN, E. D. *Intervention in Human Services.* St. Louis, Mo.: Mosby, 1974.

———. *Intervention in Human Services.* 2nd ed. St. Louis, Mo.: Mosby, 1978.

SCHULMAN, J. L., and S. STERN. "Parents' Estimate of the Intelligence of Retarded Children." *Amer. J. Ment. Defic.* 63 (1959): 696–98.

SCHWEBEL, M. "Role-Playing in Counselor Training." *Personnel and Guidance Journal* 32 (1953): 196–201.

SEARL, S. J. Stages of Parent Reaction. *Exceptional Parent* 8 (1978): 27–29.

SEARS, R. R., E. E. MACCOBY, and H. LEVIN. *Patterns of Child Rearing.* Evanston, Ill.: Row, Peterson, 1957.

SELIGMAN, M., ed. *Group Counseling and Group Psychotherapy with Rehabilitation Clients.* Springfield, Ill.: Thomas, 1977.

SHAPIRO, L. J. "Teachers and Schools, Don't Be Afraid—Parents Love You (A Survey)." *Journal of Teacher Education* 26 (1975): 269–73.

SHERTZER, B., and S. C. STONE. *Fundamentals of Counseling.* 2nd ed. Boston: Houghton-Mifflin, 1974.

SHIELDS, D. "Effects of Clients' Social Class, Race, and Religion as Perceived by Hospital Speech Pathologists." Doctoral dissertation, University of Pittsburgh, 1974.

SLAVSON, S. R. *Child-Centered Group Guidance of Parents.* New York: International University Press, 1958.

SOLNIT, A. J., and M. H. STARK. "Mourning and the Birth of a Defective Child." *Psychoanal. Stud. Child.* 16 (1961): 523–37.

SONSTEGARD, M., and R. DREIKURS. "The Teleoanalytic Group Counseling Approach." In *Basic Approaches to Group Psychotherapy and Group Counseling,* edited by G. Gazda, pp. 468–510. Springfield, Ill.: Thomas, 1975.

SPIEGEL, J. P. "The Resolution of Role Conflict Within the Family." *Psychiatry* 20 (1957): 1–16.

STERN, C., and E. R. KEISLAR. "Teacher Attitudes and Attitude Change: A Research Review." *Journal of Research and Development in Education* 10 (1977): 63–75.

SWICK, K. J., and M. L. LAMB. "Development of Positive Racial Attitudes, Knowledges, and Activities in Preservice Social Studies Teachers." (ED 073 025.) Carbondale College of Education, Southern Illinois University, 1972.

TAYLOR, F. C. "Project Cope." In *Professional Approaches with Parents of Handicapped Children,* edited by E. J. Webster. Springfield, Ill.: Thomas, 1976.

TELFORD, C. W., and J. M. SAWREY. *The Exceptional Individual.* (3rd ed.) Englewood Cliffs, N.J.: Prentice-Hall, 1977.

TRUAX, C. B. "An Approach to Counselor Education." *Counselor Education and Supervision* 10 (1970): 4–15.

TURNER, R. H. *Family Interaction.* New York: Wiley, 1970.

ULIN, R. O. *Death and Dying Education.* Washington, D.C.: National Education Association, 1977.

WALLER, W. *The Sociology of Teaching.* New York: Russell and Russell, 1961.

WARNATH, C. F., and J. L. SHELTON. "The Ultimate Disappointment: The Burned-Out Counselor." *Personnel and Guidance Journal* 54 (1976): 172–75.

WHITMORE, J. R. "An Experimental In-Service Teacher Education Program for Distressed Elementary Schools." (ED 087 777.) Palo Alto, Cal.: Stanford Center for Research and Development in Teaching, Stanford University, 1974.

WILLIAMS, F., J. L. WHITEHEAD, and L. M. MILLER. "Attitudinal Correlates of Children's Speech Characteristics." (ED 052 213.) Austin: Center for Communication Research, University of Texas, 1971.

WIRTZ, M. A. *An Administrator's Handbook of Special Education: A Guide to Better Education for the Handicapped.* Springfield, Ill.: Thomas, 1977.

WITTMER, J. *The School Survey of Interpersonal Relationships.* Linden, N.J.: Remediation Associates, 1971.

WITTMER, J., and R. D. MYRICK. *Facilitative Teaching: Theory and Practice.* Pacific Palisades, Cal.: Goodyear, 1974.

WRIGHT, B. A. *Physical Disability—A Psychological Approach.* New York: Harper and Row, 1960.

WUNDERLICH, C. *The Mongoloid Child: Recognition and Care.* Tucson: University of Arizona Press, 1977.

YALOM, I. D. *The Theory and Practice of Group Psychotherapy.* 2nd ed. New York: Basic Books, 1975.

YALOM, I. D., and M. A. LIEBERMAN. "A Study of Encounter Group Casualties." *Archives of General Psychiatry* 25 (1971): 16–30.

ZACH, L., and M. PRICE. "The Teacher's Part in Sex Role Reinforcement." (ED 070 513.) Research in Education, 1973.

ZUK, G. H. "The Religious Factor and the Role of Guilt in Parental Acceptance of the Retarded Child." *American Journal of Mental Deficiency* 64 (1959): 139–47.

Index